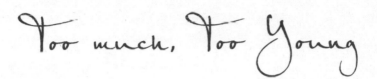

Too much, Too Young

To Molly and Lilly Sue

Too much, Too Young

KERRY KATONA

WITH FANNY BLAKE

WITHDRAWN

EBURY
PRESS

First published in Great Britain 2006

1 3 5 7 9 10 8 6 4 2

Ebury Press, an imprint of Ebury Publishing.
Random House, 20 Vauxhall Bridge Road, London SW1V 2SA

Random House Australia (Pty) Limited
20 Alfred Street, Milsons Point, Sydney, New South Wales 2061, Australia

Random House New Zealand Limited
18 Poland Road, Glenfield, Auckland 10, New Zealand

Random House (Pty) Limited
Isle of Houghton, Corner of Boundary Road and Carse O'Gowrie,
Houghton, 2198, South Africa

Random House Publishers India Private Limited
301 World Trade Tower, Hotel Intercontinental Grand Complex,
Barakhamba Lane, New Delhi 110 001, India

The Random House Group Limited Reg. No. 954009

www.randomhouse.co.uk

A CIP catalogue record for this book is available from the British Library.

HB ISBN 9780091913892 (after Jan 2007)
HB ISBN 0091913896

PB ISBN 9780091914516 (after Jan 2007)
PB ISBN 0091914515

Printed and bound in Great Britain by Mackays of Chatham Plc

Mixed Sources
Product group from well-managed
forests and other controlled sources
www.fsc.org Cert no. TT-COC-2139
© 1996 Forest Stewardship Council
FSC

Acknowledgements

Writing this book has been a sometimes painful but definitely rewarding journey as I have relived some of the most difficult parts of my life. I want to thank everyone who has made it possible, most especially my mum who has shared her memories about her own past which I know was a particularly hard experience for her.

I also want to thank everyone else who has helped me remember: my Nana Betty, Uncle Andrew, Fred and Mag Woodall, Lisa Rhodes, Andy McCluskey, Max Clifford and my fantastic manager, George Ashton.

A huge personal thanks is also due to all the people who have been there for me in my life when times have been tough – you all know who you are.

Most of all I want to thank my daughters, Molly and Lilly Sue, for being everything to me and last but not least, Mark, who has given me back my love of life. Together, the three of them have made me happy again.

'And the Queen of the Jungle is....'

The silence seemed to drag on for ever. Jennie and I sat on the log in the jungle clearing, arms around one another, waiting to hear which of us was the winner of ITV's *I'm a Celebrity Get Me Out of Here*. I couldn't have felt less like a queen if I'd tried, all hot and sweaty, with my unwashed hair tied back in a ponytail. I knew it had to be her. As the other contestants had been voted off one by one and I'd been left behind, I'd begun to think the producers hadn't been showing me on the telly. They must have forgotten I was there, otherwise surely I'd have gone days earlier.

'Jennie, Jennie, Jennie,' I whispered. She had lain under-ground with rats and eaten every mouthful of a bug-eating bushtucker challenge.

'Kerry, Kerry, Kerry,' she whispered back. I hadn't even completed my challenges successfully, fumbling in a bath of eels and leeches, gagging on witchetty grubs. And when they'd wanted to cover me in sixty million cockroaches, I'd refused point blank.

'Jennie, Jennie.' I knew my breath must stink.

'Kerry, Kerry.' Hers didn't. And her make-up looked good, too.

'...KERRY!'

What? They must have made a mistake. I stared in disbelief. 'Oh my God!'

All the other contestants who'd been evicted had come back to the camp for the result: Katie Price, Peter Andre, 'Razor' Ruddock, Mike Reid, Diane Modahl, Lord Brocket, Alex Best. Everyone but Johnny Rotten, who'd walked out halfway through. They all leaped to their feet and crowded round us, cheering and hugging us both. Then before I knew where I was, they'd all disappeared again, leaving me alone in the jungle, wandering around the empty camp, shaking and trying to take on board what had happened.

Two weeks earlier I had left my husband and two baby girls for what I had honestly thought would be two weeks on the piss with Ant and Dec in a studio somewhere. Instead I'd found myself in the middle of the Australian jungle with a bunch of celebrities I hardly knew, surrounded by creepy crawlies that terrified me and, worse still, which I was made to eat. I'd taken days to find my feet and spent most of them jumping out of my skin or in tears. I'd been such a whinger. Why would anyone have wanted to keep me in the show?

They say when you're drowning, your life flashes in front of your eyes, and now I know what they mean. During those last minutes in the jungle, before I was taken away to be crowned with my plastic crown, pictures from my childhood raced

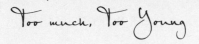

through my mind. Without a dad, I'd had to survive as best I could with Mum. Sometimes I'd lived with her and sometimes, when she wasn't able to look after me herself, I'd stayed with relatives or friends. Mum had attempted suicide several times, and I was often the one who had to look after her. I'd never lived in one place for longer than three years and by the time I was eleven, I'd been to seven different primary schools At thirteen I was taken into care, staying with four sets of foster parents before Mum and I were finally reunited. God knows how we came through it in one piece, but we did. During all the hard times I can remember feeling guilty, responsible for my mum's depression, confused about who I was and most of all unloved, but now millions of people had shown they wanted me, Kerry Katona, when only ten years earlier no one had wanted me at all...

1

HERE COMES FREDDY

THE NIGHT HAD BEGUN quite normally for us: in a pub. I'd just turned thirteen and had been living with Mum and her boyfriend Dave Wheat in London's East End for a couple of months. She'd been out all day 'kiting'. She'd taken orders from friends and neighbours, then gone to different shops using stolen credit cards to buy £50 to £100 worth of stuff in each one. Afterwards she'd sell everything on at half the price. While she 'worked', Dave would wait for her with a drink in a pub nearby.

They'd had a good day and we'd gone to the Three Rabbits to round it off with their friend Barbara, who was a heroin addict at the time, her redhead husband Micky and their eight-year-old daughter Sharon. The Three Rabbits was a smoky old-fashioned pub on the Romford Road, in the heart of London's East End. In those days it was a real gangster haunt, where men carried guns or knives in their leather jackets and weren't afraid to use them. There were worn stools by the long wooden bar, a patterned carpet that had seen better days, tables covered in glass stains, beer mats and overflowing ashtrays, and two pool tables. Seeing the film *Moulin Rouge* when I was older reminded me of what it was like, because the guys who drank there were all such weird

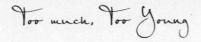

characters. There was the midget; the one who kept passing out; the one who was a bit of a lunatic; the funny one; the psycho – all of them dangerous to know. After a couple of hours' drinking, a fight kicked off between Barbara and Micky. Being close to a fight was like a drug to Dave when he was pissed. He drank every day, and would be fine for days on end until suddenly, for no obvious reason, he'd snap and want to start in on one himself.

Dave had always scared me. All he needed to do was give me one of his looks and it would stop me dead whatever I was doing. Although we'd had plenty of good times together, I'd seen what he was capable of. I knew that he was a gangster who'd been inside more than once, and in that summer of 1993 he was on parole from Parkhurst. I also knew his reputation and I didn't like it – Dave wasn't a man to mess with. I'd heard that when he was in America, he'd taken a woman back to his room only to discover 'she' was really a man, so he'd shot him dead on the spot. I'd also been told how he'd hung a guy who'd crossed him off a roof by his ankles. I didn't want that happening to me. That night he reminded me of Freddy Krueger, the killer from *A Nightmare on Elm Street*, thanks to what I called his 'Krueger hat'. Underneath it he was a tall good-looking bloke in a black leather jacket; he was slim with a black Mexican moustache, long black hair and a lazy right eye.

When we left the pub, we climbed into his red Cortina to go home. I shrunk down in the back seat listening as Mum and Dave started shouting at each other. As he drove off in the dark, Dave started punching Mum in the face with his fist – I could see she was bruised and bleeding in the orange light of the street lamps as we passed beneath them. I screamed at him to stop, but I knew he'd hurt me if I tried to get between them. Suddenly she yelled at me to get out of the car, so as he slowed down at some traffic lights I opened the door and got ready to jump.

'Shut the fucking door,' Dave shouted. 'Shut the door.'

What else could I do? If I jumped he might come after me and hit me, too. I shut the door and sat as still as I could, pulling my woolly orange-red-and-blue-striped coat (I called it my 'techni-coloured dreamcoat') around me, wishing the back seat could swallow me up.

The fight seemed to blow over as quickly as it had started, but Dave was still angry, and kept smacking the wheel with the palm of his hand. He pulled over to let Mum get out to have a pee behind a tree on the grass verge and I hopped out after her. At the beginning of the evening we'd been looking forward to going out and she'd got all dressed up in her off-the-shoulder top with a V-necked front and back, leggings, stilettos and bright red nail varnish. I couldn't understand what had gone wrong. She crouched down at the side of the road, one of her heels sinking into the mud, and I stood there watching her, my body tense as I shook uncontrollably with fear.

'Mum. We've got to run.' I was frantic. 'He's going to kill us tonight. I know he is.'

Mum seemed completely cool. I don't know how she managed it, but I suppose she knew that if she lost it I'd be even more frightened. 'He'll be fine, Kerry,' she reassured me. 'Just keep him calm.'

'But, Mum, he'll kill us,' I insisted.

'Just keep him calm,' she repeated, 'and it will be all right.'

I realize now that she knew however angry Dave got he

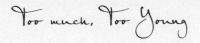

would never kill her, but back then I didn't know that. Dave had lost it with her once or twice before so she knew the signs. She also knew we would make things a lot worse if we played it wrong. I followed her back to the car where he seemed to have cooled down a bit. We started off home again, but then he pulled over as we were passing Stratford bus depot. 'Out you get, Kerry. Go and get in one of the buses. See if you can drive it.'

I was only thirteen, but I knew he was playing mind games with me. Everyone said I was old-headed even then. I realized that we had to go along with whatever he said if we wanted to survive. 'Great idea, Dad.' He always insisted I called him that even though he wasn't my real dad. I tried to sound as if I thought he'd suggested the coolest game ever. 'I'll have a look around and see if I can find one.'

'Go on, Kerry. Get in one and see what you can do.' He was laughing, thinking of all the damage I could cause. As I walked around the depot I was tense with fear. I worked my way along the lines of big red buses that loomed out of the darkness, but none of them had an open driver's door. 'Dad,' I called. 'I can't find one that's open. Let's go home and get some sleep.' I was trying so hard to control the situation and be the grown-up, the calm sensible one. For some reason, I felt it was my responsibility to make things right.

By that time he was bored with the idea and got back in the car. The light was off but he looked at Mum as if he was seeing what he'd done to her for the first time. 'I'm sorry,' he muttered. 'I was out of order.'

She lit another cigarette, her hand shaking, saying nothing.

'It's OK, Dad. Let's go home,' I said as he switched on the

ignition and turned the car round. I could see from the car clock that it was just past midnight. As we reached our house in Gough Road, the last one in the street, his mood seemed to change again. He couldn't find anywhere to park so he stopped the car in the middle of the road, got out and shouted at me, 'Park the car, you little bitch. I've been driving since I was eleven so it's about time you started.'

Of course I couldn't, so I just said to Mum, 'I'm going in, can I have the house keys, please?' She dug into her bag and handed them over. To my relief, Dave didn't try to stop me. As soon as I was through the front door, I slammed it shut and raced through the small living room into the kitchen, where I took the key from the back door. I had a gut feeling we were going to be in for a long night and I wanted to be sure Mum and I could escape if we had to. After about ten minutes there was still no sign of them – surely, they couldn't be arguing again. I looked out of the front window but the street was empty. I wanted my mum, but was too scared to go out into the badly lit street and find her. I had no choice, though. I had to look out for her.

Despite being near West Ham, Gough Street reminded me of Coronation Street, with rows of two-up two-down houses on either side of a cobbled dead-end road. Opening the front door I could see that the car was parked, but both doors were wide open and there was no sign of Mum or Dave. I crossed the street and walked towards the junction with Trevelyan Road. Just round the corner I could see Mum lying where she'd fallen on the pavement. She was curled into a ball with her arms covering her face, protecting herself, while Dave kicked at her, trying to make her get up.

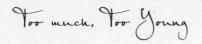

He looked up for a moment, and as soon as he saw me he stopped. 'Your mum's drunk again, Kerry. She's fallen over. Come and help me with her.'

I went over to help her up and our eyes met. After so many years of being together in bad situations, Mum and I didn't need words to communicate. We knew we were in for it that night. Once we got inside, she almost collapsed onto the carpet of the small living room, sobbing while Dave went through the archway to the kitchen, where the bags of shopping from earlier in the day still lay on the floor where they'd left them. He helped himself to a piece of chicken that we'd left on the side after dinner.

'What are you crying for, Susan?' he asked. 'You're drunk. Look at her, Kerry.' He sounded disgusted. 'Why are you crying?'

Between her tears, Mum choked out, 'You don't understand how much I love you, Dave.'

Then I chipped in from where I was on the couch, 'Can I say something, please? I think I'd be crying if I'd just been beaten up in the street.'

Big mistake.

I should have kept my mouth shut. Dave's mood changed as if I'd flicked a switch, and he turned back into the living room with that look in his eyes.

'Run,' screamed Mum. 'Run, Kerry.'

I shot up the stairs into my bedroom and slammed the door. There was nothing much in there, just the single bed and chest of drawers that had come with the house when they'd rented it. I hadn't stuck anything on the walls; I hadn't lived there long enough to make it look as if it was mine. I curled up on the bed, trying to block out the screams coming from downstairs.

'Kerry!' Mum shrieked my name so loudly that I forgot everything and ran back down to help her. From the bottom of the stairs, I could see her lying on the kitchen floor, and there was blood on the lino. She had a deep cut on her ankle and the black handle of a carving knife was sticking out of her thigh, just above the knee. The blade had gone right through her leg.

'Kerry. For God's sake help me,' she cried. Dave was in the living room, watching us as I pulled at the knife, which came out as easily as if I was cutting butter. Blood was pouring from Mum's leg. I was too scared to stay with her, but was only halfway back up the stairs when I heard him shout, 'I'm going to kill the little bitch now.' I looked back to see him standing on the bottom step waving the bloody carving knife and another serrated knife with a sharp forked tip. 'Here comes Freddy,' he said, his face twisted. 'I'm going to cut off your feet so you can't run away. I'm going to cut off your hands so you can't phone anyone ever again. Then I'm going to cut off your tits and chop you into pieces which I'll put in the fridge so no one can find you.'

'Please, please don't hurt me, Dad,' I begged. 'I've done nothing wrong.' I took a step down.

'Freddy's home,' he growled, lunging at me and swinging the knives at my ankles. I jumped back as he swung again and ran for the safety of my room. I sank down onto the floor near the door, my back against the wall, hugging my knees and shaking with fear. I thought I could see my Grandad Denis, walking like a ghost through the heavy panelled door of my built-in wardrobe towards me. This is it, I thought. I'm dead. I could picture my funeral with Maria Carey's 'Hero' belting out as my coffin disappeared behind the curtain. I wanted all my friends to be there,

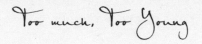

everyone from Padgate High, as well as our Pat, my dad Arnie, Nana Betty and my best friend Lisa. Enough. I stopped myself from going any further.

I jumped up and crossed to the window. I could see West Ham cemetery over the back wall, the gravestones shadowy in the darkness. I was only one floor up, so maybe I could jump down into the yard, climb the wall and run for it, but I was scared Dave would be waiting for me when I landed. And if he wasn't, I was sure that once I was in the cemetery a dead body would climb out of one of the graves and get me instead. I tried knocking on my bedroom wall, not loudly enough for Dave to hear but so that Trevor and Julie next door would know something was wrong and come to help us. Nothing. I went back to the window, steeling myself to jump, but as I tried to raise the bottom sash I discovered that it was nailed shut. The only way out of the house now was down the stairs and through the back door.

Downstairs the shouting had died down. All I could hear was my mum crying and crying as if she'd never stop. I stood up and crept over to my bedroom door, slowly opening it, then inched my way to the top of the stairs. I couldn't see Dave or Mum. Pressed against the wall, I tiptoed down the stairs, praying nothing would creak and give me away. I held the back-door key tightly in my coat pocket, repeating, 'I've got the back-door key. I've got the back-door key,' over and over to myself as if it would keep me safe. If I could get to the back door without Dave noticing me, I could go for help.

I edged around the curve of the stairs and stopped still with several steps to go. From there I could just see Dave's legs in their jeans and white trainers. They were stretched out in front of him, crossed at the ankle, as he sat back out of sight. I saw the glint of steel as he cut the air backwards and forwards with the two knives. He was making Mum crawl across the brown carpet, round the coffee table, as blood ran from the gash on her leg. I willed Mum not to look at me and give me away, but just then she turned her head and saw me. I put my finger to my lips, but she was too far gone to understand. 'Kerry. Oh, Kerry,' she shrieked.

She'd blown our last chance. Dave slowly leaned forward, looking at me long and hard. I froze. I knew he was going to kill us both.

Over the years, I've replayed that moment over and over again in my mind. Mum might have known that Dave would never have touched me, and he certainly would never have killed her, but I was just a kid and I was terrified. Now I can see that Dave was a bully who enjoyed having power over people. He loved playing mind games, seeing how far he could push you before you cracked. Yet at the same time, strange as it may sound, he did love my mum, and she loved him. On a normal day their roles were reversed. Mum admits that she could be a bitch to him, flirting with other men in front of him or arguing, while Dave would do anything for her. When he wanted to be, he was one of the nicest guys around, a gentleman who would help an old lady over the road, but he had his hard-man reputation to keep up.

Through my childhood, I'd often felt that I was the mum and Mum was the daughter. And as Dave leaned forward and looked at me, I knew that this was one of those times when it was up to me to be the adult. It was a role I'd automatically take on, adapting myself to whatever circumstances we were in. I could charm the police, look after her if she self-harmed or had a panic attack,

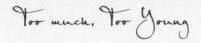

cook her supper, give her a cuddle when she was down. I looked at her now and saw her mouth, 'Please be nice. Please be nice.' I knew I didn't have a choice.

Dave leaned back again, half-shutting his eyes. Was he drifting off or was he thinking about what he had just done? 'Dad,' I said gently, and went towards him. He stopped swinging the knives as I knelt on the couch beside him and started stroking his hair. 'Come on, Dad,' I said gently. 'I love you. We've had a great day.' I put my arms around him, hugging him tight. 'Can you imagine what your Danny [his son] would say if he saw you now?' I could feel his body begin to relax, and behind his back I gave Mum the thumbs up so she could see I was OK. I kept talking to him, bringing the temperature down, changing the situation. He didn't resist as I took the knives from him and put them back in the kitchen, all the time pretending I was calmer than I felt.

Dave followed me into the kitchen, then, for no obvious reason, he snapped again, grabbed back the knives and held them to my throat, saying, 'Don't think I don't know what you're doing.'

'I don't know what you're talking about, Dad,' I protested. And I didn't.

He started slicing bits off the chicken and cramming them into my mouth. I couldn't work out what was going through his mind so I went along with him and ate as much as I could. Then he had another random idea. 'Go and lie on the sofa, Hot Lips.' He often called me that. I went through and sat on the scruffy brown couch opposite the fireplace.

'Sue, hold her down,' he ordered. 'I'm going to put a finger in each of her nostrils and rip her face apart.' He was talking dead nice, as if he was saying something really ordinary.

'Dad, I don't want you to,' I pleaded. 'Don't you think my nose is big enough already?' Sometimes I could joke my way out of a situation, but not this time. When Mum refused to help him, he told me to lie down anyway. Suddenly he turned away from us, stabbing at the door with the carving knife, 'I'm dead hard, me.' Neither of us were going to argue.

I lay still, pretending to be asleep, keeping my eyes closed even when he put a blanket over me, but I couldn't stop shaking. I wanted to stay downstairs so Mum wouldn't have to be alone with him. I could hear him threatening to knife her and chop her up again. Then I heard her voice. 'If that's what you want to do, Dave, do it now. If you want to kill me, then kill me. But don't you touch my baby. Do it now but don't kill me in front of her.' I heard them both stand up. What do I do? I asked myself. Oh my God, oh my God, what do I do? If he takes her into the garden, I can't run out of the front door and leave her. Then I heard him say, 'Sit down.' In that second I knew she was going to be all right.

After a while, I finally dared to look out from under the blanket and saw they were both asleep. Mum was over in the chair by the window while Dave was stretched out on the other couch opposite her. I thought Mum must be unconscious because her leg was bleeding so badly. This was my chance. I felt so angry; all I wanted to do was to get rid of Dave. I hated him. I got up quietly and picked up the carving knife to stab him. The only thing that stopped me was the sudden idea that he might come back and haunt me. It sounds so stupid now, but at that age the idea was so real to me. Then it occurred to me that if I didn't do the job properly, he might wake up and kill Mum and me after all, so in the end I put the knife down, tiptoed to the back door and let

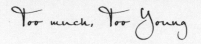

myself out into the garden. I climbed over the side fence and knocked quietly on Trevor and Julie's door. Too terrified of waking Dave, I didn't knock hard enough to wake them either. Now what was I going to do? I couldn't leave Mum on her own – I needed her – so I went back into the house, locking the door behind me and leaned over her, trying to wake her up, but Dave woke first.

'Hiya, Dad.' I tried to sound normal, but I needn't have worried. The storm finally seemed to have passed.

Mum moaned quietly as she came to. Her top had slipped off her shoulder; her hair was all messed up and her make-up had rubbed off, so her skin was grey with mascara smudged under her eyes. She looked exhausted.

'Come on, Susan.' Dave sounded tired and I could see him holding his temper in as she took her time coming to. 'Let's go to bed.'

As we climbed the stairs it was almost daybreak. Mum came into my room to reassure me that she was OK, though I could still see the thick red blood gluing her leggings to her skin. But it didn't matter what she said, I still couldn't sleep. I could hear them having sex through the wall and that killed me. How could she? I couldn't understand why she stayed with him, and I still don't really understand their relationship. If I'd been her, I'm sure I'd have left him, but I know that she loved him and believed that all the good times they had made it worth putting up with the bad times. Random nights like this one were the price she paid. It was as if in some strange way the violence tied her even more closely to him. Besides, if she had left, where would she have gone?

The next morning, the house was a mess. The sun shone through the kitchen window and you could see the blood on the floor. Yesterday's shopping was still in bags beside it. Mum was up, emptying the ashtrays and straightening the living room as if nothing had happened. When she'd woken me up, she'd begged me to be nice to Dave for her sake. That was reason enough for me. We sat in the living room drinking my favourite mini Cherry Cokes as Dave told us how sorry he was and how it would never happen again. I didn't believe him, though, and still felt that we'd be safer if we got away from him and his moods. We didn't have a phone of our own, and our chance came when Trevor called round to say there was a phone call for Dave next door. As soon as he'd gone, I begged Mum to leave, but she didn't want to go. I was so shocked.

'No, Kerry. We can't. He's all right now.' She tried to reassure me. 'Anyway, where would we go?' She was in a lot of pain and her leg looked awful. I could see the yellow fat inside the cut. What could I do?

That evening, the Three Rabbits was the same as always – everything felt so normal it was as if last night had never happened. Both pool tables were being used and there were quite a few people up at the bar. An old man with no teeth was sitting in one corner with his pint of Guinness, rolling his baccy. I remember noticing that his wife on the stool beside him was wearing a wig. It's seems funny that I can remember that when I was so edgy. We sat at a scratched, beer-stained table while Dave bought a pop for me, a Bacardi and Coke for Mum and a Coke for himself. He chatted with the regulars as usual while I played with the beer mats. After a couple of drinks, Mum said she felt faint and wanted me to go with her to the toilet. He didn't look happy but let us go together. The toilet was a tiny room that stank

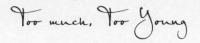

of air fresheners, smoke and shit. Fag burns marked the lino floor. We'd only been in there a minute when Mum, who had been leaning against the wall, slid down to the floor as if she was going to pass out. She'd lost a lot of blood the night before and I suppose she was still in shock. The colour drained from her face. Panicking, I ran the tap and flicked her with water to bring her round. 'Mum. Please don't do this to me. Not now, while Dave's here and I'm on my own. Please.'

'I need to go to hospital, Kerry,' she managed. 'You've got to help me. Look at my leg.' Dave had put some padding over the cut but it looked really nasty and was still oozing blood.

'What do you want me to do?' I asked. 'I can't tell Dave that he's got to take you to hospital because he stabbed you. He'll never do that. What if he gets into trouble?' Even at that young age I knew that if something went wrong while he was on parole he'd be in serious trouble. 'We'll have to think of something else.'

She moaned.

'Stay conscious, please,' I begged her as I raced through the options in my mind. OK, I'm thirteen, I said to myself. I can do this.

'Mum, we've got to go back out there.'

Gradually she came to and hauled herself up off the floor. She leaned over the washbasin, holding its sides and breathing deeply before we went back to Dave.

Mum sat down with another Bacardi. She looked awful. Trying to take control again, I knew I had to convince Dave to take her to hospital. There was no way Mum was up to persuading him.

'Mum's had an accident. She's fallen over and badly cut her

leg,' I said, crossing my fingers that he'd listen to me. 'We need to take her to hospital.'

'How's she done that, then?' Whether he'd really forgotten or was pretending I don't know, but I didn't question it. More of his mind games I suppose. Perhaps he was testing us to see how far we were prepared to go in order to get round him.

'I don't know but we need to take her. It's hurting and she thinks it might be infected.'

'That's all right. I can sew it up,' he offered. He wanted us to go home so he could get a needle and thread out!

By the time Mum had practically drunk the entire bar, we had managed to persuade Dave to take us to the hospital. She told me afterwards that she wanted to get drunk enough to pass out so that someone would have to help her, but the drink wasn't taking effect. On the way to the hospital, I remember us stopping to ask for directions. I was curled up on the back seat of the Cortina willing the couple who were telling Dave the way to the hospital to rescue me. I don't think they even saw me.

The rows of seats in the brightly lit busy A&E department of King George Hospital were packed with drunks, young and old. Dave wouldn't let me go in with Mum, so while she was taken into a cubicle to be examined by a nurse I sat absolutely still beside him, watching the numbers on the wall click round as one patient after another was called. After Mum came back, we had to wait for a doctor to come and stitch the wound. Occasionally someone would go up to the desk and complain that they'd been waiting for ages. The receptionist dealt with them all in the same dead patient way, explaining how they would be seen as soon as possible but that they had to sit and wait their turn. A couple of

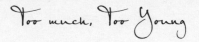

men were sitting near us, and one had a bloody bandage round his head which made him look a bit like a pirate. Every now and then, a trolley carrying a patient would wheel by, and black-shoed nurses walked briskly in and out of the cubicles, swishing the curtains behind them. Doctors in white coats swept through on their way to see someone, but it was never us. I hated the weird medical smell of the place. After about an hour of waiting, Dave began to get pissed off, so I volunteered to go with Mum to see if we could find out why it was taking so long. He yanked me back by my hair. 'I'm only going to make sure she's OK,' I assured him and he let me go.

We both knew exactly what we were going to do. Looking around, I whispered to Mum, 'Keep walking. Just keep walking.' Once we'd got through a pair of heavy double doors she yelled, 'Run.' We ran as fast as we could, although Mum was in agony, along wide grey corridors, up and down stairs, past nurses and patients in dressing gowns, through more doors until we ended up in a geriatric ward. We were wondering where to go next when the sister came over. 'Are you OK? Are you looking for someone?'

'My boyfriend stabbed me last night,' said Mum. 'We've got to get out of here. Please call us a taxi before he finds us.'

We must have looked terrible so she was probably glad to get us off the ward by telling us where to find the taxi rank.

The only money we had was my thirteenth birthday money, which I was keeping carefully in my purse until I found something I wanted to buy. We spent all of it getting to Barbara and Micky's.

Micky's brother lived in a huge council block nearby, so we stayed the night there, somewhere Dave wouldn't know to find us. The next day they took Mum to get her leg stitched properly and we went back to Barbara and Micky's shabby Victorian terraced house. I was so scared Dave was going to come round that every time I heard a car stop outside, I'd race to the window, hopping over the kids' toys and mess on the floor, to see who it was. But he never turned up. For most of the day Mum was on and off the phone to him, panicking about what we were going to do, crying over cups of tea in the kitchen. I stayed in the living room, watching TV and playing with their baby Jack in his walker. *Gladiators* had just begun when Mum came in to talk to me.

'I've been talking to Dave, love,' she said. 'I'm going to see him.'

I couldn't look at her. I didn't want to hear what she was saying. I sat on the couch facing the wall with my back to her as she told me he'd promised not to drink again and that everything would be all right.

'Mum, you can't,' I whispered in tears. 'Please don't.'

But she had made up her mind and nothing I could say would change it. She wanted me to go with her.

'You can go through that a thousand times if you want to, Mum,' I said. 'But once is enough for me. I'm not going back with you. I'm not going back to Dave. I want to phone our Pat.' My step-sister Pat, at home in Warrington, would know what to do.

'I love you, Kerry,' Mum said. I know she meant it, but I couldn't make myself say it back. I couldn't take living with her and Dave any more, even though I was frightened at the thought of what might happen to me if she left me behind. Mum didn't say she'd stay with me as I so badly wanted her to, instead she said a sad goodbye and left. Why couldn't she have chosen *me* for once? Didn't she love me? What did I have to do to make her love me? What was going to happen to me now?

I phoned Pat and when I heard her voice I burst into tears. 'I've done something bad. I've done something really bad.' I felt as if I was somehow to blame for Mum leaving.

'You've not been stealing, have you?' was her first question.

I had held myself together for three days for my mum's sake, but now I was on my own. The whole story tumbled out as I told her how I was alone in a heroin addict's house, babysitting an eighteen-month-old baby while watching *Gladiators*, and I was sure that Dave was coming back to kill me. I told Pat everything, and Pat told the Warrington police, who in turn contacted the police in London.

By the time a policeman and woman arrived, Micky had warned Dave and Mum that the police were on their way. Mum called me to try to convince me to tell the police I'd made the whole thing up. 'If you tell them you were lying, you'll be able to go home and live with your nan.' But I knew Nana Betty hadn't got room for me any more. There was nowhere for me to go, and Mum knew that. I couldn't believe she was asking me to cover up for Dave, either. I'd covered up for *her* many times, but I'd never cover up for him. It was too late anyway.

I was hysterical, begging the police to get me out of the house. The tall policewoman with big blue eyes and long blonde hair tied back in a plait took charge. She told me her name was Rosalind, then took me upstairs, sat me on her knee and held me while I cried, asking me all about my family. Downstairs, her colleague questioned Micky. I'll never forget how good Rosalind was to me. At last someone else was in charge and I could be a child again, letting her take over and make decisions for me. It was such a relief to know I was safe and that nothing could hurt me. Downstairs, on our way out, Micky yelled at them, 'You can't take her away.'

But Rosalind stood her ground. 'Try and stop me, then. Come and get her.'

Micky knew when he was beaten and quickly backed off.

I had to duck down on the back seat of the police car in case Dave and Mum were on their way over to fetch me. If they saw me, there would be trouble. First, I had to take the police to Gough Street and show them our house, then I lay with my cheek against the scratchy blue serge of Rosalind's skirt while they took me to the police station.

It would be weeks before I saw my mother again, and years before I was allowed to live with her.

2

MUM'S THE WORD

OF ALL THE UPS and downs Mum and I have been through together over the years, those three days in London were the worst. But whatever's gone on, I've never stopped loving her; after all, she's the only mum I've got. We're flesh and blood and that means everything to me. At times living with her has been tough as she's battled with bouts of manic depression and the fall-out from the way she was brought up. My childhood may not have been easy but she didn't exactly have it easy herself.

Our story really began forty-six years ago, on 29 October 1960, in a dark back alley in Warrington. An eight-month-old baby girl was found wrapped up in blankets in a pram in an alley just off Densham Avenue. Her mother was a prostitute who'd left her with a friend while she went to work. At least that's the story Mum was always told about her beginnings. In fact, the truth wasn't quite so romantic. Her mother was a prostitute but had left her with a friend while she went to work. When she didn't come back, the friend called the police. The baby was then taken to the police station and admitted to the National Children's Home in nearby Frodsham. That was the start Mum had in life.

She was quickly fostered by Betty and Ken Kewley, a part-time hairdresser working from home and a cellarman in the local brewery, but her real mum, Irene Hill, didn't waste time before making contact with them. She started calling round without telling Social Services, sometimes bringing Denis Katona, Mum's father, with her. She was always asking for clothes, coal, money or even shelter, and she'd cause a nuisance, shouting and smashing their windows, and threatening to take Mum away from them if they didn't stump up.

Of course Mum was too young to remember any of this, but her Social Services record notes how she was affected. Apparently she had doubts about her identity and was confused about who her real father was. Eventually, when she was four years old, Mum had to be put into Statham Avenue children's home in Warrington because social services felt it would be a more secure environment for her. They didn't want to run the risk of Irene taking her because they thought she was an unsuitable mother. Apparently Mum was very upset by the move, but over the next seven years she settled down, getting used to Lil and Tom Burge who ran the home. Even in the Sixties the kids were controlled by strict discipline, mostly given out, as Mum remembers, by one particular old dragon. Once one of the other girls, Julie, pushed in front of Mum in the morning queue for a wash and cod liver oil. Mum gave her a shove out of the way and was rewarded with a bite on the hand from Julie's sister. You had to look after yourself in there, so Mum bit Julie. The old dragon was so mad that she bit Mum on the ear – can you believe that? – and made her stay in the corner of the playroom all day, even when she wet herself. If she didn't eat the vegetables she hated they'd be served up again and again. And if she still didn't eat them, she'd be given nothing but jam butties for the rest of the week and sent to bed early every night. Once, when she refused to eat her rice pudding, Auntie Win held her nose and forced spoonfuls into her mouth until she threw up all over the table. For that, she was slapped and sent to bed.

She must have had to become pretty tough to survive there. I hate hearing the story of how one of the girls held her down on her bed, stopping her from putting her fingers in her ears, as another girl told her about the headless man who roamed the corridors at night. She never dared to go to the toilet in the night after that and was always wetting the bed, which earned her more punishment. Even now, in her mid-forties, she has to have the TV on for company as she goes to sleep.

What was weird was that, despite everything, she always did well at school, especially in maths and English. Apart from being a pretty blonde scrap of a girl, she must have been a bright little thing, too. Everyone thought she was really sweet, but she had that extra spark that charmed everyone around her. The Burges adored her and said they wanted to foster her themselves. She even got to be bridesmaid to their daughter. Being a favourite was good for her in many ways, but it made some of the other kids jealous and they picked on her. Among the other children in the home were two of her four half brothers and sisters, who she hadn't known existed. They all spent much of their childhood in homes, too, because Irene wasn't able to look after any of them.

Betty Kewley, who we came to call Nana Betty, never forgot about Mum. For seven years, she visited regularly, coming at least once a month and writing several times to ask if she could foster

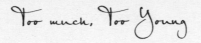

Mum again. During that time, Nana Betty had divorced and remarried. She'd fallen in love with Denis, Mum's real father, who she'd met occasionally when he'd come round with Irene. They now had two children of their own, Andrew and Angela. Then one day when Mum was eleven, Nana Betty turned up as usual, but the Burges were out. She asked the relief carer on duty whether she could take Mum out.

'Do Mr and Mrs Burge allow you to?'

'Oh yes. All the time,' lied Nana Betty.

Permission granted, she took Mum on a bus and told her that she was taking her home to meet her dad. Mum remembers being dead nervous on the way there. As far as she knew, this was the first time she'd seen him. Her dad was a stocky handsome man with olive skin, bright blue eyes and a tache. With his mouthful of silver-capped teeth and a heavy Hungarian accent she couldn't understand, he frightened her to death. At this first meeting he gave her a fiver, so then she thought he was just great. He worked at the nearby factory where they made cardboard boxes, while Betty did cleaning jobs to bring in money. The family had a good day together and, for Mum, being with them and their four-year-old son and one-year-old daughter was like being in a real family at last.

They lived in a clean and comfortable terraced house with a posh front room where they could sit on the orange three-piece and listen to the radiogram. They'd bring the tin bath into the back kitchen, which was lined with formica-topped units and glass-fronted yellow cupboards, put it in front of the coal fire and take it in turns to use the same bath water. There was a TV in there too, and the toilet was down the yard – it was a proper family home at last. Mum begged Nana Betty not to make her go back to the children's home, so Betty asked Social Services if Mum could stay. She and Denis were told that they wouldn't get any money if they took her, but they didn't care about that, they just wanted Mum. This time she took her dad's name too and became Sue Katona.

Mum's dream soon went up in smoke, though, when she saw that Denis was easily excitable and had a fiery temper. When he lost his rag, he could get violent and would sometimes hit Betty. Mum had never seen anything like that in the children's home and the violence frightened her. They'd used the slipper there when kids were naughty, but they'd never resorted to real violence. Once she had to complain to the Social Services after Denis had lost his temper when she and Andrew had come home late from the baths. In his anger, he had picked her up and thrown her against a wall, hurting her leg. The social worker took her back home, giving Denis a warning about what would happen if he ever hit her again. I suppose he was given a second chance because he was Mum's real father but I often wonder whether it was the right decision.

So Mum had got her real dad but her real mum was still out of the picture. Nana Betty was, and still is, everything to her, but she must have wondered who and where her real mother was, especially at moments like that. It seems to me that families are like jigsaws. Not having a mum or a dad is like having the most important parts of the picture missing. Nobody else can fill those gaps. I've never known my real dad and I've always wondered what he was like, so I can imagine Mum having the same thoughts about her mother. What did she look like? What would she be like? What sort of relationship would they have? What difference would she have made to her life?

One day, her questions were answered. Soon after moving in with Nana Betty and Denis, Mum came back from school one afternoon to find a large woman with black hair and lots of make-up, her eyes outlined in thick black eyeliner, sitting in the living room. She was only about five foot three inches tall and she was wearing a big black fake-fur coat. Betty looked very nervous.

'Pleased to meet you,' said Mum, suspecting nothing.

'Hiya, love,' said the woman drunkenly. 'I'm your social worker, Irene.' I've never understood why she didn't tell Mum who she really was straight away.

When she went into the back kitchen, Betty whispered, 'That's your real mother, Sue.' Mum didn't know what to say. She felt uncomfortable and wanted the woman to leave, even though she'd given her a sixpence. Nana Betty fretted that Denis would be home from work soon and would go mad when he saw Irene there. After everything that had happened when Mum was young, he didn't want her calling round. When Betty asked if Mum would babysit Angela and Andrew while they went out for a drink, she immediately agreed. She was glad to get them out of the house, even when Irene asked for the sixpence back.

Despite all that, I'm sure she didn't forget about Irene. I know I couldn't have done. Knowing who your real parents are matters, because they give you a place in the world. If you know them, you know where you're coming from. They give you boundaries that help you in life, and teach you what's right and what's wrong. At least they should do.

Mum didn't see Irene again until she was nearly fourteen, when things broke down at home with Denis. He ran the house very strictly and had high expectations of his children. If he felt

Mum had let him down, he'd let her know it all right. The final straw came when she and a friend missed the bus home after they'd been to the pictures; they had to walk and didn't get back until late. Denis answered the door looking furious, then just as she was about to step inside, and without listening to her explanation, he hit her hard across the face. She ran off in agony, her face covered in blood, even though she had nowhere to go. In the end she spent the night sleeping on the floor in a corridor in a block of flats. The next morning, feeling terrible and with her face all swollen, she went home to find Denis sitting in the kitchen, crying. He apologized and wiped her face. She hadn't slept much the night before and wanted to go to bed, but Denis asked her to dry the dishes first. When she had her back to him he whacked her across the back of the head with a frying pan and told her to go upstairs. Despite being in agony for two weeks, nothing was done about her broken nose. To this day you can still see the lump on its bridge. According to Mum, she was no worse than any other teenager; she was just a kid who liked hanging out with her mates, drinking and smoking. But two weeks later he threw her out, accusing her of stealing a Giro cheque.

For the next fortnight she slept under a park bench. I hate thinking about how scared and lonely she must have felt. No child should be forced into living like that, without a home or anyone to keep them safe. Every day, Nana Betty would meet her at the market and buy her some clean underwear and something to eat. Nan was scared of what Denis might do if she insisted Mum come home. Forced to live on the streets and with nowhere else to go, Mum decided to find Irene and ask her to take her in. Irene's flat was filthy, and had broken windows, but it was the

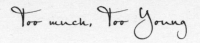

obvious and only place to go. When Denis relented, she moved back home, but again things didn't work out, so she moved back in with Irene for good. She loved being with her real mum. Irene allowed her to do whatever she wanted. There was nobody laying down the law, saying when she had to be in or what she was and wasn't allowed to do. She could drink and smoke as she pleased, and if she didn't feel too good the next day, Irene would pop her a purple heart (an upper that was easy to get hold of then) and she'd soon feel better.

During the Seventies, Irene was still working as a prostitute, so she often brought men home on the job. While they were doing the business, she'd get Mum to rob the money out of their trousers, then afterwards the two of them would go to the Irish Club, where there was a good cheap bar. It had long wooden tables down the middle of a scruffy room and a few round ones to the side. A jukebox blared out the latest hits whenever someone could be bothered to put money in it and an empty stage waited for the next entertainment. All the drunks went there when the pubs shut at three-thirty. Mum was a beautiful young woman who looked a bit like Goldie Hawn, with big blue eyes, blonde hair and a top figure. Not surprisingly, she would have a constant stream of drinks bought for her while she watched Irene pick up men.

One of the regulars in the Irish Club was Dave Wheat. His mum was a friend of Irene's and, like Mum, he'd spent much of his childhood in a children's home. He was five years older than Mum and was already a hardened criminal with a reputation for bullying, maiming and stealing. A regular Jack the Lad, he fancied Mum. He was always on at her to go out with him but he was too much of a gangster for her; she never wanted anything to do with him – until one night when everything changed.

Mum was in the club with Irene as usual, and they'd been joined by six Pakistani men, who were chatting them up and buying them drinks. They were all laughing and joking, but Mum couldn't help feeling slightly awkward because of the way they were looking at her. She didn't think too much of it until she came out of the toilet and looked around for Irene, who was nowhere to be seen. Mum went back over to the guys and asked if they knew where she'd gone.

The way they were smiling at her made her feel very uneasy. 'It's OK,' one of them said. 'Don't worry. She's gone home. We've paid her a hundred quid.'

'What for?' She asked as they closed in around her.

'So that we can take you home and fuck you,' said another.

She was a seventeen-year-old virgin and her own mum had sold her to a group of men for sex as if it was the most natural thing in the world for a mother to do. In that moment any feelings Mum had for Irene must have been completely destroyed. How could any woman do that to her daughter? Mum must have been so frightened. She was alone and no match for six men. How was she going to get out of the situation in one piece?

Hearing that story makes me feel so bad for her. Her relationship with Irene was a bit like the one she and I had when I was that age. They were more like best mates than mother and daughter, but like us they were also flesh and blood. Never in a million years, however desperate we got, would Mum have done something like that to me. Imagining her in that situation, a young woman sold out by her mother and surrounded by those

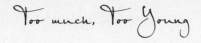

men, upsets me even more than thinking about my own life. I can't imagine how Mum got through something like that.

Fortunately her guardian angel must have been looking out for her, because at that moment Dave Wheat came through the door. He saw her crying and went over to find out what was going on. When he heard, he took on the men single-handedly, battering the lot of them, before getting her out of there. From that day on he was Mum's knight in shining armour, and he never let her forget it. That was the beginning of a relationship that was to continue on and off over the next twenty years – including those nightmare three days in London – until his death.

To begin with things between them went well. Dave would come over to Irene's and they'd have a laugh and enjoy them-selves, drinking every day – Mum's tipple was Pernod and blackcurrant then. I've never understood how she managed to forgive Irene for betraying her like that, but I suppose she didn't have much choice. Where else was there for her to go? Besides, Dave was always with her, which I guess made her feel safe.

But Mum started drinking too much and it was only when she got the DTs, and was convinced that creepy crawlies were running all over the house that Irene finally took notice and called the doctor. Mum was admitted to Winwick Hospital, an old county asylum that had become a psychiatric hospital. She was really young to be in a ward full of strangers. She was in there to dry out but must have been so frightened by the way her life was going. When she came out, she was briefly put back into residential care until she was eighteen, then as soon as she could, she went back to Irene's before getting her own council flat and working for a while as a machinist in the local shirt works.

That was the first of many times that Mum would be admitted to Winwick. Since I've grown up, she's told me that much of the time she felt there was no point in living because her life was so shit. She felt like no one loved her, least of all her own mother, and that she was worthless. Dave couldn't offer her stability, either, so she looked for security in alcohol and relationships with other men. At times she felt so low she wanted to die, and it wasn't long before she slit her wrists in the first of several suicide attempts over the following ten years – by the time she was nineteen, she'd attempted suicide four times. She had nothing – no money and no close family who could give her the support she needed. Being involved in a serious car accident when she was eighteen can't have helped, either. She was thrown through the windscreen, leaving her face and head badly cut. A piece of glass lodged in her head, giving her terrible headaches until it was found by doctors months later. None of us really knows whether the effects of the accident are related to Mum's mental problems, but it's certainly true that after the crash she began to see-saw between incredible highs and severe bouts of depression – a pattern that's been part of the rest of her adult life.

Despite everything life threw at her, Mum still kept on trying to find stability. Always after a steady job, she and a friend found work on a Warrington building site together, cooking breakfasts and dinners for the men. That's where she met my real dad, a jobbing builder, and I was conceived during a weekend of passion while his wife was away. When Mum found out she was pregnant she was thrilled. By this point in her life, she was desperate to have a baby of her own to love and be loved by. My father was horrified. The only question he asked when she told him the news

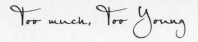

was, 'Is it mine?' She must have been having an off-patch with Dave then, so my father couldn't have been anyone else, but he had a wife and family of his own and he didn't want to leave them. Mum decided to go ahead with the pregnancy anyway. She was so excited about the idea of being a mum and promised herself that she would be the best mother in the world. She knew that my birth would make all the difference to her life.

On 6 September 1980, she went into labour and was admitted to Warrington General. She'd been drinking lager the night before and had a hangover that she still claims was worse than the labour pains. Nana Betty and our Angela went with her. Because Angela was only ten, the hospital staff wouldn't let her into the labour ward, so Mum was alone when she gave birth to me at twenty to ten that night. The hospital radio was playing Stevie Wonder's 'For Once In My Life', which has been her song for me ever since. One of the nurses took me off to be weighed and measured, and the first thing she said when she looked at me was, 'Oh my God. You want to see this baby's eyelashes.' Apparently they were so long they brushed my cheeks. The other thing Mum remembers noticing is that I had my father's coal-black eyes. I weighed 6 pounds 13 ounces and measured eighteen inches.

I was eight weeks old when my dad came to see me. Mum had popped into the nearby Farmer's Arms for a quick one and was told that someone wanted to see her. My dad had brought his brother and a friend along for moral support and asked if he could see me. They all came back to the house where Nan was looking after me. I was wrapped tightly in a shawl and apparently already looked the spitting image of him. He must have been drop-dead gorgeous! They all crossed my palm with silver, and as he held me, he cried and told Mum he loved her. She wasn't having any of it. 'Don't stand there and tell me you love me when you're going home to your wife,' she snapped, 'but you can come and see your daughter any time you like.' That was the last time she saw him, and of course I've never seen him at all. I guess you could say he's the missing piece of my jigsaw.

Mum's told me that by the time I was born Nana Betty and Denis had divorced, leaving Nan alone in Vulcan Close with fourteen-year-old Andrew and ten-year-old Angela, so Mum was able to move back there, taking me with her. Angela loved having a baby to play with and they love telling me how Nana Betty once persuaded Mum to go out to the Farmers with her for a half of lager while she had a half of Guinness. A half pint has never disappeared so fast in all of Mum's life because she was that anxious about leaving me with our Andrew. When she got home, she went straight to the carrycot. No Kerry. Our Angela was calling her from upstairs and Mum raced up there to find me lying on the floor dressed in Angela's dolls' clothes. She didn't leave me with them again. In fact, for three months she didn't touch another drink, sticking to water and tomato juice and dipping her crisps in that instead.

My dad had made it clear from the start that he wasn't going to stick around to support us, so Mum started seeing another boy, Vic Ferrier, while she was pregnant. He was a quick-witted lad who was a big fan of Rod Stewart and had the same spiky blond hair. He adored Mum and would do anything for her. Before long the three of us moved into a small second-floor flat in Grasmere Avenue on the Greenwood Estate, a pretty rundown part of the Orford area. Poor Vic had taken on more than he'd realized when he'd hooked up with Mum. He found it hard to deal with her mood swings and the way Mum would go out drinking, leaving me with him, Nana Betty or friends. She'd got a job back at the shirt works as a machinist by then and had found a whole new bunch of mates. The neighbours were always complaining about the noise and parties in the flat. Worst of all were the malicious anonymous reports made to the police saying that cigarette burns had been seen on my body. Imagine Mum's feelings when Nana Betty called her home from work because an NSPCC officer had called round while she'd been babysitting. Mum may not have been around much, but she would never have done anything to hurt me. All she could do was watch, crying her eyes out, as they laid me on the kitchen table and stripped me to check she was telling the truth.

Mum found it hard to cope sometimes, and things came to a head when a fire was lit in the rubbish bin just outside the flat by a lad who fancied her. She hadn't known he was a local arsonist when she turned him down! Fire engines and police arrived on the scene just in time to rescue us through the front window. Mum was badly shaken up by what happened. She was suffering from terrible depression and cut her wrists more than once. In addition to that her depression took away her appetite, so her weight dropped to six stone, nowhere near enough for a woman of five foot six. When she couldn't cope any longer she was read-mitted into Winwick Hospital, where she was finally diagnosed as manic depressive.

While she was there, either Vic looked after me in our new home, a modern purpose-built two-bedroom flat at 19 Guildford Close, or I was taken over to Nana Betty's, who always treated

45

me like one of her own, with Angela's help, of course. I was too young to know what went on then, but I'm not surprised to hear that those difficult times became too much for Vic. He was a young man and he must have felt that he'd taken on much more than he'd bargained for and certainly more than he could be expected to cope with. He stuck around for as long as he could, but in the end he couldn't take it any more, and after two years he left us.

Mum didn't let the grass grow under her feet. By then she'd got to know Vic's dad Arnie. Arnold 'Arnie' Ferrier had often babysat me when Mum and Vic went out. He was a truck driver who was thirty years older than her, divorced and living alone on the same estate at number 27. His five children were all older than Mum and didn't live with him any more. He worshipped Mum and very soon he asked her to marry him and, to all her friends' amazement, she accepted. So Mum's ex, Vic, became my step-brother and mum's step-son. How weird is that? Arnie knew Mum didn't really love him because she told him so on their wedding day. She truthfully admitted to him that she was going through with the marriage just so there would be some security for herself and, most importantly, for me. But he didn't care; as far as he was concerned he had a beautiful young bride. He must have hoped that she would grow to love him, so they went ahead and tied the knot on 26 November 1983 at Warrington Registry Office. Afterwards, Mum and three-year-old me moved into 27 Guildford Close to start our new life with Arnie, my 'Dad'.

3

FAMILY MATTERS

I'M THREE YEARS OLD. I'm wearing a short red pinafore dress over a long-sleeved white blouse. My white socks are pulled up to my knees above my shiny black patent shoes. My blonde hair is in bunches, tied with pink ribbons, and I've got a long fringe that goes over my eyebrows.

Mum and Dad have been rowing. I don't know what about, but the sound of them shouting is familiar even at that age. Mum has gone into their bedroom and I've gone to find her. I'm sliding in along the wall, worried by what's going on. She's sitting on the double bed crying, her legs hanging down next to the nightstand. She's very thin with slightly spiky, longish blonde hair. I'm facing her but she's too involved in what she's doing too take any notice of me. I see the light glint off something in her hand. I stand and watch as she runs a razor blade across her wrist once, then twice. Not understanding, I watch the blood streaming from her arm onto her tight blue jeans. I'm screaming and crying. Then suddenly our Pat, my step-sister who's two years older than Mum, rushes in behind me and carries me into the living room. I'm left there alone, feeling confused and scared.

That's my very first memory, and it's something no little girl

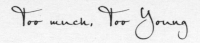

should ever see. Whenever I relive that scene, I'd like to reach out and pick that kid up and put her somewhere safe. I was the same age then as our Lilly, my youngest daughter, is when I write this. I could never do something like that in front of her. I couldn't put that burden on her. Just seeing my mum do that made me feel so unwanted, so unloved.

Mum would try to kill herself at least eight times throughout my childhood, so it was something I was going to have to learn to deal with. You can never get used to something like that. Every time she attempted suicide I'd feel guilty that I wasn't doing enough to make her want to stay alive, and confused because I didn't know what more I could do. Now I know that it would need an elephant gun to take my mum down, so looking back I think she was really crying out for help. Her depression made her believe she was a bad mother and that I'd be better off without her. But that was never ever true. Every child needs their mum, don't they?

Although Dad let Mum do pretty much what she wanted, or perhaps *because* he did, their relationship was stormy. She was so much younger than him that I bet he couldn't believe his luck at marrying such a good-looking young woman, and he was prepared to do anything to keep her, even if that meant allowing her to go out and enjoy herself on her own. He retired soon after they married and spent most of his days in a nearby pub, the Bear and Star. Mum worked long hours as a machinist during the day and was always going out in the evenings, sometimes having affairs behind his back and, during her manic periods, even disappearing for two or three days at a time without saying where she was going. I think Mum was just crazy to be loved. That's all she wanted. And I understand exactly how that feels. I think she thought she'd find love by being with other men, and I see that, in a way, Dad used me to get to Mum. As long as he had me at home, she would always come back. As far as I was concerned, her coming and going was just the way it was. If you're not brought up different, you don't know different.

I can see Dad now, sitting in the kitchen on his favourite black swivel chair by the breakfast bar, looking through to the living room on the other side, smoking one of his Old Holborn roll-ups, a whiff of Old Spice in the air. A car accident some years earlier had left him with a limp, and the keys he wore on a chain at his waist rattled when he walked. Behind his glasses he had beautiful blue eyes, and his white hair was always slicked back in a quiff. He was country and western mad, and wore cowboy shirts, boots and belts. I was brought up on his music, which was always blaring out of the stereo system, and it's because of him that I love George Jones, Neil Diamond, Motown and all those golden oldies from the Fifties and Sixties.

You could see the breakfast bar from the front door when you came into the flat, with my stool waiting right beside his. We'd sit there together while he taught me how to tell the time with a paper plate marked with a felt tip, using a knife and fork as the hands. On the other side of the bar was the living room with its patterned red carpet and a comfortable red velvet foam sofa. The flat was full of Eighties-style ornaments, the worst of them was a pottery horse pulling a pottery cart on the window sill. Mum's a big reader, but there weren't any books to be seen apart from some red leatherette-bound books which were actually video covers. The fireplace was really old-fashioned, with an electric fire that had red lights spinning under the plastic coals to make them look as if they were glowing. In front of it was a rug where every Saturday morning I'd sit with a bowl of Rice Krispies and half a cup of tea with three sugars, watching *Going Live* on the BBC. I loved all the cartoons that were on then – *She-Ra, He-Man, Jamie and the Magic Torch* and *Danger Mouse*. Over the fireplace there was a beautiful greeny painting of a naked woman and child on a velvet background that had been specially painted for Mum by a friend.

Best of all, I had my own bedroom, right beside Mum and Dad's room. It was tiny, like a boxroom – my bed just fitted the width of the room with a small window at its foot – but it was mine. Weeping Pierrot clowns looked down sadly from the pink wallpaper at the matching quilt cover. I had clown masks hanging on the wall too. Mum had made sure that I had a pretty place of my own to go to, just as she would whenever she could in all the different homes we shared.

Although I had all the Little Ponies and Barbies I wanted, I was a tomboy at heart. More than anything, I wanted a toolbox I'd seen in the Argos catalogue. I loved guns, too, because Dad and I watched old westerns together, and I dreamed of being a cowboy. I'd dress up and play cowboys and Indians whenever I could. I had a pop gun and I cut the cork and string off so I could push the tops of felt-tipped pens down the muzzle and fire them at playing cards lined up along the radiator. Once Dad even took me and one of his friends to a cowboy weekend at Peterborough Showground. We travelled in his lorry, so I slept in the bed at the back of the cabin. I was so excited about being dressed up as a proper cowboy with a scarf, hat, spurs and gun. It was brilliant.

People came from all over the world and there were marquees where different shows were laid on, while outside people sold western gear. I was even allowed to ride on the horses.

If Mum and Dad went to the pub together, the evening would often end in a fight. They would shout and hit each other while I hid in the closet in the corridor wishing they'd stop. Once she called the police for help and they turned up at the door to give Dad a warning. That frightened me. The police were often on our doorstep, but whether it was the neighbours who called them or Mum or Dad, I've no idea. I don't really remember Mum and Dad ever being happy together. Either Mum was out at work or with her mates or they were fighting. The only peaceful times I remember were Saturday and Sunday mornings. I wasn't allowed to get up early on my own so I'd sneak into their room, crawl under their bed so I came up on Mum's side in the gap between her and the sunbed she had against the wall and ask if I could go and watch telly. She'd whisper, 'Mmmm, OK, chick. Shhhh.' and I'd crawl out again. Dad would almost always catch me and I'd quickly run back to bed before there was any trouble.

Although their relationship was unpredictable, Dad never took things out on me, though if I did something wrong, he could go right over the top. Once I took one of the breakfast stools from the kitchen and turned it upside down on the living-room floor, then I sat inside it cross-legged, pretending to drive it like one of Dad's trucks while I watched a video of *Pinocchio*. He asked me to put the stool back in the kitchen so he could sit down, and when I refused, Mum supported me. 'Leave her, Arnie. She's all right.'

'Put it back now,' he insisted.

'Can't I stay in it for a bit longer?' I begged.

He took no notice but angrily snatched the stool and turned it upright.

'You're not my dad. You're a bastard.' At that age I hadn't a clue what I'd said. I didn't know he wasn't my real dad and I didn't know 'bastard' was a swear word. He was furious. To begin with my mum laughed as he chased me round the living room until I hid under the glass coffee table. He reached underneath and dragged me down the corridor by my hair, smacking my bum so hard that he left a red handprint there, then he threw me onto the bed in my room and I hit the wall beside it, shrieking. By this time, Mum was really upset. In all her life she's never once raised a hand to me. Never. And she wouldn't let anyone else, either.

Mum has always fought for me like a lioness fights for her cubs. When I was a kid, she wouldn't let anyone take advantage of me or do me down. Once, when I came home from school upset about something the head teacher had said, Mum wasn't having any of it. She stormed into school, found the head, took her by the lapels, angrily pulling her across the table, nose to nose, and threatened to hit her. Nobody was going to talk to our Kerry like that. I don't remember the head making the same mistake again.

Mum always made sure that I was dressed neatly and that I had all the toys I could have wanted. She was firm with me about how I behaved at home and when we went out, and never let me mess with any of the ornaments in the house. I got a reputation with her mates for being a good little girl. She and Nana Betty were proud as punch of me winning the *Warrington Guardian*'s Charming Child competition when I was three. The one thing she could never do, though, was persuade me to eat vegetables. Sunday dinner was always potatoes, meat and gravy. That was it, and it still is to this day. I was always a fussy eater. She even took me to the doctor when I went through a phase of refusing to eat anything but breakfast cereal. He reassured her that the milk and cereal would be enough until I decided to try something else, and of course I did in the end.

Whatever problems Mum had at home, we always enjoyed ourselves when it was just the two of us. If she had some spare cash, she'd take me on the bus for a day out to Blackpool. She was as much of a kid as me when it came to the rides at the Pleasure Beach and we screamed our heads off. One time, when she took me to Chester Zoo, I desperately needed a wee but we couldn't find the toilet. She told me to crouch down in a quiet spot by the lion's cage, which seemed like a good idea until the lion got wind of someone on his territory, strolled over, lifted his tail and sprayed me. I stank for weeks, but we've laughed about it for years. We share a wicked sense of humour and could talk to one another about anything. Because I was all she had, she treated me like a grown-up. Even when I was little I was more of a mate than a daughter to her. When times were good, I honestly wouldn't have had it any other way.

Nana and Grandpop Ferrier, Dad's mum and dad, lived in the flat directly below ours. Their flat was exactly the same as ours except that they had patterned glass by the breakfast bar so you couldn't see through into the living room. I would go down there whenever my dad or Mum went out. Nana Ferrier was a complete lady. Her thick white hair was immaculate and she always looked smart in one of her dresses, tights and high heels. One of my

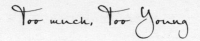

favourite games was sitting on her knee and playing with her big old-fashioned tin full of buttons. I used to tip them all out onto a beautiful antiquey wooden tray decorated with gold paint and arrange them in patterns.

Grandpop had been a sergeant in the army and a boxer as well. He was very tall, very smart and always smoked a pipe. I loved the smell of the smoke that crept into every corner of the flat. He'd sit content in his chair across the fireplace from Nana. Sometimes when I sat on his knee he'd make a penny appear from behind my ear. Or he'd say, 'Go check the rug.' And I'd jump off to find there was nothing there. Back on his knee, he'd make the penny disappear behind my ear, then tell me to check again. This time the penny would be under the rug. I was always amazed as to how he did it. To this day, I still don't know. He taught me how to skip and how to colour, so we'd spend ages at the breakfast bar with crayons and paper. In the living room, they had a red pouffe with a gold braid round it which I used to drag around the flat, pretending it was my horse or dog. But what I loved doing most was making up songs, which I'd sing all the time. Performing came easy to me, especially when I was egged on by their clapping and requests to sing something again.

Pat, their daughter, lived there too at the time. She was everything to me. If she could hear things kicking off upstairs, she'd come up and rescue me. I was with our Pat whenever I could be. Her auburn hair was like a fairy queen's and I'd press the flesh-coloured mole on her chin because it was my magic button. I was gutted when she had it removed. She used to take me to the gym to watch her training to become a body builder. We never dreamed then that she'd become Miss Universe in 1992.

There was a beautiful chest in our Pat's room, and with a turn of the key the sides opened out and the top came down releasing a gorgeous wood and leathery smell. I would sit there, pretending to be a secretary, and Nana would knock and say, 'Miss Ferrier. Would you like a cup of tea?' 'Yes, please,' I'd say. And she'd bring me half a cup with three sugars. Then I'd sit there writing and copying things out of their old books for ages. I loved staying there.

Christmas at Guildford Close was really special. I remember being dead worried that Father Christmas wouldn't come because we lived in a flat and there wasn't a chimney, so we'd leave a key for him under the mat outside, as well as a carrot, mince pies and a note. I'd go to bed early but be far too excited to sleep. I'd stare out of my bedroom window watching for him, convincing myself I could hear sleigh bells in the distance until I fell asleep exhausted from waiting to see him appear over the rooftops. In the morning, he would always have been, though I never saw him. We'd open our stockings and have Christmas dinner in the flat before piling downstairs to Nana and Grandpop's for drinks and a buffet with more of their family. Then we'd all sing karaoke. That was the bit that I loved most: I was in my element showing off to the grown-ups with them encouraging me.

The flats at Guildford Close were beautiful. We were in a quiet respectable area, surrounded by greenery, in one of three blocks of flats. Not many other children lived there, though, so if I played out it would be tennis on my own against the wall or riding my go-cart on the grassy hill over the wall behind our block.

One of the great excitements of the year was Warrington Walking Day, and Dad would draw me a little calendar, so that when he woke me up in the mornings we could cross off another day as we counted down. The whole town used to shut down for a day in July and us kids would walk through the streets in our school uniforms (ours were blue-and-white check), along with various church congregations, while people gave us money. Then we'd go to a big fun fair on the edge of town before all the family ended up in the pub.

If Nana and Grandpop Ferrier, our Pat or Nana Betty couldn't look after me after school or at weekends, Dad would take me to the pub with him. I spent so much time there that I decided I'd be a barmaid when I grew up. Dad would stand in a corner with his arm on the bar, drinking pints of Carling Black Label, while I played with the tough skin on the back of his hand, moving it around over his bones. He eventually taught me to play pool. I got so shit hot at it over the years that I can still beat most men. There were other kids there, too, who I'd run around with. Then in the evening I'd go to sleep on one of the pub's long padded seats covered by everyone's coats.

While Mum was married to Dad, I had an almost normal childhood. As far as I knew, I lived at home with my mum and dad, just like my friends. So what if I sometimes went to stay with my grandparents? I had no real idea of the difficulties my parents were going through. All that mattered to me was being with them, playing with my toys and being able to enjoy school with my friends. Everything changed in January 1987. Mum and Dad had been married for just over three years when he finally threw Mum out. I was only six. Mum would say she deserved it because of the way she treated him. She was drinking heavily and had even referred herself for treatment once but never kept the appointments. For nearly three years after that I lived with whoever would have me, sometimes with Mum but most often with Nana Betty or Dad. For the first six months or so after they separated, Mum lived on the streets, dossed with friends or came back to Dad's. By the summer, she was living in the Salvation Army Hostel. All she'd wanted was the best for us, but it had all gone wrong. Her marriage was over, she had nowhere to go and she didn't even have me with her. She's since told me that while she was living on the streets she tried to commit suicide more than once. She took an overdose and another time slit her wrists, believing I'd be better off without her. Now she knows that wasn't true, but at the time she believed it.

I was used to Mum not being around much and not knowing what was happening to her. Until I knew better, Dad and the Ferriers were my real family, and when I didn't have them, I had Nana Betty. Both of them gave me stable loving homes where I was allowed to be the kid I wanted to be. Mum moved me back and forth between the two of them as it suited her. According to her Social Services record, I was 'being used as a weapon whenever she [Mum] falls out with Mr Ferrier or Mrs Katona' and was 'constantly moved by her mother on a whim'. They also say that until Mum found somewhere more permanent to live, I was looked after occasionally by her friends. In the first six months of 1988, I lived at five different addresses as people tried to sort out a permanent arrangement for me. I knew that not every child moved about like that, but I was used to it. I didn't think twice about where I was sleeping. But wherever I went I almost always ended up back with Nana Betty.

I remember one episode that sums up what went on then and how torn I was between everyone. I must have been living with

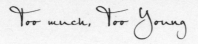

Dad when there was a sports day at Padgate C of E Primary School. All my friends and I were really excited about our families coming to watch the races. The sun was shining and I kept looking out for Dad, Nana, Grandpop and our Pat, who I knew would be there: I was in all the races for my year and wanted to do well in front of them. As the afternoon went on, I looked harder and harder for my family, sure they must be somewhere and that I had missed them. Everyone else had their mums and dads, brothers and sisters cheering them on, but as hard as I looked, no one came. At last, when all the races were over, our Pat turned up. She looked upset and hardly spoke to me until she broke the silence as we walked across the car park. 'You've got to go and live with your Nana Betty.'

'Why?'

'Because your mum wants you back,' was all she could say.

'Doesn't Dad want me any more?' I was so upset and didn't understand why I had to live with one or other of them. I was perfectly happy with my dad and desperately wanted all the fighting to be over. Why couldn't we just live with Dad?

We arrived home to find a police officer there with Mum, Nana Betty and our Ange. Dad was sitting in the kitchen at the breakfast bar, crying. A police officer took me and Mum into the bedroom to ask me whether I wanted to live with my mum or my dad. The officer was being kind, trying to put me at ease, not asking me to make the choice myself, but what a terrible question to ask a young kid. What could I say? I loved my mum, but I loved my dad, too. How could I choose between them? I don't know that I understood the full significance of what was going on, but I do remember feeling desperately sad and confused.

Mum was in the room with me, so of course I chose her. When they took me out of the flat Dad was screaming and crying, hugging me and holding on to me as if his life depended on it. My hands had to be unclasped from behind his neck as I was pulled away from him. As we got outside, I turned sobbing to see Dad standing at the glass-fronted stairwell looking down at us. Tears were streaming down his face as he waved me goodbye.

Being moved by the police seemed so final, as if I'd never see Dad again, but I loved living at Nana Betty's, too. She is the kindest woman in the world and would help anyone if she could. She and I used to have to share her double bed when I was little. I'd be squashed up against the wall, listening to the click of the snooker balls on the telly downstairs. Then when the match was over, she'd come up and climb in beside me wearing her nightie, hairnet and her star of David round her neck, and the three dogs – Candy, Cretia and Gismo – would jump on top of us. Nana was such a petite woman that there was easily room in the bed for all of us. She would lean back in bed with her arm behind her head so that I could just get a glimpse of her tit and her hairy armpit. Sometimes she'd lie there having a fag with a cup of tea and a ham and homemade pickle sandwich, occasionally scratching her upper lip with her little finger.

Nan makes the best brew in the world, leaving the teabag in right till the end and adding five sugars. Sometimes she'd even slip in a drop of whisky. She liked her sherry and dark chocolate as well. Candy, Cretia and Gismo, ran all over the house so it smelled of a mixture of dog and Shake 'n' Vac. There were loads of daft little dog ornaments everywhere. Meals were served on the dining-room table using paper plates with white plastic cups in

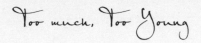

brown plastic holders so there wouldn't be any washing-up. My favourites were her Hungarian goulash and Sunday dinner, just before the *EastEnders* omnibus, but she never sat and ate them with us. She'd always be in the kitchen wearing one of those aprons that went over her head and tied at the sides, occasionally swishing in through the beaded door-hanging when she wanted to put something on the table, the slap of her flip-flops warning us she was coming. My nan loved a bargain and lots of our clothes came from car-boot sales. When I got veruccas once we all blamed a pair of trainers she'd bought me from a jumble sale.

I could never get enough of her stories about how she'd been a tap-dancer and a member of the Flying Ballet when she was young. The only thing that stopped her going off and touring with them was her mother, who was very strict and didn't like the idea of her daughter being part of a touring theatre company. To this day, Nana Betty has a picture of her self aged seventeen in pantomine costume hanging on her living-room wall opposite one of me in Atomic Kitten. Perhaps that's where I got my love of show business. I was certainly always performing for her, showing off, singing and dancing, just like our Molly does today for anyone who'll watch. Nana Betty would sit and clap for as long as I wanted her to, and when there was nothing on the telly, she'd switch it off and I'd dance in front of it, so my reflection made it look as if I was on TV. I'd happily entertain her and her friends for as long as they'd put up with me.

Nana worked at the Wasp Club, a club for six- to ten-year-olds that met once a week at Fernhead Youth Club. She'd give me 50p for crisps and pork scratchings and take me there to paint and play games. Sometimes we went to Blackpool, where we rode the donkeys on the sand and went on rides at the Pleasure Beach. The highlight of all the things we did at Wasps over the four years I went, though, was appearing in their production of *Cinderella* when I was about ten. I played Buttons and took over the show completely when everyone forgot their lines. I knew all the words and all the songs, so I just ad-libbed until I had everyone in the audience, including the Mayor and Mayoress, in stitches. That was the first time I got to show off to a proper audience, and it gave me a real taste of performing, so I guess I can thank Nana Betty for giving me the acting bug.

Andrew and Angela were much older than me. Andrew was nearly twenty by then and dead quiet and handsome. The only time we really got on together was when we drew tattoos on each other's arms with a pen, otherwise he was always busy doing his own thing. He'd recorded loads of films from the TV, which he kept filed in alphabetical order in his very tidy room, and we'd watch my favourites, *Some Like it Hot* and *Annie*, together sometimes. I idolized our Angela and she doted on me. I often wore her hand-me-downs and she was like a big sister watching out for me. Occasionally Nana Irene, Mum's real mum, would come round, although there wasn't much love lost between her and Nana Betty. Although I thought she looked just like my Mum, even as a kid I didn't get on with her. She was full of stories like the one about her being up in court for robbing a fur coat and getting off because she slept with the judge the night before. That was Nana Irene all over. Hearing about her adventures made us laugh, but Mum and I were what she used to be and she didn't like that – I could feel her jealousy even as a kid. My mum still had her looks and her youth, and I think our close

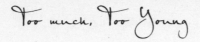

relationship must have reminded Nana Irene of what she'd missed out on with Mum.

There was a great community spirit on the estate where Nana Betty lived and there were loads of children who ran in and out of each other's houses. Every Bonfire Night we'd have a big fire in the yard in the middle of all the flats, which was just over our back garden fence, and the whole neighbourhood would get together and have a fantastic time. Nana would get out her accordion and play everyone's favourites all night, and we'd have competitions with nearby Valiant Close as to who could make the biggest bonfire. My godmother Hilda, an old pal of Nana Betty's, lived next door, and in the summer my nan used to put a blanket on the floor out the back of the house so we could have picnics out there together.

Everyone knew Nana Betty. She was always out and about on an old sit-up-and-beg bike, with a basket at the front; they kept getting stolen but she'd just buy another one cheap from Slippery Sid, a guy who dealt in dodgy stuff. I remember riding behind her while she warned me to mind my feet, as she pedalled down the road, taking me to Padgate C of E Primary, which was just over the road from where I used to live in Guildford Close. Then afterwards she'd pick me up and take me back home or to the Ferriers'.

Meanwhile, Mum hadn't limited her search for love to men, and had been seeing more of Tina Bates, a lesbian friend of hers and Vic's. By the end of 1987 she and Tina were living together. Dark-haired with very dark eyes, Tina had loads of tattoos, including a cross on her forehead and a devil on her neck, and later my initials on her leg and Mum's name across her toes. As far as I could see, Tina dressed like a bloke, thought like a bloke, sat like a bloke and behaved like a bloke. Perhaps Mum thought Tina would be more loving towards her than a man and that the relationship would be more caring. All I knew was that Mum and Tina couldn't have me with them all the time, although I stayed whenever she wanted me to. I don't remember her being around all that often and I don't think I really minded or noticed too much.

Mum and Tina were eventually given a one-bedroom council flat together in Greenwood Crescent. She wanted me to move in with them, but they didn't have room, so I'd just go and stay at weekends, sleeping in the little spare bed in their bedroom. I always looked forward to it. I got to know a few kids there so I could play outside and climb trees until it was time to go home, but it wasn't the same as being at Vulcan Close. The flat was small and Mum was obsessively house proud, so the red-and-white kitchen and large beige-and-brown living room were always spotless. I didn't think anything of the fact that she and Tina lived together. If that's where Mum found love, that was fine by me. Other people were less open-minded.

On my ninth birthday they let me have a party. I invited ten friends and Mum had worked hard in the kitchen so the table was covered in plates of food – sandwiches, biscuits and crisps – as well as a fruitcake with nuts round the side and a cherry on top. I was gutted because I didn't like it. I've still got a photo of me looking like a right little tomboy standing beside it all. My aunt was there with Mum and Tina. Together we waited for my friends. One o'clock came and went. Ten past. Quarter past. Then it was two o'clock and still no one came. So I sat there and

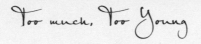

opened the pass the parcel and blew out my candles alone. None of my friends were allowed to come because their parents didn't like my mum being a lesbian. But Mum put the music on anyway and we danced without them. It would have been nice if they'd been there, though.

4

ALL
CHANGE

AFTER THREE YEARS of being moved from pillar to post, every-thing suddenly changed. I was only nine and I hadn't realized that Mum and Dad had been fighting a bitter custody battle over me. Dad wanted to have responsibility for me and challenged Mum's right to custody. He thought that because she was living with a woman she wasn't a suitable parent, and he didn't like the idea of me sharing their only bedroom. What he was offering was a much more conventional, stable set-up. All I knew was that I was taking it in turns to live with my mum, my nan and my dad.

As the battle had worn on, Tina pushed Mum to tell me that Arnie wasn't my real dad, pointing out that, as I was eight by then, I would find out one day and blame her for not telling me. Mum was adamant that she didn't want me to know but finally agreed. It can't have been an easy thing for her to do.

The three of us were in the garden at Nana Betty's when Tina suddenly announced, 'Arnie's not your real dad.'

I couldn't believe what she'd just said. If it was true that meant that Grandpop and Nana Ferrier, our Pat and her sister Jane, and most importantly Dad, weren't family at all. They were strangers. Everyone had lied to me.

'Well who is then?' I immediately wanted to know.

That's when Mum told me the truth: that my real dad had been married and had a little girl who was the double of me. Apparently he was a very nice man who had met me when I was eight weeks old but we hadn't seen him again since. I made her tell me over and over again. She was upset at having to go over it all but I was excited by what she was saying. Wow! Maybe there was someone somewhere who looked like me, because I certainly didn't look like anybody in Dad's family. They all had blue eyes, except for his son, Glen, from his first marriage. I was always asking, 'Is that where I get my brown eyes from then?' And everyone had always answered, 'Yes. That's where you get them from.' Now I knew that wasn't true.

I was so curious to meet my real dad that whenever I walked down the street, I'd be watching out for someone with blond hair and brown eyes like me. To this day I wonder what he looks like and how he would have been as a father. Mum said she thought a friend of hers might have a picture of him, but although I've asked her for it several times over the years, I was never shown it. I wonder if he loved my mum? I'd like to believe I was made out of love. I used to see my friends playing with their fathers who loved them. Would he be like that? I wondered what his daughter, my half-sister, was like. Endless questions ran through my head, and from that day on I wondered about him. As I grew up, I longed to be a daddy's girl, I wanted a different relationship to the one I had with Mum, one where we could share secrets and laugh at them together. Would he be proud of me? Would he understand when I felt down? I missed him then and I miss him now.

I didn't tell Dad that I knew he wasn't my real dad until after my ninth birthday. I didn't want to hurt his feelings, so I went on pretending nothing had changed until one day when we were sitting at the breakfast bar and he suddenly came out with, 'I believe your mum has told you a story about how I'm not your dad?'

I didn't know what to say. 'Yeah,' I murmured uncertainly. 'So what?'

'How do you feel about that?'

I felt very uncomfortable talking about it. 'Well, you're my dad and I love you,' I muttered. 'That's it.'

'Well I brought you up,' he said, taking my hand. 'And as far as I'm concerned, you're my daughter.'

Then we carried on with whatever we were doing. We didn't need to say any more, we knew where we were with each other.

The custody battle came to a head at the end of a weekend in April, 1989, when I'd been staying with Mum and Tina and had cried and cried because I didn't want to go home. Mum said simply, 'Well, you don't have to if you don't want to,' and immediately got in touch with Social Services. I don't think anything bad had happened at home, simply that we'd had a fun weekend and I wanted it to go on and on. That's what kids are like – they never want the good things to end. After that, I remember being taken out of school for the day. Mum, Dad and I were asked along to a meeting in the Winmarleigh Street Social Services offices. When we got there I was made to sit down and draw pictures. Then a man who must have been a family counsellor or child psychiatrist asked me what I thought my drawings meant. God knows what I drew but I couldn't understand what he was on about. They were just pictures to me.

Mum was finally awarded custody before Christmas just after I'd turned nine. At the same time, Cheshire County Council put me under a supervision order because of my 'unsettled life' and 'experience of several carers', both while I was with Dad and after their marriage was over, while Social Services continued to be concerned about Mum's 'anxiety attacks and bouts of depression'. I had to stay with Nana Betty for a few more weeks until Social Services rehoused Mum and Tina in a two-bedroom flat on Alder Lane. Now that they had a child they had to have an extra bedroom.

The area around Alder Lane was much rougher than Guildford Close, and I learned early on that you had stick up for yourself if you wanted to survive. There was a field at the back of our block where I often played with our Jack Russell, Pip, in full view of Mum, who watched me from the kitchen window. All the kids played there and someone had hung a rope and an old tyre from a tree to make a swing. A girl pushed me off it one day and refused to let me have another turn, so I ran home crying. But all Mum said when I went in was, 'I'm going to smack you if you don't go outside right now, push her off and get back on it yourself.' She'd never smacked me and I didn't want her to start, so out I went and head-butted the girl, just as Tina had taught me. The moment I felt my head smack into her face, I regretted what I'd done. I felt so sorry that afterwards I went round to her house and apologized to her mum. Perhaps Mum wasn't always right.

We soon settled down in Alder Road as a family, but it wasn't a family like everyone else's. For a start, I was living with two lesbians, even if one of them was my mum. There was always drink and drugs about the place and lots of parties, laughing, shouting and fighting. Everything revolved around the pub, but I loved going there. There was always a great atmosphere and everyone was pissed and seemed so happy. True, those evenings often ended up in fights when we went back to someone's house, but to me that was just a way of life. Sometimes when Mum and Tina were partying or things were kicking off between them I'd stay at Nana Betty's – I was in and out of there all the time. Now that I was older I no longer slept with her but in one of the bunks in our Angela's room. I never minded going round there and some of my happiest memories are from those days.

With Mum and Tina I was expected to be much more grown up than I had been before. Dad and Nana Betty had always let me be a child, a free spirit. Now, if I wasn't at school, I was expected to join in with Tina and Mum. They were both on the social so money was always tight, and if we needed cash, we'd rob the TV metre. Somehow we had a key for it and could open it and take out what we wanted. Sometimes Mum would get dodgy £50 and £20 notes from one of her mates and send me to spend them in the shop so we could get the change. No one ever suspected a nine-year-old blonde kid of passing off fake currency. I didn't really understand what I was doing at the time anyway, so I always looked dead innocent. Sometimes we'd rob little things we needed from shops – I remember doing runners from places all the time. Quite a lot of our stuff was stolen from cata-logues. Mum just used false names so that when the debt collectors turned up, we could honestly say those people didn't live there. When the bailiffs turned up, as they frequently did, we'd hide or plead poverty. Looking back, I'm horrified by what we got away with, but I didn't know enough to question it. I was just a kid who did whatever her mum told her to, and Mum was just trying to get by.

Tina gave me a mountain bike for Christmas. I was over the moon about getting something I'd wanted for ages, but I didn't have it for long before the bike got a slow puncture. Our Pat used to come and pick me up every fortnight to spend the day with her, and she took me off to buy a new inner tube from Warrington Market. I was dead excited that I'd soon be riding the bike round the estate again, but when we got home I saw a girl riding my bike down the street.

I ran after her shouting, 'Hey. What are you doing? That's not your bike. It's mine.'

'No, it's not,' she said, wheeling to a stop.

'It is mine,' I insisted. 'I've just been out buying a new tyre for it.'

'Well, your mum's just sold it to my mum.' And she cycled off home.

Mum had needed the money so she'd got rid of the one thing that really mattered to me. How could she? At that moment, I really hated her. I was left gutted, holding the inner tube while the girl pedalled away.

I remember being left alone a lot of the time while Mum and Tina went out. I just looked after myself, eating tomato ketchup sandwiches, watching TV and going to bed when I got tired. I was perfectly happy until it got dark when, thanks to all the videos I'd watched, I began to hear poltergeists and ghosts in the flat. Then I was scared stiff and had to hide in bed or put something else on to take my mind off it. I still loved watching *Annie*. I identified with the little American orphan girl who wins over the heart of millionaire Daddy Warbucks as she looks for her real parents. Although I may not have realized it at the time, I think I knew in my heart of hearts that life could be better than the one we had. My friends weren't left alone at night or taken along to pubs and parties like I was. All I wanted was for my own Daddy Warbucks to come along and make everything OK.

One of the good things about living there was that I had my own proper bedroom. Instead of weeping Pierrots gazing from the wall there were rainbows and clouds racing across a blue background with a big blue paper lampshade hanging from the ceiling. I could lie in my pink-sheeted double bed watching the big old TV I'd been given or playing Centipede, Space Invaders and Pac-Man on my Atari. There was even room for a dressing table.

All my toys were kept in there, but Mum used to get dead angry when I didn't tidy them up when she asked me – show me a kid who does! While I was at school, she'd go in there armed with a black bin bag and fill it with anything that wasn't neatly put away, so that when I came home from school everything would be in the bin. She threatened to keep on doing that every fortnight until I started cleaning my room, but in the end she'd always replace what she threw away. My room was just the tip of the iceberg when it came to keeping the flat tidy. Mum was forever doing housework, washing, dusting, hoovering. She once refused to let me make a sandwich because I'd make crumbs. Her cleaning got so out of control that she had to be treated at Winwick again, this time for obsessive–compulsive disorder, which was related to her manic depression.

Now that I was older, I was more aware of how much I had

to tread on eggshells while living with Mum. Tina and I had to be so careful not to upset her. Times when she was happy would be followed by stretches when she was so low she couldn't see any point in carrying on. I realized she'd slashed her wrists again when she rolled up her sleeves to wash the dishes once and I saw the bandages, but I was also aware that if I wasn't around, giving her a reason to live, she'd be dead. That felt like a big responsibility for a little girl. But in a weird way, because I was always there, I learned what to do when she was down, and that made us even closer.

When she had to go into Winwick, I'd stay with Tina. She was very good with me, a bit like a big sister. She'd let me swear and we'd have a laugh together, especially when we teased Mum about her obsessive tidying up. She used to take me to the pub with her, and to Blackpool, but a lot of the time we'd just stay at home playing cards or Frustration and drinking Coke.

We used to go and visit Mum in hospital together. Once we found a wallet with fifty quid in it on the way there and split it between us. I hated visiting Mum. Her arms were bandaged and she was shaking and crying, apologizing and telling me she loved me. I didn't feel upset, just awkward, as though I had to play the grown-up again and be sensible. 'Don't worry, Mum. It'll be all right. Don't worry. I love you, too.' She made me feel lonely, no good and unwanted. I thought that if she had wanted me she would never have tried to kill herself. I should have been enough to make her want to stay alive. I hated seeing her cry and couldn't wait to get out of there. Of course I didn't understand then about manic depression and what it can do to people. Now, having had my own battle with depression, I can sympathize much more because I know better what she must have been going through.

As well as changing homes, I had to change schools, and was soon enrolled at St Ann's Primary. I never found it hard going to a new school. I went to so many – eight by the time I was thirteen – that I got used to it. School became a great escape from what went on at home. I always loved art, drama and music and whenever we put on a show at school I was there, singing and dancing. We did a great rock 'n' roll show one year at St Ann's where we did the jive and the twist and sang 'Yellow Submarine' and 'Ob-La-Di Ob-La-Da'. It was brilliant. I found it easy to make friends and always settled in quickly. I had to. My best friend at St Ann's was Louise Appleby. After school, we'd go to each other's homes and shut ourselves in the bedroom for hours with a 'keep out' sign on the door and play Atari, watch telly, or dance in front of the mirror to the Jackson 5.

Although Mum and Tina's relationship didn't bother me, I'd learned that other people didn't like it one bit. I've always thought this was really unfair. After all, Mum's a human being just like the rest of us, and if she wanted to be loved that way, that was fine by me, and as far as I was concerned it ought to have been fine with others too. What I didn't like was the way people judged her, and then judged me because my mum was a lesbian. And kids can be the worst.

One of my school friends came round to the flat and went home to her parents full of the 'perverted' paintings my mum 'the lesbian' had in the house. She meant the velvet painting of the naked woman and child that we'd had when we lived with

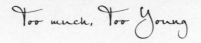

Arnie and a popular Eighties painting from Woolworths of a swan carrying a naked man and woman on each of its long wings. Hardly hard porn! Without seeing the pictures for herself, her mum went straight to the school gates and told all the other mums.

On the way home from school the next day, two girls started following me, calling my mum and Tina names. I tried to ignore them but it was impossible, then they grabbed hold of me in full view of the headmaster and gave me a good hiding. I made sure I gave as good as I got until one of them held me down while the other one bit my bum. That was their victory. I arrived home and showed Mum the teeth marks. She burst into tears when she saw the state I was in and went straight round to see the girl who'd spread the rumour about the pervy paintings and her mother.

Her father put her off, saying he was going out, but Mum shouted, 'You're going nowhere. Not until you've spoken to me.' She walked past him into the house, so he had no choice but to follow her and apologize for his daughter's behaviour.

The next day I begged her not to come to school with me but she wouldn't listen. She marched into school and insisted on confronting the head, and when he wasn't as apologetic as she thought he should be for not having stepped in, she punched him. I was standing outside the office, dying of embarrassment as I listened to what was going on behind the door. She went right over the top but I guess her only concern was for me. We had to stick together.

Perhaps having Tina as a father figure made me become more tomboyish. My hair was long at the back, shaved at the sides and spiky at the front, and one of the dinner ladies even mistook me for a boy. I much preferred hanging out with the lads. I also joined a brass band called Free Spirit which used to meet in the park behind Alder Lane and enter competitions. Pictures show me standing proudly in my black-and-pink uniform with neatly pressed white trousers, black jacket, a pink-and-white sash over one shoulder and a white stetson. I was ace on the triangle and cymbals! And eventually I learned to play the drums too. Tina once organized for us to go and play outside Mum's window when she was in Warrington General having a hysterectomy.

Over the months, Mum and Tina's relationship became more and more explosive. Tina was very possessive of Mum and seemed to grow jealous of her relationships with other people, even with me, so that I wasn't even allowed to give Mum a kiss or a cuddle in front of her. They'd have terrible rows that seemed to start over nothing but would soon turn violent. Once she threatened to kill us both. But it could go both ways: Mum completely lost it one night when Tina hit her. Mum picked up a knife that was lying on the side in the kitchen and, when Tina turned away, she stabbed her in the back, screaming, 'You'll never hit me again.' Mum sobered up bloody fast when she saw Tina pouring blood and phoned the ambulance immediately, telling them she'd knifed her friend. Fair play to Tina, though, because when the police and ambulance men arrived, Tina didn't grass Mum up. 'No, she never. She's making it up,' she insisted. 'Someone jumped me when I came out the pub.' They were taken to the hospital together where they were told that if Tina hadn't been turning away when the knife went in, it would almost certainly have punctured her lung. That's one of many incidents that Mum will admit she's not proud of. But that's

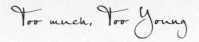

what life at Alder Lane was like: unpredictable and violent, but never dull.

Our stay at Alder Lane ended after about eighteen months when Dave Wheat came back into the picture. I know now that Mum had seen him on and off while I was a kid, but up until then I'd never met him. The first time I saw him was a few months after Tina and Mum finally split up, after Tina stabbed Mum's hand with a hunting knife. Don't ask me where that came from!

Mum had been out as usual and I was in bed when she got back and came in to talk to me. Dave followed her, so drunk that he fell on the floor, laughing. I stood there, dressed in my all-in-one red zip-up pyjamas, staring at him and thinking, Oh my God.

My first impressions were confirmed when, a few nights later, I was alone in the house and Mum brought some friends back from the pub. They were laughing and shouting in the living room when she came into my room to tell me Dave had asked her to marry him. I don't know why but I knew she shouldn't and I said, 'Please don't, Mum. Please don't. He's going to hurt you.'

'Don't be silly, Kerry,' she reassured me. 'He won't. I've known him for sixteen years and he's never laid a finger on me.'

I wouldn't give up, though. Something told me it wasn't going to work and I kept on at her, 'Mum, please don't. He's going to beat you up bad. I know he is.'

She wouldn't listen. But later that night, everyone had gone except an ex-girlfriend of Dave's. She was a proper down-and-out heroin addict known as Crater Face and she wanted money for herself and for her six-month-old baby, who she'd brought with her, claiming Dave was the father. I'd gone to bed but I could hear raised voices – not that that was anything new after a few drinks.

Apparently she told Mum that Dave had slept with her the night before and that did it. Mum slapped her and Dave went mad, dangling the baby out of the window and threatening to drop him. I could hear Crater Face screaming while I lay in bed, burying myself under the bedclothes and putting my fingers in my ears. I knew Mum and Dave were bladdered and there was nothing I could do.

Dave set about this woman, beating her up until she passed out. When everything went quiet, I got up and went down the corridor into the living room where the baby had been left to cry. I took him back to bed with me, changed his nappy and gave him some of the bottled apple purée that was tucked under his blankets. When his mum came round she trailed down the corridor behind us and I let her crawl into bed with us, despite the fact that she'd wet herself and stank of alcohol. She murmured that she knew my real dad before drifting off to sleep. 'He's in a pub nearby,' she said. 'He's always watching out for you.' She hadn't been there long before Dave and Mum came in to take her and the baby away. The sound of Dave hitting her again as they left made me feel sick, and I slid down my bed, breathing in the smells they'd left behind and thinking about what Crater Face had said. I wondered if she really knew my dad or if it was just drunken ramblings. I couldn't forget what she'd said, though, and started thinking all over again about how much I missed him. It was hard not to wonder how different things might have been if he'd still been around.

The violence scared me, even more so when Mum was on the receiving end of it. A few nights later, I was watching *Chancer* on TV, totally gripped by all that wheeler-dealer stuff. I had no idea where Mum was but guessed she was out with Dave. I heard the front door slam and turned to see her stagger into the room. She stood, propping herself up against the doorway, her left arm in plaster. She was in a terrible state, bruised and crying, as she tried to tell me what had happened. They'd been out drinking and had gone back to his flat to bed. For no reason she could remember, he had another Jekyll and Hyde moment, and without warning, he pulled her out of bed onto the floor and jumped on her, bruising her badly and breaking her arm. Then he made her sit naked in a chair while he held a sawn-off shotgun to her head. God knows what was going through his head. Although Nana Betty was only seconds across the road, Mum couldn't get out of there. She was in agony but still confronted him: 'Go on then, Dave. Shoot me. Just do it. Do it, because I'm not scared of you.'

He looked at her, put the gun down and started crying. Then he got up, put Dr Hook on the stereo, singing 'Like the Movies', opened the door and said, 'You can go.'

We hurriedly packed a few things and went to stay with a friend of Mum's and her husband who lived nearby. When they heard what had happened they agreed that we could stay for a couple of weeks, but the next morning the police turned up at the house to see us. The one thing Mum would never do was grass Dave up, so she was horrified when she realized that someone had anonymously tipped them off. They took her to the station where they photographed her bruised breasts, face, neck, back and broken arm. At the time she agreed to press charges of assault against him, but Mum could never go through with something like that and as soon as she left the station she dropped the charges. They fought like cat and dog at times, but

Mum isn't a vengeful person and would never be responsible for Dave going back inside. We were both frightened by the idea of what Dave might do when we returned to Alder Lane. Mum was scared that he would think she'd grassed him up, and we both knew he wasn't a man to cross. Social Services recognized the danger too and arranged for us to be taken into hiding somewhere he wouldn't be able to find us.

The next day Tom, one of the Child Protection Team assigned to our case, picked us up and drove us away from Warrington to our new home. As usual I was the one who was in control, trying to act the grown-up and comfort Mum. But how could a ten-year-old properly understand what was going on in her head. I had no idea what she really felt about Dave and about leaving Warrington. On the way, I remember we stopped at a BP garage where Tom bought me a packet of Maltesers. He was a gentleman. He took us to a Women's Aid refuge, a large five-storey Victorian house somewhere in Harper Hay, Manchester. Mum was nervous and still very shaken by what had happened, but Tom kept saying there was no chance of Dave being able to track us down. I was scared too but at the same time, a bit of me was dead excited to be going somewhere new, away from everything that had happened at Alder Lane. This was the new start I'd hoped for.

5

REFUGE

WE TURNED INTO A DEAD-END street in a rough-looking part of Manchester where the houses were all really run-down and bags of rubbish overflowed onto the pavement, then we pulled up outside a large red-brick house. It was much bigger and more imposing than anywhere we'd lived before, but paint was peeling off the front door and dirty, scrappy curtains hung at the windows, giving nothing away about what was going on behind them. The basement windows were so dirty that I couldn't even see inside. We took the little luggage we had into the hallway, where we were welcomed by Sally and Heather, the women who ran the refuge. They immediately made us feel at home, explaining the rules of the house and showing us our room, the shared kitchen, dining room, living room and bathrooms. I'd seen one or two kids staring at us in the corridors, and I soon went off to explore and discovered a supervized play area in the basement. There was always a member of staff down there, or one of the mothers. They made sure we were properly looked after, and if any of the mothers went out at night, there were always at least two of them left behind to babysit – everyone was especially careful because of the risk of someone coming and taking or harming one of us kids.

We were given our own room, which Mum made as comfortable as she could for us. We had a big double bed that we shared at night. Mum refused to use the second-hand bedding the refuge gave us and used her money from the social to buy all new. We had a telly and a video, so it was almost like having our own little flat. I was never allowed to mess up the room. In fact, Mum kept it so tidy that everybody else, whose rooms were always messy, wanted to spend their evenings in comfort with us. We had no idea how long we'd be there, but from now on this was our new home – just the two of us alone together.

Inside the refuge were women of all ages and nationalities and from all walks of life. There were prostitutes, addicts, and people like us – all of us suddenly homeless because we'd all had to run away from someone who was violent, threatening or abusive. We met some of the loveliest women in there, and everyone had a story to tell. Hearing them made us both feel a little bit better about our own situation – perhaps we weren't so badly off after all. I especially remember an Indian woman who was in the refuge with her beautiful little daughter. Her husband had sexually abused the little girl before pouring a kettle of boiling water over her private parts, causing her lasting physical damage. At least we hadn't had to deal with anything like that.

Mum's injuries were already on the mend, although looking back on it I can see that the damage Dave had done to her must have gone a lot deeper than I realized at the time. She had felt rejected by people all her life as she battled for survival; she must have felt so worthless and unloved. Falling in love should have been the saving of her, but when Dave treated her so violently, I imagine she felt total despair, as if she had no one. There she was, a single mum, living alone in a strange city, with no money and no home. This wasn't like the other times when things had gone wrong for her. She must have been at a loss for what to do next and exhausted by the thought of having to start over. I'd have felt like giving up: the future must have looked so bleak.

Going back to live in Warrington wasn't an option now, so Mum applied for housing to Manchester Council and we waited for them to come up with somewhere permanent for us to live. Meanwhile Tina came to visit every now and then, and one weekend Mum went to visit her, but something went wrong and they had another of their fights. Mum came back to the refuge bruised and frightened that the refuge workers would throw us out. In fact, they were sympathetic when they heard what had happened, but our stay at Harper Hay was over and we were moved to another refuge.

This time we went to large modern building in Longsight in another part of Manchester. It had marble floors and large open rooms with plenty of light shining through the net curtains. There were also two kitchens. Mum decided to use the cleaner of the two, of course, and carefully locked our supplies in our allocated cupboard. There was a big garden where they held parties on warm evenings. We got on really well with everyone there and I was happy, going to a new school in the day and playing with friends in the house at night. Although she was only thirty-one, Mum became known as 'Top Dog', just like Bea in *Prisoner Cell Block H* – people were always doing things for her. You weren't supposed to drink in the house, but when they got to know and like Mum, the staff even smuggled in two bottles of cider for her one night. They spoiled her rotten.

Too much, Too Young

One morning I woke up as usual in our bunk beds to the sound of the TV, which Mum kept on all night. Suddenly Dave's name leaped out from a news report. I jumped out of bed and turned up the volume so we could hear. He had escaped from jail and was on the run. The police were warning the public not to approach him because he was dangerous and might be armed. Mum was stunned but kept quite calm, confident that if Dave did find us, he wouldn't hurt her. How she was so sure I'll never know, perhaps she just said it for my sake. The police turned up at the refuge, wanting to know if Mum had any idea where Dave might be. She hadn't. They even bought her some hair dye so she could dye her blonde hair jet black in an attempt to disguise herself, and I had my hair permed. It all seemed pretty stupid to me, since I was sure Dave would be able to recognise the two of us together whatever our hair looked like. Fortunately there wasn't a chance to be proved right because they caught up with him in Blackpool after he stabbed a security guard with a pen. This time he was banged up in Parkhurst. He wouldn't be bothering us for a bit.

At long last Manchester Council found us emergency housing in New Moston – our very own house with stairs – and yet another school for me. Julie, one of Mum's friends from the refuge, came and lodged with us after she'd got kicked out of her house, which was great company for Mum. Thanks to the decorating grant she was given, Mum and Julie did the whole place up and filled it with all her bits and pieces from Alder Lane, including the famous 'pervy' pictures, which had been in storage. Outside in the garden, they cut back the knee-high grass so I could play there. Plenty of other girls from both the refuges we'd stayed in had been rehoused in the same area, so they often came round for a drink or we'd go to theirs.

But despite everything going well on the surface, Mum was increasingly miserable. All I knew was that she was out drinking all the time. Once she didn't come back for three days. I had no idea where she'd gone so just stayed at home. I didn't even go to school until she came back. One night she went out drinking with some women she knew, leaving me to babysit one of their children. By the time she came home, I was in bed. When she came into my room and leaned over me to give me a kiss, I could smell drink and fags on her breath. I was going to sleep when suddenly I heard her scream from the bathroom. Julie ran to see what had happened and found Mum had slit her wrists again. Together we comforted her and bandaged them up before Julie took her to the hospital.

Every time this happened I wished I could run away. I just wanted to escape from the life we had, so she wouldn't want to attempt suicide again. I longed for the ordinariness of life with Nana Betty or Dad. Why couldn't Mum be like them? I didn't get it. At eleven years old, I felt helpless but I also felt responsible. I thought that if I was a better daughter, she might not want to kill herself, but I didn't know how to be better. Afterwards, she would have forgotten what she'd done – only the bandages reminded her – and she was always so sorry. I'd stroke her hair, trying to make her see that everything was all right, but it was as if I could never do enough. She would sit crying, drinking, saying what a bad mother she was and wishing she was dead. She couldn't help herself. If I couldn't make her feel better, I'd stay in my room out of the way so I didn't make things worse.

On her thirty-second birthday Mum went out all day. Left at

home alone, I decided to do something special for her. Wearing my red all-in-one pyjamas, I sat cutting out coloured paper I'd found upstairs and gluing it together to make paper chains. Then I made a big poster that read 'HAPPY BIRTHDAY MUM'. I waited for her to come home, knowing she'd love the things I'd made for her. Eventually she came back, but she was with some bloke and they were both pissed. She was pleased with the decorations and we were having a laugh, but the next thing I knew this guy started poking fun at me. Mum thought he was joking and went along with it, but then he turned round and spat in my face. It was as if time stopped still in that moment and Mum and I just looked at each other. I was so shocked that I burst out crying and couldn't stop. The whole day was ruined. Mum never said anything to him or threw him out. I escaped to my bedroom as soon as I could, and while I lay there, I could hear them having sex in the next room. That wasn't the first time I'd heard those noises, and whenever I did, I felt sick and alone and longed to be back in Warrington.

Our life veered from one extreme to another, bad times alternating with good. Mum's down times would be replaced by periods when it was as if she was flying, she was so up. I didn't understand at the time that these mood swings were symptoms of her illness; I just looked forward to when things would get better, which they usually did.

Mum and I have the same quick wit and we've always bounced off each other, making each other laugh with things that no one else finds funny. Once she took the ladder away when I was up in the loft, sitting in my 'jamas with my legs dangling down through the hole. I cried as she teased me: how was I going to go to the shop now that I was stuck there? How would I be able to do the dishes? To get back at her, I hid in her wardrobe one day so that when she opened the door I was standing there with a monster face and my hands like claws. I honestly thought she'd die from the shock. I know it sounds weird, but they were the kinds of things we couldn't stop laughing at.

Once we were walking home from school playing a rhyming game.

'Book,' I said.

'Hook,' she came back.

My turn. 'Fook.'

'Kerry!' she protested, laughing.

'But Mum, it rhymes,' I insisted, laughing too.

And another time we went canoeing on the canal on an outing organized by the refuge, and she tipped up my canoe. Very funny. And so we went on.

As part of the refuge's aftercare service, we got taken on our very first holiday. I was so excited. I knew that proper families went on holiday together, sometimes abroad and sometimes to the seaside. Mum and I had never done either – that was what *other* people did. We had great days out, like trips to the zoo or Blackpool Pleasure Beach, but we'd never stayed anywhere for a whole week. Six other women and their kids from Manchester refuges were sent to Pontins in Blackpool for a week. We were given spending money and our fares were all paid for. I'd never been anywhere like it. Although Mum and I had been to Blackpool on day trips, Pontins was something else. It was dead exciting. Mum and I had our own apartment and, like the others,

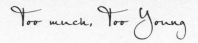

we were close to all the action so I was free to join in with the kids' activities and see the shows. I entered all the competitions I could and won the lot. Mum begged me not to enter any more because she was sure the others would think it was a fix. I was the best Kylie Minogue and won best dancer three times. I loved getting up on stage in front of an audience – singing and dancing was what I did best. We had the most brilliant time ever, and there was nothing to remind us of what we'd left behind. Mum was relaxed and happy, enjoying herself with the other women, and I could just go off and enjoy being a carefree kid for a change.

We'd only been in our house for six months when Mum arranged a house swap with someone who particularly wanted to be in New Moston. We packed up our stuff and went off to Viola Street in the Clayton area, where we had a two-up three-down red-brick Victorian terraced house. All the houses in the streets around us were the same, and my seventh school, Seymour Street Primary, was just around the corner.

In that one year in Manchester I went to four different primary schools, so as you can imagine I didn't make any lasting friends. I just learned to get on with the kids I was with and enjoy the moment. If my schooling suffered, I wasn't aware of it, and in any case, I was learning other things that would set me up for life. I still love meeting new people and making new friends, and the fact that we never stayed long in one place gave me the ideal background for being in a band because it meant I didn't mind being on tour. I was used to being on the move. As for Mum's mood swings and the way they affected me? I learned that though things get bad, they also get better again.

Life was far from the one I imagined my schoolfriends had. I don't suppose their mums went off for days without warning. Once she'd signed the income support book, I doubt they had to go down to the Post Office on Tuesday to cash it. I'd give Mum her spends then hide the rest so we'd have enough for the shopping. I went out and bought what I needed when I needed it and mostly lived off tomato ketchup butties, though I tried to get food in for when she came home. The only thing I regularly bought for myself was a Dime bar.

One time, Mum had been gone for a few days and I had to go out and get some food. I remember walking past Seymour Street School and looking in at the kids in the playground. I so wished I was in there with them, where I should have been, instead of going down the road for the shopping.

When I got home from the shops the house was still empty. I didn't have a key but I was sure Mum would be back soon. I had to sit on the step for an hour in the freezing November cold and wait for her to come straggling up the street.

'Where have you been, Mum?'

'None of your business,' she replied, opening the front door. 'I'm starving, Kerry. Make me my tea.'

'No I won't.' I was so angry with her. 'You've not been here for three days and now you want me to make your tea. Well, I'm not going to.'

'Make me my tea or get up those bleeding stairs now,' she shouted. 'You're grounded.'

I slammed upstairs. I was furious she was so unfair. I hated her right then. After a while I was so hungry that I crept back down again. 'Where's my tea?' was all she could say to me, so I made us chips and a tinned steak and kidney pie. We had half each, but she didn't even finish hers.

Life limped along in the same up-and-down way. I went to school when I wasn't needed at home to look after Mum, and she did her best to provide a home for me. We had a special Christmas that year. She managed to get us a small tree but we didn't have any money for proper presents or decorations. She was so upset that she hadn't been able to get anything more than one or two tiny tokens for me. Then, on Christmas Eve, someone arrived from the refuge laden down with two big black bin bags stuffed full of food and presents. Mum and I were made up. We got a Batman game, a love-heart teddy, a recorder, smelly sachets to put in our knicker and sock drawers, toiletries and perfume. Amongst all the food, there was even a festive tin of corned beef! On Christmas Day, Julie and Mum brought the table from the kitchen into the front room, lit candles on the mantelpiece and table and put up a couple of paper chains. Then we had a proper Christmas dinner surrounded by decorations and the tree. It almost felt normal.

Every fortnight, our Pat would come and collect me so I could go back with her to Warrington or stay with Nana Betty. I used to cry a lot for our Pat when she wasn't there. Sometimes I couldn't wait to get out of the house and away from Mum, who was on so much medication for her depression that she wasn't herself. My 'relatives' in Warrington were all very worried about how I was being looked after, but as Social Services reported, I was a kid who always 'bounced back'. Once, when things were bad in Manchester, I went off with Pat and phoned Mum from Warrington to say that I didn't want to come back. Mum knew that she wasn't in a fit state to look after me, so she let me go back to Dad's for a few weeks. Perhaps not having me on the scene was a relief to her and one thing less to worry about or feel guilty over. Not being around her was certainly a relief to me, although I cried a lot with guilt. I hated the idea that I'd left Mum all alone when I was all she had. I could imagine her coming home pissed all alone to an empty house and felt a huge sense of responsibility for her.

I've since learned that kids who find themselves in a situation like mine often feel that they are the only ones who can look after their parent and make sure they're safe. I certainly didn't think that anyone else could look after Mum like I could. Nobody understood her the way I did, and I was afraid that something would happen to her if I wasn't there. I suppose I wanted to be needed by her, because if she needed me, I'd never lose her, even if we weren't always living together. In a way, we fed off each other's needs.

Just after my twelfth birthday I moved in with Nana Betty again. She offered to foster me, but she didn't want to do anything that might upset Mum. She knew that Mum trusted her and relied on her to look after me. I was so happy to be back there at last with people I knew and loved, and where life was ordinary. I started at secondary school, Padgate High, just a short walk from Vulcan Close. It was the eighth and final school I would go to.

I made some good friends there, including Lisa Rhodes, who's my best friend to this day. She lived round the corner from Nana Betty with her mum and dad, two brothers and sister. She had been in and out of my life since we were babies, even briefly

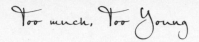

coming with her mum to stay with Mum and me in Guildford Close. She was taller than me, with straight brown bobbed hair, her train-track braces showed when she spoke or smiled and she dressed trendily, even then. She was in the year above me and used to boss me around like anything. I've made up for it since though! We used to take it in turns to say sorry whenever we fell out because it happened so often. She and her mates used to make me stand in the middle of a circle and egg me on to sing Michael Jackson songs and moonwalk for them. I loved that they thought I was good at it. They'd make me do it again and again and I happily would – any chance to show off was fine by me. We had loads of friends on the estate and we used to play out all the time around the houses. For the next three months I finally got to lead a normal life, doing the things most kids do, until things went pear-shaped again at Christmas.

As far as I can remember, I hardly saw Mum during that time. She was living with a new boyfriend in a caravan somewhere and there was no room for me. What I do know is that she was re-admitted to Winwick Hospital at the end of 1992, suffering from alcohol abuse. As we were having our Christmas dinner that year, there was a knock on the door. It was Mum, looking dead tired and thin. Our Andrew didn't want her causing any trouble so he refused to let her in, but I went outside to see her. She gave me a big hug and a fiver for Christmas, but I gave it back to her because I knew she didn't have any money. When she left, I sobbed my heart out. I didn't want her to be on her own; I wanted to go with her. Christmas was ruined.

I wasn't getting on too well with Nana Betty then. It wasn't anything I can put my finger on now, probably just the same stupid rows all teenagers have with their parents over nothing much, but I know that at one point I stole some money from the jar she kept in the kitchen. When I was found out, she kicked off and was quite rightly furious. But now Mum was back on the scene, having moved to the Salvation Army Hostel for the Homeless on Liverpool Road in February 1993, I knew that I didn't have to be with Nana Betty any more. Mum was on her own again and wanted me back with her, although children weren't really allowed in the hostel. She got away with murder when it came to bending the hostel's rules and soon persuaded the Salvation Army captain to let me join her. She'd been given a big room which she'd transformed so it was like a flat, just like when we stayed in the refuges, so there was room for me to live there too and space for me in her double bed.

We muddled along together until the day I came back from a week's summer holiday – the second holiday I'd had – in Wales with our Jane, Arnie's daughter, and her family. Mum wasn't at the hostel and I was told she'd gone shopping, but as the week went on she didn't return and no one had any word from her. I just assumed she was doing one of her usual disappearing acts and would be back when she was ready, but this time there was no sign of her. Then she phoned me from London. Dave Wheat had been released on probation from Parkhurst and was living in London's East End. She'd gone to see him and had decided to stay there. She couldn't resist. After all those years he still had a hold on her, going right back to the day he rescued her in the Irish Club. Despite everything, she still loved him and believed he had the power to rescue her from her shitty life. Never mind about me. I felt a confusing mixture of anger, sadness and jealousy that

Mum as a little girl

Me with Vic – my 'dad' who
became my step-brother!

Mum (left) with my step-
dad Arnie and a friend

Me (aged 3) with our Angela and one of Nana Betty's dogs

Nana Betty (right) with her best friend and my godmother, Hilda

I feel so warm inside when I remember living at Nana Betty's

Mum, Pat and me in our Alder Lane flat

A normal night – fast asleep in some pub

My musical side! Marching with Free Spirit on Warrington's Walking Day

Me with Tina

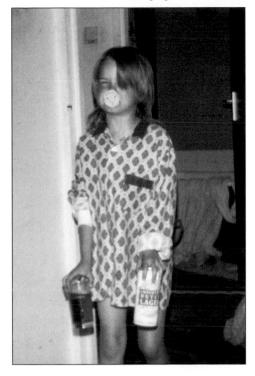

At home with Mum
in the Salvation
Army Hostel

Dave Wheat in my bedroom in London

Visiting Mum in London in my
'technicoloured dreamcoat'

Just one of the lads at Padgate High!

Friends – Jeanette (left), me and Lisa when we were about 14

With Carl Dundon, my first love

When I looked good!

Just got the good news – I'm the first member of the band

The Kittens on tour – me, Tash and Liz mucking about

she'd gone without me. Deep down, I hated Dave for always being able to take her away from me.

When she left me in the hostel, I don't know that she even gave me a second thought. But if she did, she knew that the other down-and-outs in there would look out for me. I didn't mind living there on my own, but I felt a bit awkward in the presence of the other women, so I kept myself to myself and stayed in our room. I was comfortable and had everything I needed, but before I could get too comfortable, Mum and Dave came back to get me. They wanted me to live with them in London. I packed what I needed and once again I was on the move. I was wary of going anywhere with Dave after what I'd seen him do, but I wanted to be with my mum. The weird push-pull relationship I had with her, where we both relied on each other, meant I felt I had to stick with her rather than go back to Nana Betty's again. Of course at the time neither of us had the slightest idea how bad life was going to get.

Before we moved to Gough Road in the East End, the scene of the big showdown, we stayed briefly in a grotty rented flat above a record shop on the Romford Road. The rooms were quite big but the whole place felt cold and damp, with its peeling wallpaper and sagging, chipped old furniture. The few nice bits and pieces we'd had in Manchester had been left behind. Mum and Dave were often to be found in the Three Rabbits next door, but I used to nip home to watch videos quite a lot. My favourite was *The Jacksons: An American Dream*, the story of the Jackson family and how the boys formed the Jackson 5, turning to music to get away from their violent father, and what happened to them after that. The idea of escaping their life by being in a band really appealed to me for some reason and I couldn't get enough of Michael Jackson. I was mad for him. Of course, having only just arrived in London I didn't have any friends there, so I watched a lot of TV. I was thrilled when I saw we had a channel called Carlton. Did that mean we had Sky TV at last? I was dead upset when I worked out that Carlton was much the same as Granada.

Mum and Dave managed to lay their hands on most of the things we needed and we had some good times, although I still held what he had done to Mum against him. I don't think he knew or cared what I thought of him because he was very protective of me. He used to call me Hot Lips, but he wouldn't let me wear too much make-up or anything he thought was too revealing. Even though I was only about to turn thirteen, he didn't want me to go to school when the winter term started but thought I should get a job in one of the London markets instead so I could bring in some money.

I still didn't see what Mum saw in Dave. Plenty of people believed he was my dad and he certainly told them he was, although all three of us knew it wasn't true. Sometimes I liked him saying it, though, because his reputation meant I got respect from people. If trouble kicked off in the pub, just a look or a click of his fingers was all that was needed for me to have a bigger team of bodyguards than President Bush. He wouldn't let anything happen to me.

My thirteenth birthday, held in the Three Rabbits, was probably one of the most memorable birthday parties I've ever had. By that time, even though we had moved to Gough Road by then, Dave and Mum were regulars. All the regular hoods were there and someone had made me a sponge cake with thirteen candles. I celebrated by playing pool with all the gangsters and whooping their asses. There was even a woman who claimed to be a psychic and Mum insisted I talk to her. Out came the Tarot cards and she did a reading for me where she foresaw that one day I'd be a big, big star. She would, wouldn't she?! I was pleased by the idea that my life might change for the better some day though. Perhaps it was then that I began to feel sure I'd be famous one day. I hadn't a clue what for, but it was a dream to cling on to when times got tough. It was quite a night – just madness.

But there was no madness like the nightmare that happened soon afterwards in Gough Road when Dave threatened to kill us both. That was the night when our world went crazy after we'd left the Three Rabbits and Dave flipped completely, knifing Mum in the leg and frightening us half to death. Mum and I ran away from him while we were waiting for her leg to be stitched in hospital and ended up hiding out in their friends' house, terrified he would find us. Eventually she decided to go back to Dave, despite everything he'd put us through, leaving me alone to be picked up by the police.

After Rosalind, the policewoman, and the other officer had taken me from the house and I'd shown them where everything had happened, I was taken to the police station. I had no idea where Mum and Dave were and I didn't care. All I knew was that I didn't want that man anywhere near me ever again. I was so relieved to be out of the situation, to be safe and looked after, that I didn't stop to feel nervous about exactly what was going to happen next. The police looked after me, making me some toast and jam while they waited for Social Services to organize somewhere for me to go. When I heard that Mum and Dave had come to the station, I was terrified. Rosalind went out to talk to them and I sat waiting. I felt really alone at that moment and desperately didn't want to go back to live with Dave. But I was almost as terrified at being left alone in a room with a male police officer: seeing what Dave had done to my mum made me nervous of being alone with any man, even a policeman.

When Rosalind came back, she told me that Dave hadn't come to the station, just Mum and her friend Barbara. I couldn't leave with them because of what had happened, but that I was going to be OK. She said she knew that one day I was going to be someone because she could see it in my eyes. Whether she was just saying that to keep me calm or whether she meant it, I don't know, but whatever the reason it made me feel better. She did her best to take my mind off what was happening and asked me if I'd heard of foster homes. Of course I had. I hadn't watched *Annie* all those times for nothing. 'Well, we're going to find a nice one for you,' she told me. Any anxiety I had about what was going to happen to me vanished. Suddenly I was really excited. At last I was going to be like Annie. I was going to my very own version of the grand mansion owned by Daddy Warbucks. Everything was going to be all right at last.

6

IN CARE

IT WAS THREE O'CLOCK on Sunday morning when I arrived at the emergency foster home, and as we pulled up outside all my excitement vanished and my nerves kicked in. Even in the dark, I could see that it wasn't the mansion I had dreamed of. What a disappointment. Where were all the kids? Where was the dormitory where we'd all sleep together? And where was Daddy Warbucks? This was just a normal semi-detached house owned by a normal family in Dagenham.

The next morning, after a few hours' troubled sleep, I woke to find myself lying on a mattress on the floor of a bedroom with two strange girls staring down at me.

'What's your name?' asked the younger buck-toothed one with black hair tied back in a ponytail. 'Mine's Anne-Marie.'

'Why are you here?' asked the other, older one. Her blonde bob and tracksuit made me think she was a tomboy like me. I found out later that her name was Jo.

They had also both been fostered and quickly made sure I knew who was boss. I didn't know what to do. The night before I'd been excited at the idea of being fostered, but now that I was facing the reality, I didn't like it one bit. Everything was very

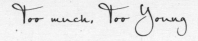

different from the way I'd imagined it. It was so ordinary and I was scared – not of the family, but of what was going to happen to me next. I was used to not being with Mum, but until now I'd always had my family to look out for me. This was the first time I'd been completely on my own.

Anne-Marie and Jo took me downstairs to meet my new foster family – a mum, Jan, and dad, George, with two sons of their own, Sean and Paul, and an adopted daughter, Tammy. I'm sure they did their best to make me feel at home, but I was still traumatized by the events of the past few days and felt too lost and confused to be able to respond. Although the police had explained everything to me, I still had no idea how long I'd be there and desperately wanted to go back to Warrington.

As the days went by, I felt more and more lonely. Nana Betty had moved house and didn't have room for me any more. Grandpa Denis had moved back in with her, but he'd had a stroke and his bed was now in the dining room, while our Andrew had the other bedroom. Dad couldn't take me because he was in his sixties, and in any case Social Services would never house a young female teenager with an older man. And Mum had chosen to be with Dave. I would sit on the sofa, pretending to watch TV, wondering over and over how she could have made that decision. I didn't understand her circumstances, or the crazy decisions love can drive people to make. But back then, to me aged thirteen, it looked as if she'd made a straight choice. She didn't want me any more; she wanted Dave. And nobody else wanted me either.

It wasn't until years later that I could see that, as far as Mum was concerned, there hadn't been a choice. In a way, Mum's whole life had led up to that moment. She wasn't a bad person.

From the time she was abandoned as a baby, through to her days in a children's home and the way her natural parents, then Tina and Dave, had treated her, her life had been all about survival. That's what she knew how to do best. All Mum wanted was to be loved. But however hard I tried, I couldn't give her enough of what she needed. Although early on she had worked as a machinist, her manic depression and drinking made it impossible for her to hold down a job, so for most of her adult life she had depended on the social for money and had nowhere of her own to live. She had wanted to be the best mum in the world to me, and in her eyes and most other people's she had failed. She went back to Dave after he attacked us because she had nowhere else to go but the streets, and she knew she wouldn't be able to look after me: she wouldn't have been able to cope. By giving me up, she was trying to give us both some sort of a future. She would be with the man she loved and there was a chance that I would be properly looked after.

During those weeks in Dagenham, I was the loneliest I've ever been in my life. When I went down for breakfast in the morning, it was: 'Morning, Kel,' or, 'All right, Kel? Make your own breakfast.' Kel? Who was Kel? Who were they talking to? I looked over my shoulder to see who was behind me then realized that 'Kel' was me. I never got used to that Essex accent. However hard they tried, I always felt excluded from the family. Often it was just the little things, like us foster kids being given supermarket own-brand Frosties when everyone else got Kellogg's. I suppose it's to be expected that parents will favour their own kids, but I felt like nobody cared about me and that I had no one to talk to. When one of the kids had a birthday, Jan got out a big knife to cut the cake.

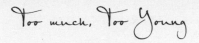

For a moment I froze in my seat: seeing it brought back memories of my last night with Dave and Mum. Not surprisingly, I've had a phobia about big knives ever since. I couldn't stop shaking, not that anyone took any notice. Perhaps they didn't know how to deal with me or felt that ignoring me was the best way, but whatever their reasons, I ended up feeling very unloved and alone.

I was told that I couldn't go to school or play out in case Dave found out where I was and kidnapped me. Instead, I stayed at home with Jan, doing bits of schoolwork in my room, watching TV or doing my chores – cleaning the skirting boards, the bathroom and the toilet. Sometimes I went shopping with her, but every time we went out I was scared that Dave might appear around the next corner, or be in the next aisle of the supermarket. I was always relieved to get back home, however boring it was there. Once Rosalind, the policewoman, came to see how I was doing. She even took me to the cinema to see *Sleepless in Seattle*, and slept all the way through it!

Us kids got on fine together most of the time, just bickering and bitching like most children do. One of them complained once to Jan that I'd been out calling one of his friends names. When I denied it, she turned on me angrily. 'Are you calling my son a liar?'

I wasn't taking that. 'You know I'm not allowed out so how can I have seen any of his friends? I don't see anyone except you.'

She let fly: 'I don't know who you think you are. You're Queen Shit, you are.'

This was my foster mother talking, the woman who was supposed to be caring for me. All I wanted at that moment was to get out of there, but where would I go?

When I went to sleep, I'd have a recurring dream that Dave had been arrested. I saw Mum waking up to find herself alone and running into my room to find that I wasn't there either. Then she would walk downstairs to a Christmas tree and start opening the presents all on her own. How anxious must I have been feeling about her? For the first time I felt so low that I thought about killing myself.

Fortunately something happened that stopped me feeling so sorry for myself. I was looking through one of my foster mum's magazines that was full of real-life stories about terrible things that people had been through. I remember one of them was about a kid of about my age who had been kept locked in a cupboard and was fed on bread and scraps. She was only allowed out twice a day so her father could abuse her. Reading that and the other equally nasty stories made me realize, 'I'm dead lucky, me. Really, really lucky.' Suddenly life didn't look so bad. I did have people back home in Warrington who loved me; I knew Mum loved me really; I looked OK; I could play pool with the best of them; I would be going back to Warrington soon. I knew deep down that my life didn't have to be like this. I didn't have to be the same as Mum. I could try and make things better.

Meanwhile the Social Services had been busy finding me an emergency set of foster parents in Warrington so that I could be near to my friends and family again and go back to Padgate High. It was only a matter of weeks before they found Alison and Ian. We wrote and spoke on the phone before I moved back north to live with them and their two little girls in Padgate. I remember them asking me what I wanted for Christmas. More than anything I wanted an encyclopedia – I loved learning and taking things in,

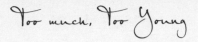

but I knew I'd missed out on a lot of my education. They bought me one and I spent all that Christmas poring over it or watching my video about Princess Di. She was a fantastic person who gave so much to other people. I loved the whole romance with Prince Charles and the fairy-tale wedding – she was an inspiration to millions of people, including me.

Alison and Ian were a lovely couple who made me feel at home with them. She was a big, friendly woman with dark curly hair who talked quite posh. He was tall, thin and quieter, happy to take the back seat while Alison ran the roost. I was the first child they'd fostered and I don't think they knew what had hit them.

Soon after I moved in with Alison and Ian, I was asked by Social Services to travel down to London to see Mum for the first time. I travelled first class with my social worker Jenny Peake. She was a diamond, so easy-going and willing to listen to everything I wanted to talk to her about. She would do anything she could to help; I was so lucky to have her. I was really nervous for the whole journey. I knew Mum was still with Dave, and I still constantly asked myself why she couldn't have chosen me over him. At the same time I didn't feel angry or upset, just relieved that I was away from it all. Jenny took me to a café somewhere in the East End – a right greasy spoon where Mum was sitting in a corner dressed in her leggings, a T-shirt and a waistcoat. Despite all my worries, she looked well and we were made up to see each other. Our meeting was all a bit awkward because Jenny had to sit there as Mum had a coffee and I tucked into a fry-up and a Coke. Then when Mum asked me about Alison and Ian, I felt bad saying they were nice because I didn't know how she would feel. Her face said it all: she was gutted.

Jenny let us go to the toilet together. Alone for a moment, Mum whispered, 'Dave sends his love.'

I couldn't believe what she'd just said. 'I'm not interested, Mum.' I carried on washing my hands and we went back into the café as if nothing had been said. Why would I want to hear from him? There was no way I was putting up with any more of Dave's mind games. But at least she'd let me know that she wanted me back and for us to be a family again. When the meeting was over and we'd got back to Warrington, Jenny told me that I'd be allowed supervised visits from Mum, but I still didn't think I'd ever live with her again. We kept in touch, though, and on her birthday in January, I sent her a card and a gold cross and chain, which she's always kept.

Mum ended up moving back to Warrington not long after, lodging with friends until the council came up with a flat. Dave stayed in London at first. I was happy that she was back on the scene, but at first I was only allowed to see her for supervised visits. To be honest, I was glad I didn't have to be part of all that chaos any more. She was my mum and I loved her, but I felt more secure with my foster parents and happier being a teenager with my friends than I'd ever been living with her. At last I'd got some of my childhood back.

The first thing I had done when I got back to Warrington, after putting my stuff in my room at Alison and Ian's, was put on my technicoloured dreamcoat and go round to my best friend Lisa's. Her younger sister Nicola answered the door, but when Lisa heard my voice she ran down the stairs and jumped on me. We were made up to see each other again. She never changed. We

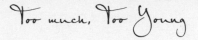

caught up on what had been happening and then I rushed round to see Nana Betty, who had moved round the corner to Valiant Close. Lisa couldn't believe everything I had to tell her, and I couldn't believe everything she told me either. I was really shocked to discover that in the short time I'd been away most of my friends had started drinking in the street – twenty or thirty of them hanging out together – and some had already lost their virginity. I was in the year below most of them at school and was still a real innocent.

Back home at last, all I wanted was to be out with my mates again, doing what they were doing. I wanted to be part of the gang. I'm not proud of all the stuff we got up to but this was the way it was. Jenny Barnes, Jeanette Burgess, Lisa and I used to hang around with loads of other kids, either in the park or at Vulcan Close, huddling under the covered alleyways between the flats. Sometimes we'd sneak to the phone box and make 999 calls or phone ChildLine and tell them my uncle Andrew had beaten us up. He never had, of course – you couldn't meet a nicer, more gentle person – and they never believed us anyway. I was the youngest and I never smoked or drank or swore. All my mates would stand round me going, 'Go on, Kerry. Say shit. Go on,' they'd insist. 'Say it.' Eventually I'd come out with it – 'Shit.' – and they'd think it was hilarious.

On Fridays and Saturdays we were allowed to stay out later. Sometimes we'd go to the junior disco at Mr Smith's Night Club, and that's where I had my first proper kiss. I was still dead tomboyish, very insecure about my looks and not really interested in boys in that way – yet! – but I wasn't going to be the only one who'd never had a kiss. Jeanette and Lisa kept egging me on, 'Go on, Kerry. Kiss someone.' I spotted this lad we'd seen a few times, wiped my mouth with the back of my sleeve, walked over, grabbed him and kissed him long and hard. When we'd finished, I wiped my mouth again and went back to the others. Mission accomplished. I don't think the poor lad knew what had hit him.

One of our favourite places to hang out was the Venny Park. It was a kids' playground that was down a little lane and off to the right, slightly hidden by the surrounding bushes. That was where I first got properly drunk. I'd been dying to do it and be just like the others; I thought being drunk looked fun and I didn't think I was the fighting sort, like Mum. That night, somebody had got hold of some bottles of White Lightning cider and we drank the lot. At last I was drunk! Everyone was throwing up and kissing boys, and so was I. It was all a big blur to me afterwards, but I thought being part of it all was great. Dead mad. When it was time to go home – Social Services had agreed a nine o'clock curfew with my foster parents – we chewed gum to get rid of the smell of drink and fags and tried to act sober. Almost every week-end we'd be down there, sitting on the arms of the spider's web, under the heavy wooden climbing frame or hanging off the swings. If it was raining we'd sit underneath the slide with our bottles of White Lightning and Mad Dog. We got caught by other kid's parents more than once, but I don't think Alison and Ian ever really knew what was going on. At least if they did, they never said anything.

Social Services finally found me a third, and this time permanent, foster home with Jeanette Burgess's mum and dad, Janet and Steve. We all thought it was a brilliant idea because she was one of my best friends and we went to the same school. What

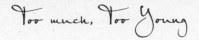

could be better? They lived in Padgate, round the corner from Alison and Ian, and Jeanette and I hung out together doing the same old teenage things as the others.

As time went by, getting hold of drink became more of a challenge. We'd hang around outside the off-licence, getting people to buy it for us, but when it got harder to persuade them, we had to be cleverer, so we told Nana Betty that a new kind of pop called White Lightning had come out. She bought several bottles for us honestly believing she'd bought lemonade. When that didn't work any longer, we used to raid our parents' drinks cabinets, mix up the spirits in a Coca-Cola bottle and take it back to school.

Not surprisingly, it wasn't long before we got in trouble. Pissed on White Lightning in the park – thank you, Nan – Lisa and I had tried to hug each other and missed. She fell over backwards, smacked her head on the tarmac and was out cold. I got up, having hit my forehead and danced around her shouting, 'She's dead. She's dead.' Somebody must have called the police, because suddenly they appeared with Lisa's mum, who dragged Lisa away as she came round. Moments later Jeanette's mum, Janet, arrived and packed me into the car. Next thing, Lisa and I were in next-door hospital beds. Needless to say we were grounded for weeks and weren't allowed to see or speak to each another. Janet took Jeanette and me to school every day and was waiting at the gates to collect us every afternoon. Oh well, at least we didn't have to walk!

Another big craze we went in for was shoplifting. I remember the first time I stole something, a gang of us had gone into town and they were egging me on to take a lip liner. I was so nervous – I knew it was wrong and that there'd be big trouble from Social

Services if I got caught, but I still did it. From then on I was hooked – the combination of a sense of danger as we made sure no one saw us and the excitement of getting away with it made it seem fun. Lisa and I would go round school making a list of what everyone wanted, then we'd go round the shops with our bags open and knock stuff off the shelves into them. Mum was in on it, too, which as far as I was concerned gave me the OK. When she came back from London, leaving Dave down there, she didn't bring much with her, so she took us into the big chemist shops to steal stuff for her. Lisa and I would follow her round as she picked up what she wanted and put it down on the ends of the shelves. All we had to do was slip the things into our rucksacks and get out of the shop.

Shoplifting was like a game; it was just a way of passing a Saturday afternoon. Of course it was wrong, but when you're a kid you'll do what it takes to earn the respect of your friends. Most kids test their boundaries by doing stuff their parents' won't approve of, seeing how much they can get away with. If we'd thought about it at all we'd have said we weren't doing any harm and that it was just something everybody did. Nobody else got hurt. But as you grow up, you learn what's right and what's wrong, and I know better now. Times change. If I left a shop today without paying for something by mistake, I'd go straight back in and cough up. And if I ever catch my kids shoplifting or drinking under age, I'll be absolutely furious. Of course, I don't want them to break the law, but back then, the stores never caught us and we didn't have a conscience until someone else found out.

One day, Lisa insisted on taking the rucksack filled with our takings home with her. I tried to put her off because we knew her mum was getting suspicious, but she wouldn't listen. Early that evening she'd called me and we'd had an odd, very awkward conversation about meeting up later. Little did I know that her mum had found the stuff and was standing right beside her. As I was walking down Padgate Lane to meet her, I saw her mum standing in the middle of the road. Knowing I was in trouble, I just said, 'Hiya. How are you, Karen?'

'Car. Now,' was all she said.

As we drove back to theirs I got the giggles, which always happens when I'm in trouble, and that didn't help the situation. When we got back to the house, Karen put all the make-up she'd found in the rucksack in front of us.

'What's all this?' She was so angry that neither of us dared say anything. She picked up the phone. 'I'm going to tell the Burgesses about this.'

Immediately we both burst into tears, begging her not to make the call.

'You can't,' pleaded Lisa. 'If you do Kerry will be put in another foster home and we'll never see each other again. Please don't.'

She was persuaded not to phone but took us into the garden where she made us watch while she crushed all the make-up under her heel. We were gutted. Thinking about that night makes us laugh now, but Karen's fury did the trick. That was our money-making scheme down the drain.

I don't know whether it was that or something else that marked the beginning of the end of my time with the Burgesses, but for one reason or another living with them didn't work out as well as we'd thought it would. There was a lot of jealousy between me and Jeanette and that made things difficult. It's enough to say that I thought I should leave before Jeanette's friendship and mine was ruined. I told Mum that I was unhappy and she unpicked the arrangement with Jenny Peake.

I really didn't want to move again. My nan always used to say, 'You're a pair of gypsies, you and yer bleeding mother.' But I didn't want to be a gypsy. I was mad that that's what she called me. It wasn't my fault that I kept on moving; I never had much choice about where I lived. All I wanted was to be settled. I didn't want to have to move schools again. I felt that Padgate High was where I belonged and the friends I'd made there, like Lisa, were the people I wanted to know for the rest of my life.

I was finally placed permanently with Mag and Fred Woodall, two of the most wonderful people I've ever met, and as they lived close by, nothing else in my life had to change. I stayed with them until I was sixteen, which is about the longest time I've ever stayed under one roof. If I could go back anywhere in my life, I'd go back there and be fourteen, moving in with them all over again.

7

HOME

THE MINUTE I walked into the Woodalls' small semi-detached house I knew it was where I wanted to be. The atmosphere was so warm and friendly, that I felt at home straight away. Mag opened the door and showed Jenny Peake and me through the porch into the living room. I went and sat by Mag on a dark blue leather sofa opposite the TV. I could see through the large window to the unfenced front garden and the other tidy little houses on the estate, while Jenny sat on one of the other two comfy chairs facing the fireplace as we had tea.

Mag and I liked each other on sight. She was a short down-to-earth woman in her forties with a great sense of humour, which you can see in her face. She remembers me in my school uniform with my green-and-black tie carefully tied so that one end stuck out of the bottom of my very short black school skirt.

It was a Wednesday afternoon so Fred, an engineer at Rylands, was at work. Jenny had brought me over to meet Mag so that we could see if we'd get on. Earlier in the week I'd been told I might be going there, so I'd been past the house several times with Lisa and Jeanette to check them out. Jenny said that I could have the rest of the afternoon off school to spend time with

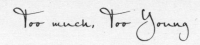

Mag, who suggested we go to the chippie. Apparently I didn't stop talking the whole time. Afterwards, she told Fred I talked so much I could 'put a glass eye to sleep'. No change there, then!

When I turned up at the Woodall's they'd only been fostering for three months. They had waited until their only son, Paul, had turned eighteen before starting. Along the way, Fred's sister had taken in two girls who would occasionally stay with them when she went away. Having them to stay and seeing how fostering could benefit kids convinced Mag and Fred that they wanted to try it for themselves. They completed the nine-month training and had had a good experience with their first child, who had just left to go back to her mother when I arrived.

Two days later, I brought round all my clothes and possessions from the Burgesses and moved in. I was given my own room, which Fred and Mag decorated especially for me. Everything was pink. They bought me a special dressing table where I could put all my make-up, and against the other wall was my single bed with a wardrobe and chest of drawers, as well as a TV and video. I had all the *Friends* videos, so I spent hours up there, laughing my head off. I was never into boy bands, so I didn't stick posters on the walls – I never had a clue what was number one in the charts. I'd only ever had one poster and that was when I was staying with Nana Betty and I pinned up a huge picture of Michael Jackson over my bed. Lisa was Take That and Bros mad and not into Jacko at all, but I was mad over him. She thought I was dead weird. I spent hours getting his dance moves right in front of the mirror. Apart from Michael Jackson, I only liked listening to the Motown and country and western stuff I'd been brought up on.

Mag and Fred were very relaxed about my coming and going and let me see my friends and family whenever I wanted. They even let me go down the Venny with Jeanette on the first night I was there. Fred immediately became a father figure to me. Quite a quiet man, with thick brown hair and a tache, he was quick to laugh. Living with them meant being in a proper family home for the first time, with a mum, a dad and a brother. They did all the things I thought families were supposed to do, and that meant I had to live by their rules. Tea was always on the table at a certain time, I had to go to school every day and on time and I had to do my homework. I watched *Corrie* and slept in at weekends, and in the summer we'd have barbecued ribs in the back garden and they'd ask round a couple of boys, Dave Cunningham and Mattie Mackay, whose parents were friends of theirs and who soon became great mates.

I was treated as family from the off. We'd go and watch Paul play football on Saturdays before going to St Oswald's Social Club together for a couple of hours. Fred and Mag would never miss anything that was going on at my school, either. They came to all the parents' evenings, to any entertainments we put on and to watch me play rugby. Yes, really! And I loved it. They got on well with Mum, too, so if she came along, there was never an awkward atmosphere. The supervised visits meant that we were back on good terms again. They put up with all the times she'd call me, upset or pissed, wanting me to talk to her or help her. Mum and I didn't always see eye to eye, but I would never hear a word against her. She was my mum and I defended her just as she had defended me when I was a little kid. I made it plain to Fred and Mag from the start that if I had a falling out with her, I

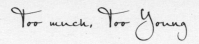

was the only one who could call her names, no one else. I didn't want to hear anyone else criticizing her.

After a couple of weeks with the Woodalls, Jenny Peake came back to make sure everything was going well and that I was happy. I couldn't have been happier. We all sat down together and agreed a plan for my staying there permanently, including stuff like how much pocket money I'd get, how much clothes allowance, what time I had to be back home every night and general house rules about how to behave. One of the many great things about Fred and Mag was the way they made me feel safe. I knew exactly where I was with them and didn't feel like I was treading on eggshells any more. They looked out for me as if I was their own daughter.

Although I wasn't allowed, after I'd had my dinner at Fred and Mag's I'd sometimes sneak out to meet Mum and Tina – yes, she was still on the scene – at Mum's local, the Old Bull, where we'd have a great time singing karaoke. Mum worked behind the bar there at the time. Once I told Fred and Mag that I was going to Manchester to have tea with my friend Jenny Barnes's dad so that I could secretly stay the night with Mum. Somehow Mag found out where I was, and when I called her our conversation was brief.

'All right, Kerry?' said Mag briskly.

'Yeah.'

'Enjoying your tea?'

'Yeah. Thanks.'

'Y're a liar,' she barked down the phone. 'Let me speak to Sue.'

Mum took the phone from me and listened. She told Mag that she understood they had to phone Social Services because we were breaking the terms of my foster arrangement so, as my foster parents, Mag and Fred had a duty to report what had happened. I stayed in the pub until we rolled home to wherever Mum and Tina were lodging. That night I hardly got any sleep: we thought every car we heard was the police coming to get me, so I'd jump out of bed and hide. The next morning Mum took me down to the police station dressed respectably in clothes I'd borrowed from Tina rather than my little dress and heels. We were locked into a room because the police knew Mum and said they didn't want her kicking off and running away. We thought that was dead funny. We always laughed when things went wrong. 'Ha ha. You're going to be grounded,' she'd chant. 'Ha ha. You won't be able to go to the pub.' Our sense of humour may have been a bit weird, but at least it was something we shared.

They finally let me out when Fred turned up to take me home. I tried to look upset for his and Mag's benefit, but he just looked at me angrily, then started to smile as he raised his hand as if to hit me. 'Why I orra...' he teased and we both started laughing. He knew and understood that I wanted to see my mum even though I couldn't, and didn't, want to live with her. He also understood that I would find a way, whatever rules were laid down. Thanks to him going to talk to Jenny, the supervised visits were stopped and I was allowed to go and see Mum whenever we wanted, provided I stuck to the 11 o'clock curfew.

I was in my element being back at Padgate High. Mrs Deakin, my head of year, had come to a case conference meeting in London when I was in emergency care and agreed to keep a place at the school open for me. I'll always respect her for that. Apart from the fact that being there was an escape – the one place where I couldn't get phone calls from Mum – I loved the routine and the

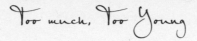

learning. The teachers all treated me as a grown-up. They knew my situation but never held it against me. I'd experienced how, in some schools, being in care automatically meant you got treated as if you were trouble, without being given a chance to prove otherwise. I was never a troublemaker, but I was cheeky. Once I jumped out of a cupboard and scared Mr Speed, my science teacher, half to death. Another time I called him a 'miserable sod', with less good results: I was suspended. Mrs Hiepko, my form teacher, was very sweetly spoken and I always felt she was very understanding. My favourite subjects were still art, music and drama. I even got a part in our production of *Annie* as a big fat maid. I had to say something like, 'No, no.' I think I even got that wrong, but at least I remembered how much I loved being in front of an audience. The trouble was I only wanted the main roles, and only the goody-goodies got those, so I didn't bother trying for anything else.

By this time I'd caught up with all my mates in most things, but I still hadn't lost my virginity. Nearly all my girlfriends had lost theirs during the hot summer when I was in London and I didn't want to be the odd one out. I was really curious to see what sex was like. I'd always got on well with the boys and had been thought of as one of the lads, but I guess things were changing a bit and I was beginning to realize I might have some potential in other ways. I wasn't very confident about my looks, but the way the boys used to stare at me and make comments made me think I had a good body. Once, when I took a message to a teacher at school, I walked into the gym and a second-year boy pinched me on the arse. The next assembly, I was hauled up in front of the whole school and the teacher said, 'I know she's an attractive girl and most of you would like to go out with her, but you do *not* pinch her bottom!' I was so embarrassed. All my friends took the mick for months.

I was never one to try it on with lots of lads; I've always been more of a one-man woman. I had a boyfriend called Frankie then, a footie player who I'd go and watch on Saturday afternoons down at Bennett's Rec or after school. We'd hang out together with friends in the street, the way you do when you're too young to go to the pub or get into clubs. Social Services would have gone nuts if they'd known because he was more than two years older than me and I was only fourteen. I liked the idea of having a boyfriend like some of my mates, but unlike them we'd never done the business. Although I was nervous, we both wanted to, but there just never seemed to be an opportunity. We finally got the chance when we went to a party at a friend's house. I got up my courage by having a few drinks and then we snuck upstairs. I thought it would take ages and I'd be making all the noises I'd seen people make on TV, but it was just in, out and pop! That was my cherry gone. It was nothing very memorable and I didn't rush to do it again, but at least I wasn't the odd one out any more.

By the time I was fifteen I'd fallen for a lad called Carl. We were both at Padgate High, where everyone thought he was a bit geeky looking with his spiky straight black hair and goofy teeth, but I couldn't have cared less. By then I knew that looks don't matter; it's what's inside that counts. Carl was really good fun and we laughed at things together. He cared about me and looked out for me and was my first true love. We were mad about each other and were like best friends with sex thrown in. You know what sex is like when you're in love for the first time? We exper-

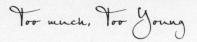

imented with everything, everywhere. We were together for about three years, on and off, arguing and making up, arguing and making up. Neither of us could let go. I had his name tattooed on my right ankle, but after we finally split for good, I got it covered up with roses. I also loved his mum and dad, and they were brilliant to me, supporting me whenever I fell out with Mum.

Drugs were definitely not on my list of things to do. I knew people took them, but I took the warnings seriously and steered clear. I'm still shocked that I was given them for the first time without even realizing – and by my mum, of all people. I'd gone to the toilet in the Old Bull one night, and she and Tina were in there with some white powder. I asked what it was and Mum told me it was sherbert. 'Want some?' She took some up with her finger and rubbed it on my gums. Mmmm. It tasted disgusting, not like sherbert at all, and sherbert certainly didn't have that effect. After a while, I felt an incredible rush of confidence and couldn't stop talking. When I got home I was still talking, my eyes were huge and there was no way I was going to get to sleep, so I felt dead ill the next day. Just as Irene had introduced Mum to purple hearts, so Mum introduced me to speed.

As the weeks went by, I began to realize that loads of people we knew were taking it and that they always seemed happy and in a good mood. After that, doing speed with my mum became a regular thing at weekends. When I did, I felt as if all my insecurities about my background and who I was dropped away. I did feel guilty about taking it, not because I was in care or because Fred or Mag might find out, but because I knew it was wrong. I think even then I knew I was letting myself down by taking it, but I wanted to be doing what everyone else was doing – peer pressure's hard to resist. On the other hand, sometimes taking it seemed normal because my mum had given it to me. And didn't that mean it was OK?

I'm horrified that my own mum introduced me to drugs, and I can't offer any excuses, except to say that speed was just what the people I knew did back then. I can see now that Mum and I didn't have a normal mother-daughter relationship. I think it's good to be friends with your mum, but although I'd like my kids to be my best friends just like my Mum is to me, I'd never encourage them to take drugs. It's not something I'd recommend to anyone in a million years, and I had to learn my lesson the hard way.

Fred and Mag were no pushover, but they couldn't have known everything I got up to. What parent does? Fred was a proper dad to me. He looked out for me and was very firm about when I had to be home. If I wore something he thought was unsuitable, he'd tell me I looked like a slapper and make me go and change. Sometimes I'd take whatever it was back to the shop, but other times I'd hide it and wear it anyway without him knowing. Well, hell, why not? He was always clear about what I was and wasn't allowed to do, but of course I didn't do everything I was told – that would make me abnormal! He never wanted me to go clubbing on Friday nights, but I just got my mates to come over and pick me up and then we'd sneak off together without him knowing. Once I took his umbrella with me and brought back someone else's. He'd told me so often not to lose his that I didn't dare confess. I'd listen to him complaining that it didn't work as well as before, but I just kept quiet. Sometimes it wasn't so easy to get round them, though. One New Year's Eve when I was babysitting at a friend's house, Fred brought me round some

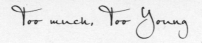

food. The problem was that I'd invited three mates to join me. He went back to St Oswald's Club, where they were seeing in the New Year, and told Mag what I was up to. She called me right then, furious. 'Enjoying yourself are you, Kerry?' she asked.

'Yeah, thanks, Mag.'

'Well, you won't be for the next week,' she snapped. 'You had no right to ask those people round to someone else's house. You're grounded.'

That was me told, except that I knew she only grounded me to keep her company! It didn't matter what happened, though, I always respected Mag and Fred and the way they looked after me.

As soon as I could, I got a job. I'd seen Mum with nothing and I was determined not to end up the same. I was only fourteen but I wanted my own money and my independence and I've worked ever since to make sure I've always had them. My first job was working in a shoe store in Warrington markets on Saturdays and in the summer holidays. While I was there I was offered a job as a glass collector at the World, one of Warrington's nightclubs. I'd get back home after a day's work, have tea and then Fred would take me to the World. I was sacked after two weeks because they found out I was too young. When I eventually wanted a change from shoes, I got a job at JD Sports. I'll always remember the day Mel C from the Spice Girls came in with her brother. All us shop staff were falling over ourselves to serve them, and after they'd gone we spent ages rewinding the CCTV recordings to look at her and examining her signature on the receipt.

Thanks to Fred and Mag, I spent two and a half years just like any other teenager. I got to hang out with my mates, go into town shopping, and on Fridays go drinking in the park. Lisa and I used to earn our beer money by charging 50p to all the first years at school who wanted to kiss me on the cheek! During this time I didn't lose touch with my other family, either. I was always popping in to Nana Betty's to say hi, and on the way home from school I'd often pop into the pub where Dad drank. He never came to see me, but I knew I'd find him there and that we could have a half of lager and a game of pool.

My relationship with Mum wasn't always easy during those years, and I was still the one she relied on for support when things went wrong. One day she called me and asked me to get round to the Old Bull as soon as possible. This was nothing new, but I legged it over there, thinking it was urgent. When I got there I found her working behind the bar and none other than Dave Wheat standing there smiling with a pint in front of him. As he turned and looked at me, my heart sank. Mum had told me he was back in Warrington and living with her, but this was the first time I'd seen him since that awful night in London. My first reaction was to run straight back out of the pub. There was no way I was going to go anywhere near him; I wasn't going to risk going through a night like that again. Mum followed me outside and told me I had to go back in.

'No way, Mum. I'm not going in there. Not while he's there.' She would have to drag me in kicking and screaming, but she had another way.

'If you don't come in right now I'm going to tell everyone about you and Dean,' she threatened.

I'd been on a couple of dates with Dean and it was nothing major, except that I was only fifteen and he was twenty-one. If Social Services had found out they'd have had a field day, and so

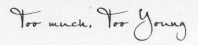

would his girlfriend. He was a cheeky chappie Scouser who worked in the local chippie. He was full of compliments, and I fell for them all. He took me out for a meal and charmed me. I quite fancied him but I soon found out what he was really like. A couple of days afterwards, I went round to Mum's and noticed a new bottle of perfume on the table. She told me that Dean had brought it round for me but that while he was there one thing had led to another between them. My Mum had slept with a lad I was seeing behind my back! How could a mum do something like that to her own daughter? She explained herself by saying she'd done it for me, to show me what sort of a bloke he was. But perhaps I didn't want to know, and even if I did, that certainly wasn't the way I wanted to find out. It felt like a massive betrayal. I would never have told Dave that she'd been unfaithful to him. Apart from knowing that he'd have killed her if he'd found out, I would never blackmail someone. When she saw how upset and angry I was, she took Dean outside and beat him up, making him promise to stay away from me. I never talked to him again; I never wanted to because I started seeing Carl soon after.

By the time I walked into the Old Bull and saw Dave, I still hadn't completely forgiven her. At the same time, I didn't want to fall out with her again by calling her bluff and walking off. I couldn't believe she was using Dean to blackmail me, but I didn't want to stand up to her and start a fight. I can see now that all through my childhood, Mum let me down time and time again but I could never cut her out of my life. As far as I was concerned, the fact that she was my only blood relative tied us together no matter what happened. Reluctantly, I went back into the bar and stood beside them. Dave carried on as if nothing had happened and we'd seen each other just the day before. I'm sure he enjoyed the atmosphere he caused between the two of us; I knew he could smell my fear.

Now that he was back in Warrington there was a restraining order taken out against him so that I could get him arrested if he came anywhere near me. Even if Social Services hadn't ruled out the possibility, I would never have gone anywhere near Mum's place when he was there. I just felt lucky to have Mag and Fred who gave me everything she couldn't.

As I got older, sometimes I'd wag it round to my mum's with friends rather than go to school. She never sent us packing, so we'd sit on the grass outside her patio doors, drinking and having a laugh, or we'd pull her old sofa round to the front of the flat and sit having a barbecue and karaoke where the cars parked.

Because of my curfew I had to go home, but some of the time my friends would stay and party at Mum's. Friends like Lisa, Jeanette, Jenny and the girls, as well as Dave, Mattie, Deano, Brian, Scottie, Sam McWilliams and another two of my mates who'd better remain nameless because they were only sixteen when Mum slept with them. She phoned me up and told me that piece of news when I was at work in JD Sports. Just when I thought I'd seen everything, she'd pull something else out of the bag and shock me all over again. I was so mortified that they all knew and I didn't. I couldn't speak to her I was so disgusted. Now we laugh about it, but then it was different.

Everyone loved my mum. If you meet her, you can't help but love her. She's larger than life and very easy to talk to, and she loves a party. I know she wasn't the best parent in the world, but I could always sit down and open up to her if I needed to – we've had a great relationship in that way. She would always listen, she never let anyone slag me off and she helped me when I needed her. She taught me how to smoke and even how to give a blow job on a carrot! I know that's not what most people expect from their mum, but I could tell her anything, and so could my friends. She was a friend to them, too, and they trusted her. She was always up for a good time and of course all my friends loved that as well. Once, when Lisa had an argument with a boyfriend, she went round to Mum's to talk in the middle of the night. Mum got out of bed, made her a cup of tea, listened to her, then put her to bed in the front room. She's a great friend – a better friend than a mother – but then I guess her mum hadn't exactly been the best role model. However kind the Burges were to her in the children's home, there's no substitute for a mum who wants to look after her own child and teach it how to grow up and get on in the world. She may not have been the usual sort of mother, but I did learn the difference between right and wrong from her. She was never like any of my mates' mums, and she never tried to be, but she was *my* mum, and despite all our fallings-out and difficulties I loved her.

The only time I went round to Mum's when Dave was there, I had Lisa with me. We were at home when Mum phoned up hysterical. 'Dave's going to kill me. Get round here as fast as you can.' We ran round to Cabul Close and knocked on the front door. Dave answered and was as nice as anything. When he disappeared inside, Mum said we had to hide in the garden and look through the patio windows of the ground floor flat so that we could watch him change. We stood outside, feeling like Batman and Robin, but wondering what the hell to do. Now that I was older and on my own turf, I wasn't as scared of Dave as I used to be. I'd got used to his presence in Warrington and knew that he couldn't do anything to me because of the restraining order. Lisa and I decided that if we went opposite ways round the block we could get round to the back patio doors, one on each side, and be able to see what was happening inside. 'Don't let him see you, Lisa, or he'll kill you,' were my last words to her.

We crept round to the back of the building and made our way on our hands and knees across the grass so that we were on either side of the doors. I don't think we had a clue what we were going to do. When we got there we peered in, hardly daring to breathe. Dave had just started in at Mum and she was sitting there on the couch, not moving, just taking it. He wasn't shouting but it was the threatening way he was talking that was scary. It reminded me so clearly of that night in London. We both burst in and immediately he stopped, acting dead normal again. The next thing, he wouldn't let us out of the house. 'Where d'you think you're going?' he asked. 'No one's going anywhere.' We sat on the couch together, not moving, saying nothing, then he left.

Mum walked into the bedroom, crying as if she'd never stop, and after a few minutes we followed her. The telly flickered in the corner and her wardrobe door was open so you could see her clothes neatly arranged inside. She was sitting on the brown bedspread with a Stanley knife on her knee, holding her hands out in front of her, blood trickling into the palms. She'd slit her wrists again. We sat on either side of her while I bandaged them, all the while talking to her like a child, 'You silly billy. Look what you've gone and done. Let me bandage them.'

'I'm sorry, Kerry,' she whispered.

'Oh, forget it, Mum. It must have hurt you much more than it

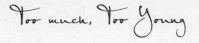

did me.' It was the same pattern that had repeated itself time and time again as I grew up, with me becoming the grown-up and Mum the child. Lisa helped, consoling her, never once losing her cool. We called on Mum's friend in a nearby flat to come over and she took her to hospital to be stitched up. The next time I saw her there were bandages round her wrist and she behaved as if nothing had happened, though I knew how ashamed and sorry she was feeling. She never wanted to talk about her feelings, it was easier to pretend, and if she seemed happy then that was fine. Except, of course, that it wasn't really. As a kid, and as her daughter, I didn't want to drag things out and make them worse by trying to get her to talk about what had happened or how I felt. It was easier for us both just to sweep everything under the carpet.

Whatever happened, Mag and Fred were always there for me. I could talk to them and they'd listen, offering advice if they could. They even took me on holiday with them. The first time we went to Butlins in Minehead and took Lisa with us. There was so much to do it was brilliant. The funfair rocked, although it was pretty basic, and we could go swimming in Splash Waterworld or bowling at MegaBowl, and just across the road from the camp was the beach. There were shops, bars and clubs galore, not forgetting all the entertainments and competitions laid on in Centre Stage and Reds. It's funny now to think that I was back there five years later performing with Atomic Kitten. Mag and Fred were very relaxed and allowed us to drink in the bars in the evenings until we got in such trouble that they brought us home a day early.

During the week we hung out with some lads, and Lisa was very keen on one of them. One night she left me in the club on my own while she went to meet him. I sat nursing my drinks and hers, having to pretend that she'd just nipped to the toilet and was making a long – very long – phone call. After a bit, Fred and Mag got suspicious and made me go and sit with them until she came back. They were furious and a bit shaken after a couple they'd just met had suggested a foursome! And then a threesome with me. I was only fourteen, for God's sake. The next morning Fred and Mag announced that we were going to leave a day early because of what had happened the night before. They stuck to us like glue all day, so we hatched a cunning plan. We'd go out in the evening with them, then once they were asleep we'd climb out of the bathroom window and go out for the rest of the night. To make sure the plan would work, we practised climbing in and out through the window. Out was easy, in was not. I was stuck on the outside of the chalet when Mag called us through for tea. Frantic, Lisa managed to pull me back in, scraping my belly all along the window ledge, but at least we were ready. Later that night, we came back as planned and climbed into bed fully clothed and ready to go out as soon as Mag and Fred had gone to sleep. The next thing we knew it was morning and we'd slept right through. We'd never looked so good first thing! They still made us go home, though. We were so disappointed.

The following year they took me and another friend, Beth, with them on holiday to Torremolinos. That was the first time I'd ever been on a plane and I was dead excited. I'd only seen those blue, blue skies with beaches and swimming pools basking under the sun in magazines and on TV, but being there, staying in a self-catering apartment, was amazing. We'd spend the day on the beach or by the pool, then go out to eat and drink every night. We found a brilliant karaoke bar on the main drag. It was packed with tables that spilled out into the street and there was even a small dance floor. Beth and I were always up dancing round our handbags and singing. I'd belt out 'Big Spender' and 'You're The One That I Want', loving the attention we were getting. In the end the manager gave us free drinks because he liked the way we pulled in the customers. He was happy for us to stay there dancing all night as more and more lads piled in. When we went home they gave me a big cuddly bear to say thank you. I even celebrated my sixteenth birthday there; they put up balloons and even gave me a cake. We were all set for another great evening when Mum called to wish me happy birthday. I was so pleased that she'd remembered and had bothered to call, but then she dropped a bombshell: she was going to marry Dave. She'd always said she never would, however many times he asked her, but now she'd changed her mind. I was absolutely heartbroken. He was the last person on earth I wanted as a stepfather. Any hopes that I'd had of eventually going home to live with her were shattered. Even though I was happy where I was, it would have been nice to have had the option of living with her – now that door was closed for ever.

I suppose I wasn't surprised when they never did get married. Our lives continued much the same until the night of 16 November 1996, when everything changed for ever. I came home from a night out with Jeanette – I remember it was pouring with rain and we were soaked – and as soon as I walked in Mag said Mum had called from Nana Irene's and that she'd sounded drunk. I phoned immediately, but could hardly make out what Mum was saying because she was so upset. Bit by bit, I pieced together what she was trying to get out. The police had come to

Cabul Close. There'd been an accident on the Winwick Road. A bad car crash. Dave and his cousin had been crossing the road in the rain and had been killed. The police had taken her to the hospital to identify Dave's body and then dropped her back at Nana Irene's. I can't think of anything worse than having to identify the dead body of someone you love.

I was stunned. I couldn't believe what she was saying. 'What do you mean? Do you want me to come round?'

Nana Irene took the phone from Mum and said no, just to stay where I was.

When I put the phone down I burst into tears and sat next to Mag on the couch.

'What's up, love?' she asked.

'Dave's dead.'

'Well at least you're free now, love.' I know she meant to be kind and was trying to look at the positive side of things for me, but I went mad.

'But Mum loved him so much she gave me up for him,' I said. 'Can you imagine what she must be feeling?' I felt so bad for her. I'd had a row with her not long before, and had told her that I wouldn't come round again if he was living there. I felt as if it was my fault, and that he might still have been there if I hadn't said that.

I couldn't believe he was gone. Just like that. Whatever I thought of the man, I wouldn't have wished that on him or anyone. I couldn't stop crying. But his death meant a number of things for us. It meant that I could stay with Mum whenever I wanted, and that I never had to be frightened of what he might do to either of us.

8

A LUCKY

BREAK

THE LAST TIME Mum tried to kill herself was when I was sixteen. After Dave's death, she went into a deep depression. When all my friends were thinking about their GCSEs, I was dealing with that. Despite everything they'd put each other through, she really did love him, and I honestly didn't think she would get over losing him. She and I were in Cabul Close one night, sitting in the living room having a drink, when she told me yet again that she didn't want to be here any more. She missed Dave so badly that she couldn't live without him; she really wanted to kill herself. For the first time something in me snapped – I'd had enough. I'd heard her say that so many times. I was shaking with anger as I went and got her sleeping pills from the bathroom and put the little brown bottle into her hand.

'Here you are. Take them,' I said. 'You're so bloody selfish. I'm your daughter and you're telling me you want to kill yourself. And then what? I'm only sixteen. What am I supposed to do?' I knew that yet again she wouldn't succeed and that afterwards I'd have to listen to her go on about being a bad mother, and I'd had enough of it. The responsibility seemed too much. 'Here are your pills, just take them.'

All the suicide attempts she'd made, all the times I'd comforted and bandaged her. What was the point? She never succeeded in killing herself, so why not cut the dramatics and get on with it? I was sick of picking up the pieces all the time. Of course I didn't want her to die, but I desperately wanted her to stop doing this because she made us both feel so awful afterwards. We both knew that if I was with her, I wouldn't let her die, so what was I doing, giving her the pills? I suppose subconsciously I was trying to make a point.

I snatched back the bottle, passed across her half-empty glass of Tennants and poured the pills onto the table, then I handed them to her one after another. I watched her take every single one of them as the tears rolled down her cheeks. 'I only want to be with Dave,' she wept.

'Well, tell him hiya when you see him then,' I said as I passed her another pill. Any sympathy I had for her had vanished. I knew I was acting like a completely different person but for once I was too angry to fall back into my usual comforting role. This time, I was really tough with her.

When there were none left, and before the pills had time to take effect, I called an ambulance. I knew that she'd be OK, after all, we'd been here before. 'There you are, Mum. I'll pick you up from the hospital tomorrow.'

Sure enough, there she was the next day, stomach pumped and waiting for me at the hospital as if nothing had happened. We went back home and nothing more was said, but if something had snapped in me, something had changed in her, too, because she never tried suicide again. She says now that she came to the decision that enough was enough. Not only that, she also decided to stop taking her medication for depression. She swore to cope with life without the tablets and she's never taken one since. That's an amazing thing for her to have achieved. The one thing she would never give up though is the booze: she likes her drink too much for that. Did she change because Dave wasn't around playing his mind games with her any more? Was it because I'd had the balls to stand up to her? Or was it because she really did care about me? To this day, I don't know. But whatever the reason, she seemed to start looking at life differently, and thank God we've never had to go through another episode like that again.

Somehow I got through my GCSEs and began a sixth-form course in Leisure and Tourism, studying hotel management, marketing, customer services, and all that. But I soon realized that it wasn't what I wanted to do with the rest of my life. Gone were the days when I wanted to be a barmaid or a cowboy, but I knew I didn't have the education or attention span that I'd need to qualify me as a doctor or a lawyer or anything like that. Anyway I didn't fancy sitting behind a desk for the rest of my life. However, I did have a 34DD chest and a size 6 waist, so I decided the way forward was to become a page-three model. I was proud of my tits and I liked the attention I got because of them, so I thought I might as well give it a try. Perhaps this would make the difference to my life. I'd seen how successful page-three girls like Sam Fox and Linda Lusardi had become.

Mum encouraged me so, without telling Fred and Mag, we snuck off to a model agency in Bolton that advertised in the local paper. It was a small studio where the photographer was obviously used to taking shots of wannabes like me. He was friendly but brisk and professional, so that once I'd done the difficult bit

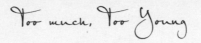

of taking my clothes off in front of a stranger for the first time –
big deep breath, just do it – I felt fine. I followed his instructions
and began to relax in front of the camera. In most of the shots I
was wearing something, so they were quite moody, and at the
time I thought I looked quite sexy and sophisticated. In fact, I
looked a cheap, tacky mess, but hey, what did I know? Mum
thought they were great, too, so we sent them off to the *Sun*. I'd
been told to expect a wait of six to eight weeks, but within hours
of receiving them, they phoned up wanting me in straight away. I
was made up. This was the break I'd been hoping for. They obviously saw me as another Sam Fox type. My age and DD chest had
done the trick.

I had to take the day off school to go to London, which meant
I had to tell Mag and Fred what I was doing. They were cool
about it, but said, 'Look. We've got to tell Social Services because
it's our job as your foster parents.' I thought, Fine, yeah, whatever. In fact, I think school had already been on to Social Services
because I'd taken my photos in to show the teachers. They said
they thought they were good but, like Fred and Mag, they had
their job to do. They knew I was in care and anything like this
had to be reported.

I was dead nervous on the train down, but Mum was with
me, so we had a laugh together. My appointment was with
Beverley Goodway, who was probably the best-known glamour
photographer in the country at that time. I thought Beverley was
going to be a woman, so I was a bit gobsmacked when 'she'
turned out to be a 'he', but he was straightforward and friendly
and made us feel at home straight away. His studio was small,
with cosy couches and chairs to sit on, while the brightly lit area

where he took the photographs had a huge sheet of white paper rolled down from floor to ceiling as a backdrop. All around the walls of the room were pictures he'd taken of all the top girls, among them Linda Lusardi, Melinda Messenger and Sam Fox. Looking at the way they posed inspired me to do my best: I wanted to get my picture up on Beverley's wall, too.

Beverley chatted away to me, making sure I was at ease, although I felt completely comfortable anyway. After all, we're born naked, so going about with nothing on has never bothered me. I did my own hair and make-up – I was always good at that – then posed in a thong in front of different backdrops so it looked as if I was on some gorgeous beach somewhere. The only thing anyone looking at the finished results couldn't see was the fact that, because I'm so short, I was standing on a pile of *Yellow Pages* all the time. The whole shoot only took about an hour and then we went straight home. I felt on top of the world, as if my whole life was about to change.

Wrong! That was the beginning and the end of my career as a glamour model in the national newspapers. As soon as Social Services got wind of what I was doing, they refused to let things go any further. There was no question of the pictures being allowed to appear in the *Sun*. Of course, I can see now that a kid in care appearing on page three wouldn't look good, but at the time I was furious, and it was the deciding factor in my leaving Fred and Mag's. I was sixteen and a half and I wanted to move out and get that court order lifted so I could do whatever I wanted with my life.

Fred and Mag were as sad to see me go as I was to leave, but we all knew I couldn't stay there for ever. I needed my independence.

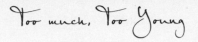

They had become such a big part of my life that, although I was moving out, I knew I'd never lose touch with them, and sure enough I never have. I still go back for Mag's eggs, chips and beans.

Over the following six months I was more unsettled than I'd been in ages. I was on the waiting list for a council flat in the Padgate area, but I had to move around until one came up. I felt as if this was the beginning of a new life. Again! I wanted to be independent and I wanted to keep trying with the glamour modelling. I didn't know where it would lead but I was sure life had more to offer than I'd had so far. I started out with a semi-independency flat – well, bedsit really – in Latchford, but I didn't last long there. The flats were dead scruffy and loads of kids in care lived there, which made me quite nervous: it was a bit like being back in the refuge, but without Mum. I made my room as nice as I could and Mag and Fred gave me a telly. I shared a kitchen and bathroom with the others, but as there was a chippie over the road, I never bothered cooking. There was a supervisor living on site who made sure we didn't bring people back after a certain time or bring back too many of them, either, and that put me right off. Sometimes Mum would come over and we'd put a blanket on the grass outside and have a drink. Whenever I could, I'd stay round at hers. We were getting on well together and I enjoyed staying with her, even though we had to share her double bed, which meant listening to her snoring and farting. That didn't last for long, though; all it took was one of our blow-ups to ruin the peace.

One night I was round at a friend's watching a film and Mum kept phoning and phoning, trying to get me to go over to hers.

The calls got on my mate's brother's nerves so much that eventually I said I'd go back to Cabul Close and see what was going on. It was two in the morning when I arrived to find her drinking with Mick, a bloke from across the road.

'Hiya, love.' My mum welcomed me in. 'Come and have a drink with us.'

I could see from the number of fag ends in the ashtray and cans on the table that they'd been at it for hours. Was that all she'd wanted me to come round for?

'No thanks, Mum. I'm knackered. I'm going to bed.' I disappeared into the bedroom, leaving them to it, and was just drifting off when Mum burst into the room. Her mood had switched from friendly drunk to absolute psycho. I knew the danger signs of old and thought the only thing to do was get out of there fast. I grabbed my clothes and struggled to get on my top while dodging her hands as she tried to grab me. 'It's your fault Dave died,' she screamed.

That stopped me in my tracks. 'What d'you mean, Mum?' She yelled that the only reason she threw him out was because I refused to visit her when he was there. But I didn't believe that because nothing I said had ever made any difference before. By this time I was in the living room, trying to get to the door where Mick was cowering, absolutely terrified by the turn the night had taken.

She picked up the glass-topped coffee table, raising it above her head and staggered towards me, yelling, 'I'll kill you. I know you think I'm a cow. I'll kill you.'

'Mum. Calm down, you're drunk,' I said, but she was on another planet. I don't think she could even hear me. I opened the

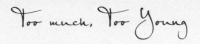

front door and ran out barefoot, despite having next to nothing on. God knows where Mick disappeared to. Mum dropped the table with a crash and chased me all round Cabul Close, screaming that she'd kill me if she caught me. I ran to a friend's house and banged on the door. Donna answered immediately. She could see I needed help, although we knew Mum wouldn't do anything while she was watching.

'All I need is a lift,' I begged, thinking I'd go to Arnie's step-daughter Jane's. A bloke appeared from somewhere behind her in the flat, wondering what was going on, and said he'd help me. We got in the car and roared off out of there, but once we were clear of Cabul Close, he slowed down and put his hand on my knee, saying, 'You know you can always stay at mine if you want to...' Could the evening get any worse? I flung open the car door and legged it down the street. I had no idea where to go as I was too far away to walk back to my flat, then I thought of Carl – who was my ex at the time – who lived nearby with his parents. I ran round to the back of his house and started throwing stones at his window, trying not to wake his parents or the neighbours. Eventually Carl heard and came down. He fetched his car and drove me back to my flat, where he stayed the night as I was way too nervous to be alone.

As soon as we got back the police came hammering on the door. I hid Carl in the wardrobe because men weren't allowed to stay overnight, and then I let them in.

'We've had a report from your mother that you've run away from home,' they said.

'What? But this is my home,' I explained. 'This is where I live, so how can I have run away?'

I was absolutely heartbroken. Although Mum and I had been getting on well, that night's outburst showed I couldn't predict when she would let fly and that I still hadn't a clue how to calm her down when she blew up. Although I knew it was her illness that made her moods change so dramatically it didn't make it any easier for either of us to cope with. Perhaps it was because she'd stopped taking her medication. I don't know. She lost it with me many times, although that was the worst, and every time was as upsetting as the last. I'd think she loved me, but then she'd threaten to kill me or herself, so I never really knew where I stood.

I honestly don't think she remembered what had happened by the next morning because she just waltzed in with a friend, acting as if everything was normal, saying, 'Hiya, Kerry love. You all right?' Then she started burrowing around in my kitchen cupboard and, without saying another word, went off home again, taking all my detergents and cleaning stuff with her. She'd do that sometimes – help herself to whatever she wanted – and that was always fine by me. I was used to her and it was just the way life was.

I was only allowed to stay at the semi-independency flat for a limited time anyway, but it got to the point where I had to move out because I couldn't bear it there. It was partly because of the place itself and partly because I discovered I hated being on my own. I still do. The trouble was there was nowhere else for me to go. Fred and Mag had fostered someone else, nobody I knew had enough room for me and Mum and I weren't getting on after the coffee-table incident. Luckily Carl's parents came to the rescue and let me live with them for a time. They were so good to me and supported me when I really needed it. After that, Lisa's

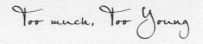

parents agreed that I could stay with them, even though, with two daughters and two sons, there wasn't much space. Lisa and her younger sister Nicola shared a room, so for a few months I shared Lisa's bed, either topping and tailing or hugging each other so neither of us fell out.

All this time I carried on with my modelling with a lovely professional photographer in Warrington called George. I liked him because, to look at, he reminded me of my grandfather Denis. George used to take topless shots of me and I got £50 for a photograph here and there. I didn't want to have to depend on anyone else so was still daydreaming that modelling might be the way to earn my own money and independence.

Neither Lisa nor I ever had much money, so whenever we went out on Fridays and Saturdays we got drinks bought for us wherever we went. We'd only have a fiver between us, but when someone offered to buy one of us a drink, she or I would say, 'Thanks *we*'ll have...' It always worked. We were shameless. Our favourite club was Mr Smiths, an old cinema that had been converted into a huge nightclub with several bars. Hundreds of people would cram in there and Lisa and I were regulars, along with lots of our friends. You know what it's like. We'd spend ages getting tarted up, trying on each other's clothes, doing our hair and make-up. Sometimes, we used to go there wearing identical little white dresses and big high heels. At the time we thought we looked the business, but looking back, I'm not quite so sure. I was known as mini Pam after Pamela Anderson. I'm sure I don't have to explain why! Then we'd pile into a cab, ready for a good evening. When we got there, we'd bolt a couple of drinks just to get us in the mood and then hit the dance floor. Dancing was my thing and Smiths was a great place for that. I loved the atmosphere, the music and the people. We were all young, free and single and making the most of it.

One night I was bet a bottle of champagne that I wouldn't get my boobs out – too right, I wouldn't! – but the DJ grabbed me and dragged me up on stage where everyone could see. They stopped the music and I looked down at the sea of faces turned up to see what was happening and could pick out Lisa grinning up at me. 'What do I do?' I mouthed down to her. I was surrounded and couldn't see a way of escaping.

'For one bottle of champagne, get your tits out.' A huge cheer went up as I stood there frozen.

'For two bottles.' Another cheer. I know I'd done page-three modelling but this was different and I really didn't want to.

'For three bottles.'

I could see Lisa shouting, 'Go on. We've got no money.'

'Lisa. I don't want to.' I don't know if she even heard me as everyone had begun chanting, 'Go on. Go on.' I knew no one meant any harm and that they were having a laugh – I'd seen other girls be put through the same sort of thing – but I still didn't want to do it.

'Go on. Go on.' By this time everyone was joining in and I knew there was only one way I was going to get out of there, so I lifted up my top, revealing all, then yanked it back down again. The roof nearly came off the place with the shout that went up. 'Hhhhheeeeeeeeeyyyyy!'

Two weeks later I got on a bus and the driver turned round and asked, 'Weren't you in Mr Smiths not long ago?'

'Yeah,' I replied, pretending not to be pleased that he'd noticed me.

'Yeah. Thought I recognized the chest.'

I was absolutely mortified but it didn't stop me going back.

Mr Smiths was the scene of some great times and we went most Friday and Saturday nights. We still laugh about the time we got involved in a fight with some girls who kicked off at Lisa, deliberately elbowing her on the dance floor. When she pointed them out to me, they started in on me as well. 'What's your problem?' I wasn't going to take any shit from them. 'Who do you think you're elbowing?' Within seconds we were rolling round on the floor, fighting, as the dancers stepped back to give us space and cheer us on. Miraculously we never got kicked out.

It wasn't long before Lisa got a job at BT with good pay. She was so generous while I was on the dole and paid for everything, lending me clothes and sometimes even buying them for me. She could afford all the best stuff then. She even bought me a deep-purpley-blue suit so I could go to an interview with BT as well. The suit cost £90 – a lot in those days – but it was worth it as I got a job as a sales adviser. Suddenly life was looking better.

Before I started there, the council had at last come up with a one bedroom flat for me in Valiant Close, just around the corner from Lisa's and my Nan's. This was the first proper home of my own and I made a big effort to do it up nicely. I had a £1,000 grant that I spent on a cooker, a bed, a pinkish fitted carpet and curtains. Everybody chipped in and gave me a few kitchen utensils, pots, pans and plates, so the flat looked quite homely. I felt dead grown-up – quite the independent, hard-working single girl. Even so, I didn't have enough money to put in my electricity metre, so when the electricity was cut off one night my alarm didn't go off in the morning. By the time I woke up, I was so late for work that I got my cards, and that was the end of my two-month office career. I didn't want another office job so I got a job at the Captain's Table, a good fish-and-chip shop. The owner liked having me there because he thought the way I looked brought in business, and besides, I was good at the work and after a while could practically wrap a bag of chips with my eyes closed. The only thing I didn't much like about it was going home stinking of chip fat. Apart from that, I carried on with my modelling, hoping to get a break.

My big break finally came when I was least expecting it: on the dance floor at Mr Smiths. Those were the days when I was a lot more daring about what I wore and had on long white pants and a bra top with ties that wrapped round under my bust. It was a look that was all bosoms really. The music was pumping and I was dancing with Carl and Jeanette. The place was really hot and sweaty. I was vaguely aware of a bloke who kept on looking over at me. He was quite well dressed with bleached blond spiky hair. I didn't recognise him so I knew he wasn't from around Warrington and just ignored him, losing myself in the music. As the night wore on I noticed him looking at me again until eventually, when I stopped for a drink, he came over and handed me an envelope. 'We're auditioning girls for a band called the Porn Kings,' he yelled over the music.

'Never heard of you,' I yelled back.

'We've had a top ten hit...' He went on, but I could hardly hear him over the noise.

'I don't know who you are.' All I wanted to do was get back to the dancing.

'We're a dance band,' was all I heard him say, but he'd lost me; I wasn't interested. I'm not into dance music now and I wasn't then. He disappeared into the crowd and I stuffed the envelope into my handbag before going back to my mates.

On the way home in the car, I remembered the envelope and got it out to see what was inside. Carl wasn't happy about the way the bloke had come up to me, so he grabbed the letter, screwed it up and tried to throw it out of the window.

'Hey, that's not yours, it's mine.' I snatched it back. I was so annoyed at him being so possessive that I got him to drop me off at my mum's, saying I'd stay there that night.

Mum was in bed when I walked in. By this time I'd read the letter properly and found out that the guy was someone called Davy T, who was part of a band looking for dancers to go on tour. 'Mum, this bloke wants me to be in the Porn Kings.' I jumped onto the bed beside her, all excited by the thought that this might be my first step towards making something of myself. I'd seen TV shows and movies where all it took was a lucky meeting with a stranger to turn someone's life around. Maybe this was my turn.

'You're not going to be in any bleeding bluey!' she screeched, immediately thinking the worst.

I reassured her that I wasn't that desperate, but the next morning we looked at the letter together. The Porn Kings were a techno dance band from Liverpool, who had toured with some other dance bands whose names I didn't recognize. Mum thought the letter looked OK and that I should give them a ring. I had nothing to lose and everything to gain, but I was dead shy about making the call. They'd probably found someone better than me by now anyway. Mum wasn't one to give up on an opportunity, though, and she pushed me until I eventually picked up the phone.

'Hiya. Is Davy T there?' I was so nervous. 'He gave me a letter last night.'

'Oh, it's you,' he said. 'The blonde one. We've been waiting for you to phone.' Oh my God, he remembered me. He asked me to meet him under the clock at Liverpool Lyme Street Station. I didn't like the idea of meeting some dodgy bloke on my own in Liverpool, so I took Mum with me. As it turned out, I needn't have worried. We got into his silver, soft-topped BMW convertible and dropped Mum at the pub while we went back to his studio so he could explain what being a background freestyle dancer meant – basically just what it sounds like. Davy T was a nice genuine bloke and was the main singer and rapper in the band. When he asked me to join them, I agreed there and then. We went back to pick up Mum, who was made up for me. She brought out her Bacardi to the car to continue celebrating. 'Mum, you can't bring that,' I said, but she did.

Davy T kept in touch until two weeks later when he called to ask if I had a passport. Thanks to Mag and Fred taking me to Torremolinos, I did. 'We're going to appear at a big awards ceremony in Berlin,' he explained, 'and we'd like you to come with us as one of our two dancers.' I was really excited and scared at the same time and went over and over it with Mum. 'Should I go? I'm too nervous,' I worried. 'No. I can't. But I want to. Oh God, what shall I do?' Although I wanted to go deep down, I couldn't make up my mind. Mum, on the other hand, knew exactly what I should do. 'You'd be stupid not to, Kerry,' she said, and I knew she was right.

Early the following morning I was standing outside Mr Smiths with my bag and passport, wondering if Davy T was really going to turn up. Perhaps he'd been having a laugh at my expense? Or perhaps he'd changed his mind? But then up he drove with Kyle, a black lad with dreadlocks, who was on decks. For a moment I hesitated – I was going on a plane with people I didn't know to a country I'd never been to; it was madness.

I couldn't eat all day, I felt so sick with nerves. I wasn't worried about what I was wearing because Davy T had OK'd my outfit – a pink all-in-one hot pants get-up with a halter neck – but what would happen if I let the band down? The time whizzed by as we arrived, checked into our hotel – I'd never stayed in such a fancy place – and went along to the venue, which was in a massive park. We hung around backstage as various foreign acts I didn't know went on before us, then finally our moment came as we were announced. I followed Davy, Kyle and the other dancer out onto the stage; I was terrified. Davy T had told me to be myself and dance however the music took me. He'd seen what I could do and that was good enough for him. Ten thousand people were out there waiting as the daylight faded. Would I be good enough for them? The lights beamed down hotly on us and an incredible roar went up from the crowd. I was stunned. 'Oh my God. How cool is this?' As I felt the beat of the music, I could feel myself changing into someone else. I felt outrageous and wild, and really got into the music, pretending to play the keyboard then crawling sexily about the stage. I gave it everything I'd got. Where were those nerves? It was the best buzz I've ever had and I didn't want it to end.

I got back to Mum's a day later absolutely full of the whole experience. I couldn't stop talking about the posh hotel we'd stayed in, the gig, the music, how I'd danced, everything. I'd had a taste of something I'd really loved and I wanted more. Davy T often asked me to work for him after that, dancing in different nightclubs and miming to songs. Lisa and her boyfriend David usually came with me and I'd get anything from £50 to £100 a night, which was really good money for me, as well as free drinks. The trouble was the cash never lasted long. I was often broke and occasionally had to resort to desperate measures. One time I was doing a gig but needed some Tampax and had no money to buy any. No one would lend me anything and Mum had nothing to spare. I couldn't do the gig without the Tampax and I needed the cash I'd earn from the gig, so me and Mum sold Alfie, my mum's green parrot. I loved Alfie – I used to sing 'Rockin' Robin' to him while he bobbed his head up and down in time – but it was him or me. We sold £700 worth of parrot for £20 to Slippery Sid, a bloke we knew who bought and sold loads of dodgy stuff in Warrington. He probably sold him on for £700, but what did I care? At least I could get back on stage and do my thing. Poor Alfie, it was such a shame. Mum was gutted.

Dancing was something I was naturally good at but it didn't bring in regular enough money, so I was going to have to find something else to do as well. That's when Davy T said, 'You know what, Kerry? You're too good to be a backing dancer. You deserve to be up at the front.' That was just what I wanted to hear, but how was I going to get there? He hadn't finished. 'I want to introduce you to someone called Andy McCluskey. He's a mate of mine who's thinking about putting a girl band together and, if you want to go for it, I think you deserve it.' Want to go

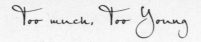

for it? Was he crazy? Of course I did. Davy told me how Andy was one of the co-founders of a band called Orchestral Manoeuvres in the Dark, who were huge in the late Seventies and early Eighties. The name didn't mean anything to me, but I decided to go along anyway and see what they wanted.

Davy T sent along a video of me dancing with the Porn Kings and fixed up a meeting with Andy and his mates Stuart Kershaw and Martin O'Shea. He picked me up in his car and we drove across to Liverpool for a midday meeting in a big recording studio in Hesketh Street. I'd taken ages deciding what to wear because I really wanted to impress this McCluskey bloke. In the end, I'd chosen a purple velvet miniskirt, knee-length boots and a low-cut top. I took my page-three pictures along, too, as I didn't know what they were after and anything might help. As we walked in, I took in the music desk, the piles of CDs everywhere, the big padded doors and the studio through the glass window. Shit! I thought. This is as real as it gets; this isn't just a few blokes playing games.

Andy was tall with dead short, tight curly hair and he had the money to put behind a group. He's a real gentleman and we clicked immediately. Like Andy, Stuart and Martin are Scousers. Stuart's smaller and more plummy than the others. Like Andy, he's very talented musically and has a wicked dry sense of humour. He'd be writing the songs with Andy while Martin, who had long curly hair and was another good laugh, was to be the manager. They explained how they wanted to put together a girl band that would be something like Banarama meets the Spice Girls meets Manga comics, and that they were looking for singers. Yeah, right! I sat down and chatted with them, getting out my pictures, and we were soon in stitches, laughing.

'This rawness is just what we want,' said Andy. 'Just be yourself. Can you sing?'

'I've sung karaoke and that's about it,' I confessed. So they gave me a CD of a studio singer singing three songs they'd written: 'Right Now', 'See Ya' and 'Whole Again'. I was to go away and learn them, then come back in a couple of days. I went home, giddy with excitement, and put on 'Enola Gay' the Orchestral Manoeuvres in the Dark CD Andy had given me. I recognized it straight away. 'Oh my God, Mum, they're dead famous. This is serious shit.' I put the other CD on her karaoke machine and thought the songs were completely brilliant. I started singing along and dancing. Here I was at 17, still performing in my mum's living room but feeling like Madonna. Mum sat there welling up with pride, a can of lager at her side. 'You'll definitely be in the band, Kerry.' She was certain.

When I went back to see the lads a couple of days later, I was ready. I loved the songs and knew them by heart. I was nervous about going into a recording studio for the first time, but I took to it immediately. I wasn't going to let this chance go without giving it everything, so nothing could phase me. I sang my socks off, giving it loads. I could see them chatting on the other side of the window before I nervously went in to see what they had to say. They were smiling. 'You're the first member of the band.' I was so excited I couldn't believe my ears. I knew I didn't have the strongest voice in the world, but at least I could sing in tune – or so I thought. I was good enough to sing live, but you have to be that much more perfect when you're in the studio, and apparently my pitch wobbles slightly, but they reckoned they could sort that out. Of course, I now know it wasn't my voice that got me into

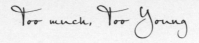

the band. Andy's told me that what made them pick me was the fact they knew instantly that I was going to be a star, and that I'd bash my head against a brick wall until I got there. He called it the Marilyn Monroe syndrome.

They asked me to go for singing lessons with a singing coach called Jenny John, to strengthen my voice and teach me how to use my vocals. Everything was happening so fast. Of course I knew that nothing might come of it, but I trusted the lads and my mum was 100 per cent behind me. I went to the lessons and practised all the boring voice exercises Jenny taught me, even though I never really had any time for them. I told myself that if the band got off the ground, I wasn't going to be the one to let everyone down. When I wasn't singing, I was busy working out the choreography to go with Andy and Stuart's songs. At least I didn't need anyone to teach me that. For a couple of months I remained the first member of an unnamed band. I couldn't wait for us to find the other two. At last I had a job.

9

SHOW TIME

ABOUT TEN GIRLS had got through the voice auditions and were sitting around the Lomax, a club in Liverpool, looking anxious. Andy, Stuart and Martin had narrowed down the girls to those whose voices would complement each other and provide a wide vocal range. Now it was time to see whether they could dance and which of us looked good together. Seeing the second stage of auditions in *The X Factor* always reminds me of that day. Some of them looked really confident, as if they'd already got it, but others looked scared stiff. I was as terrified as they were, but Mum was in her element. She'd come to watch and got chatting to the other mums who were just as anxious as their daughters. One of them was bragging about everything her daughter had done. 'I'm sure she'll get this,' she said. 'What about your daughter, Susan?' Mum was so chuffed to be able to say, 'What? Kerry? Oh, she's been in the band for the last two months.' Squashed.

A professional dancer spent the whole day with the girls, teaching them the routine that was already laid out for 'Right Now', going over and over it until they'd mastered all the moves. The guys were looking out for the girls who picked up the moves quickest and did them the best. They filmed us all doing the

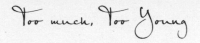

routines then put us together on computer and watched us on screen to see how we looked in a line-up and if we all moved well together. They also wanted to make sure I got along with whichever girls we chose.

One of them, Liz McClarnon, came up to me, smiling, and said, 'Hiya girl. Y'all right.' I liked her straight away. A Scouser with brown hair in plaits which she'd wound into buns, she was wearing violet contact lenses that made her eyes really blue. Liz was a year younger than me, but a couple of inches taller; she'd originally thought she would be a lawyer, but then decided she wanted to get into show business. The other girl who stood out was Heidi Range. She was taller than me, too, and was dead pretty with long brown hair, but she was only fourteen. I remember her being mad for Prince William and carrying a picture of him in her purse. When she sang, though, her girly voice disappeared and she sounded like a big black gospel singer. Amazing. She was a great dancer, too. Stuart was worried that she didn't look right, but I was sure. 'Have you heard that voice, Stuart? We'll give her a makeover if we have to. You can't let her go.' In the end, the guys agreed with me and we had our band.

Andy thought that because we were going to be working in Liverpool, it would be much easier if I lived there, too. Not having the one-hour journey from Warrington meant that, like the other girls, I could be at the studio whenever Andy wanted us there. That way he could call us any time he wanted one or all of us to try out something new. He rented a beautiful modern two-bedroom flat for me right around the corner from the studio. Compared to what I'd left in Warrington it was dead posh. Liz decided she wanted to move in so we could get to know each other better, but because she was younger Heidi had to carry on living at home with her mum in Liverpool. The lads also set up a new label called Engine Records to help us and other local bands get started before we were signed to bigger labels.

One of the first things the lads wanted to do was give us a new look, starting at the top. Liz had beautiful long hair that she could sit on, so she was in tears when they cut it into a bob – I still can't believe they did that to her. Heidi had hers trimmed and a few highlights added, while mine was layered at the sides and I was given a fringe – I looked like a Christmas tree! Then came the clothes. We went to a designer called Mary Lamb who had her own label called Automatic Kitten. She'd been briefed to give us a cartoony image based on our personalities and a designer had drawn up some ideas. I looked more like a hooker working Lyme Street Station than a pop star, with big furry boots that made my legs look like golf clubs, dead short denim hot pants that showed my bum, denim chaps and a two-tone metallic bra. I was sure when people saw me they'd ask how much I charged. Heidi had a big baggy white shell suit with a white jacket and furry hood, and Liz, who was a bit of a tomboy in those days, preferred to cover up in combats and a T-shirt. I then decided I didn't like my hairdo at all. I was so down about the way I looked that in the end they agreed I could have hair extensions. That was better. We thought we looked dead good.

But we were still a band without a name. We'd thought of all kinds of different names, including Exit and Honeyhead, but none of them stuck. I went home one weekend to see Mum and tell her about everything that was going on, including our makeover. She could never get enough of my news – talk about a

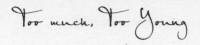

proud mum. She had her taxi-driver friend Bob the Leg round that day and he couldn't say 'Automatic Kitten'. He kept on getting it wrong and coming out with 'Atomic Kitten'. I thought it was a brilliant name, better than anything we'd come up with so far, and I went back to Liverpool to tell the others – yes, I took all the credit! They loved it and the name stuck. Atomic Kitten had been born.

When we weren't working on our image, we were kept busy working up the band, the songs and our performances until we went on the road, but until we did I was broke. Andy gave me the odd £20 here and there but it wasn't enough to live on. I desperately needed a way of making some money that would fit in around Atomic Kitten. I often went back to Warrington to see my mates where, thanks to my yet-again-ex, Carl, I met a girl called Carrie. We were in someone's flat and I was moaning about being broke when she suggested I try lap dancing. As a lap dancer working in Liverpool's Sugar Fantasy Bar, she knew what she was on about. I was doubtful, especially when I heard that it was fully nude. Doing topless modelling was one thing, but this sounded a bit too up close and personal. 'Come and see what you think,' she said. 'It's easy money and they don't touch you.' What had I got to lose? I wasn't ashamed of my body, and if the customers weren't allowed to touch you, I couldn't see that taking my clothes off would be a problem.

The outside of the Sugar Fantasy Club gave nothing away. It was just a door in a brick wall with no windows – nothing glamorous and a bit scary. I couldn't imagine what it would be like inside, and for a moment I thought I wouldn't get to find out. I almost didn't get past the front door because the doorman didn't think I looked eighteen. Once I'd shown him my ID, I was allowed in, though, and inside the club was quite a classy place that was open in the afternoons and evenings. There were big leather couches with low tables for the customers' drinks and a stage. The other lap dancers were sitting around, waiting for the first shift to begin, and I could feel their eyes on me, watching to see what I would do, although one or two of them gave me an encouraging smile. I was so scared as I stripped down to my new silver Ann Summers bikini, but at least the lights were dim as they put the music on. I was a bit taken aback at having to dance for the doorman, until I discovered he was the boss's brother. He sat expressionless, watching me. I swallowed and did my best to get into it, giving my all doing my robotic-Michael-Jackson-meets-body-popping moves. I thought that when I'd finished he'd tell me what a good dancer I was as nobody had ever had any trouble with the way I danced before. Instead, when the music stopped the guy looked at me and said, 'You need to be a bit slower, a bit sexier.' I had to dance for him again, this time standing between his open legs, nudging them with mine, pretending he was a customer as I improvised, copying the girls I'd seen on TV and in films. I can't do this, I said to myself as I tried to give him what he wanted. But I needed the money, I needed the job, and dancing had got me work before. Despite feeling completely self-conscious, I must have succeeded because I was offered the job.

I'll never forget my first dance. I'd gone in before the club opened and sat on the floor in the Ladies' with the other girls, putting on my make-up. My stomach was turning over with nerves. Then I changed into my costume – a silver thong, silver

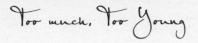

bra and a pair of knee-high boots – and went through into the club with Carrie. She passed me a glass of champagne and said, 'Just follow me.' Never have I been so glad of a drink! I knocked it back. The music was loud and the bar was starting to fill up. We sat down and waited for someone to come over. We were asked by two guys at the same time, so I kept my eye on Carrie, who started dancing on the other side of the bar, and tried to copy her moves. She looked dead sexy as she slipped off one bra strap then the other, then the bra. I followed her every step of the way, but when it came to taking my bra off, I couldn't undo it and had to ask the bloke to do it for me. I was absolutely mortified, but trying not to giggle, I carried on until I was fully nude.

Funnily enough, after I'd done it once my nerves disappeared and I began to enjoy myself. I soon got the hang of pushing into the customer's knees with my legs, bending over and blowing in their ear or on their neck. The men who came in were often on stag dos and just there for a laugh so the atmosphere wasn't at all sleazy. As far as I was concerned it was just a job. One dance for one song and we were paid for each one with a plastic token worth £5. We were meant to stick them in a box behind the bar, though I found it easier to stuff them down my boots, and cash them in at the end of the night. Because of being a size 6 with a double D chest, I soon became one of the top earners. The boss would come over because he had three blokes waiting for me, only to find I already had a queue of five already in line. One guy did slap my arse once, but he was thrown out straight away, so I knew that I was completely safe.

At last I was making good money. Lisa remembers sitting on the pavement outside her house when I came home one weekend, waving wads of notes. I wasn't ashamed of what I was doing and I enjoyed it.

I only lasted there for about three weeks. Atomic Kitten was demanding more and more of our time, so I had to leave. I can remember my last dance as clearly as I can my first. She was called Michelle. I'd just finished my shift one night and was walking out when she grabbed me. I recognized her from the bar where I'd noticed her watching me all night. She was a proper butch woman with long blonde hair and an Everton T-shirt. 'Please dance for me. I've been waiting for you all night. I've been dying for you to dance for me.'

'What's your name,' I asked her.

'Michelle,' she replied.

I danced for her – well, it was another fiver in my pocket – and did just what I did for the men as she sat there, moaning quietly. I went home to Mum and told her I'd had to dance for a woman and how it had turned her on. The Sugar Fantasy Bar was the one place Mum never came to watch me perform, but she loved the stories and thought this one was hilarious. All the same, I felt dead uncomfortable about it and handed in my notice the next day.

Although we were working hard as a band, we had a problem: Heidi had decided she wanted to leave so she could sing more rhythm and blues. Liz and I were gutted when she said she'd made up her mind, but we knew we couldn't persuade her to stay if she was unhappy. I think she found it hard being so much younger than Liz and me, especially given the fact that she still lived at home while Liz and I were having a laugh living together. She's since gone on to be one of the Sugababes, so it all worked out well for her in the end.

Meanwhile Liz and I needed another band member, so we held auditions again in Liverpool. For some reason, I wasn't there, but Liz was and chose another Scouser, Natasha Hamilton, a trendy sixteen-year-old redhead. She was at college in Liverpool studying performing arts, but had spotted our ad in the *Liverpool Echo*. Although Liz liked her, Tash and I got off on completely the wrong foot. We first met when she came round to our apartment to learn the new routines I'd choreographed.

'Hiya,' I said to her, all friendly.

'Hiya,' she replied, but when she looked at me she gave me a look that said, 'Don't mess with me,' and I didn't like that. At one point she was having trouble keeping up, and when we went through the moves again, she said, 'That's just stupid,' and gave me another of her looks. I went mad. 'Well, that's the routine. If you want to be in the band, you're going to have to do it.' I didn't feel that it was going to work out with her at all, and afterwards I went straight to Martin and told him I wasn't having any sixteen-year-old girl coming into my flat and telling me how to do my dance routine after two minutes.

Martin was really sympathetic. 'OK, Kerry, if you're that unhappy give it two weeks. If you still feel the same about her, we'll let her go.' I thought that was fair and decided to make a real effort. Liz had picked her, so it was up to me to see if things could work, and if they didn't there was a get-out. Without telling me, Martin decided to go round to see Tash and tell her how I felt. Apparently she burst into tears: she'd been under the impression I liked her and didn't know what she'd done wrong. I had completely misunderstood the way she'd looked at me. She hadn't meant anything by it. I decided I needed to get to know her, so I asked her over to Mum's. We all went on to the World, the night-club in Warrington, where we had a wild evening together. The ice was broken, and after that we became the best mates in the world. She had my sense of humour and was very old-headed for her age too. Needless to say, she stayed.

Our first public performances as Atomic Kitten were as the warm-up act at Paradox in Liverpool and then at Heaven in London. We got a good reception at both and interest in us began to kick off. We spent a lot of time in Andy's The Pink Museum recording studio, learning songs and rehearsing endlessly. Much of the time we weren't even singing together. Liz might go in for half a day, then me and then Natasha, each of us singing different parts in different ways and at different levels. I sang the high parts, Tash had the big voice and sang the lower parts, while Liz had a lovely soft voice that filled in the middle. I used to get really frustrated, because I'd have to do fifteen or twenty takes before one was good enough for Andy, Stuart and Pat, the engineer. I could see Andy twiddling with the computer and the others sitting at the mixing desks and I sang the same bit again and again, but I always got there in the end. Then Andy and Stuart would mix the tracks, experimenting until they had the finished product. After that we'd have to learn it again, just as we'd sung it on the track, rehearse the dance routines to go with it and finally put it all together. By June we had three songs, 'Right Now', 'See Ya' and 'Holiday' ready. I was made up to be able to do the choreography and had a great time creating lots of the dance moves we eventually used performing the first two singles. We used a choreographer as well when we started out, but she was quite rigid, so after a couple of gigs we said we

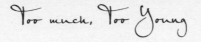

wanted to free-form a bit and interact more with the audience. I thought we should run around being crazy during the verses and then snap back into the routine for the chorus. Until then bands were choreographed from the first note to the last, so we broke the mould in that way.

We began to get out on the road, performing wherever Martin could get us the gigs, in schools, colleges and clubs. The important thing was to get our name out there, so that people knew about us when we finally released our first single. The reception we were getting built up our hopes that we'd make it big – you have to believe in yourself if you want to succeed, and we did. I knew that I stood a chance of making some real money, too, which would make a huge difference not only to my life but to my mum's and to the people who had helped us. The band was something I wasn't going to give up on, despite it being bloody hard work. Most of all, I wanted to prove to myself that I could succeed at something.

I went back to Warrington whenever I could to see Mum and my mates, and I kept in touch with them all the time by phone. The other reason I used to go back regularly was to see my new boyfriend Cluke, a doorman at Churchills, one of the clubs in Warrington town centre. I'd first met him years before when I was sixteen and used to go into the club under age. Instead of throwing me out, he asked me out on a date. I didn't see him for a couple of years after that, but then we met up again one night on the town and got it together. He was fourteen years older than me, a big good-looking guy with shaved blond hair and blue eyes. I remember how nervous I was the first time I slept with him. I was wearing his T-shirt and lay there as stiff as a board, not daring to move. Amazing that he wanted to see me again, really! He had a great body that was covered in tattoos – he had two eyes on his bum, so when he got out of bed to go to the loo, it looked like they were winking at me! When Mum met him for the first time, she chased him round the living room, trying to get his top off. I was mortified, of course, but he took it off to keep her happy. To begin with I couldn't make my mind up between him and Carl, so I two-timed them for a while, going out with one then the other, until I realized that Carl and I were definitely over at last.

Mum was as excited as I was about what was happening, and like me she couldn't believe it. She loved being part of it all, coming to a few of the gigs and saving pieces about us in the paper. I used to worry that she'd get pissed and let me down – Mum won't put on a front for anyone, which I guess is how it should be – but all the same I didn't want to be embarrassed in front of all the new people I'd met. Fair play to her, though, she hardly ever showed me up. With Dave gone, we'd become much closer again: we spoke every day without fail, often more than once and sometimes as many as twenty times because there was always something to talk about.

Once, Tash and I were having a break from the studio and were walking down to the pie shop when Mum phoned. She was upset because she'd just had a row with her boyfriend, Fox, and I tried to calm things down. All the while I was thinking, When I get famous, everything will be different. Everything will be all right. But of course I was wrong. What you don't know at that stage is that fame finds any cracks in your life and makes them bigger, takes a hundred photos of them and plasters them all over the front pages of the national newspapers for six million people to see. Your life stops being your own any more.

Soon after Tash had joined us, we went down to London to do a few showcases for the A & R men from the record labels that were interested in signing us. We were shitting ourselves. We'd rehearsed and performed together loads of times but this was the big one. It was the difference between everything and nothing. By this time we'd recorded a load of songs but chose to perform only the ones we really liked 'Right Now', 'See Ya', 'Whole Again', 'Hippy', 'Holiday', 'I Want Your Love' and a couple of others. The showcase that mattered most to us was the one we did in front of Hugh Goldsmith of Innocent Records, a division of Virgin Records, because we knew his signings included Billie Piper and Martine McCutcheon. He was the only one who had responded to the demo tape, but as soon as he'd bitten, three other companies followed suit. As usual, I was the one who fronted us, going into the studio and making everyone laugh, being the cheeky one who could push it so far and get away with it. After we'd introduced ourselves and talked about the band, we began to sing.

Halfway through the third song, he interrupted us: 'Stop, stop, stop.' Surely we weren't that bad? He beckoned us over to where he was sitting, and we went over expecting the worst. He looked at us and said, 'I want to sign you.' We all did a double take. Did he really just say that? Could he do that?

'I just have to get the head of departments to hear you, so can you stay in town and showcase for us again tomorrow? We'll foot the hotel bill?' The next day we performed for him again, and by the next day, Friday, we had seven offers of recording contracts – three from people who'd heard about us but hadn't even seen us!

As far as I knew, that was it. Four weeks later we signed a contract with Innocent. I only found out much later that he'd told our management team Innocent wouldn't sign Atomic Kitten unless they got rid of me. They only wanted Liz and Tash. Apparently they thought I was too mouthy and too much of a loose cannon. Me?! Fair play to our management, though, who said, 'Look, we've based this band on Kerry and her personality. She gives the other two confidence. She's like a secret hand grenade. Toss her into a room of strangers and they'll all be her best friend within half an hour. Either you take all three of the girls or you don't sign them at all.'

They agreed to take us all, so in the summer of 1999 we were signed to them. We were all over the moon. Everything was happening so fast; maybe all our hard work was going to pay off. We kept up our appearances so we'd have as much exposure as possible before our first single 'Right Now' was released in November, and we even started being invited onto TV shows too. The first one we did was *SM:tv*, and I remember it out of all the others because the record company went mad about what I was wearing. They made me change my pink belly top and little pink cardigan for a yellow one because they thought the pink one made my boobs look too big and that I looked like a slapper. I was really annoyed, but had no choice but to do what they said. That was the first time we met Ant and Dec and I had a bit of a crush on Dec. None of us guessed we'd all end up together in the Australian jungle three years later.

The only low point for me was in August when Andy and the boys forced me to have my tonsils out. I was often under the weather with throat infections. They put it down to me being a party girl, but they weren't going to stop me going out, so they paid for me to go into a private hospital and have my tonsils whipped out instead. After the op my voice became deeper and huskier, so we had to recut some of the songs we hadn't finished recording. That was hard. Thirty-nine – yes, thirty-nine! – different takes went into the spoken verse in 'Whole Again'. Originally I was doing all three verses, but Innocent insisted the first two should be sung. Probably just as well.

To get our names and songs out there, we were signed up as the support band on a couple of tours. The first was for 911, another band signed by Virgin, who'd released four albums and had ten top-ten hits. The band was made up of three northern lads, Lee Brennan from Carlisle, Jimmy Constable from Liverpool and 'Spike' Dawbarn from Warrington. I already knew Spike from the club scene in Warrington and all of us had a great laugh. We were big on stupid practical jokes like spraying foam all over their dressing room and putting up posters in there of A1 (another boy band). The three of us were so giddy with everything – going out on stage and seeing banners with our names on them, fans cheering for us and signing autographs. We loved it, just as we loved our second tour where we supported Steps, who gave us experience of a much more serious gig because they were so huge then.

Before long we were gigging all over the place in nightclubs, schools, universities and radio roadshows. It was unbelievably hard work and we virtually lived in a Chrysler Voyager as we travelled all over the country. In one day we could get up at four or five o'clock in the morning to travel to a TV studio in London where we'd have our hair and make-up done before appearing live on *SM:tv*. Afterwards we might change our clothes and do *CDUK*, and then we'd get back in the Chrysler to go to Birmingham to do another gig at the uni. Then it was straight off to a college gig in Manchester before getting on a private jet back to London so we could sing something for Children in Need. There were times when we'd appear at between three and five schools a day. I loved those appearances because the kids were always so excited to see us. One time we even did a gig at Padgate High – it was so special to be back there, getting all the feedback from the kids and my old teachers. Our schedule was never-ending, though, and we kept ourselves going on vodka and Red Bull. Despite all the hard work, it was the perfect job for me. I'd been moving around and meeting loads of different people since the day I was born, so it couldn't have suited me better.

Andy, Martin and Stuart never came on tour with us. They always stayed behind the scenes. It was just the three of us, our driver and security man, Carl, and Helen 'Foxy Knoxy' Knox, our tour manager. The five of us travelled everywhere together, with Foxy Knoxy watching out for us. She was in her thirties by then and was really old-school, having been a roadie with The Rolling Stones. She dressed like a hippy, always in black, and never wore make-up. She was very strict with us and did every-thing she could to make sure we didn't step out of line. It must have been a nightmare job.

The management had strict rules that meant we shouldn't be seen drinking, smoking or dating. Our image had to be kept squeaky clean for our fans. Everyone believed that if we were single, sober and smoke-free we were more saleable, so we had to be dead discreet about enjoying ourselves, so no one could criticize us or give us bad press. But we all know that rules are made to be broken. We may not have been meant to drink or party, but we always found a way, like the time we went to Will Smith's party in Planet Hollywood. We were under strict management instructions to be back in our hotel by 12.30 a.m., so the three of us did exactly as we were told. Then after Foxy Knoxy had checked that we were back and going to bed, Tash and I crept out the back way, went back to Planet Hollywood and partied till the early hours of the morning. That was the sort of thing we did all the time. Poor Foxy Knoxy was constantly harassed, but being a Kitten meant that we made up and broke the rules as we went along.

The three of us would always get dead nervous before a gig, but then we'd hear our intro, run out and everyone would be screaming. What a feeling. I've never known a buzz like the one you get from being on stage, dancing and singing, with the crowd on their feet cheering. We took our nervous energy out on stage with us, so everyone thought we were mental. The people from Innocent were always nervous about what we might get up to. They never knew what we'd say or do on stage. We were known for being in your face and outspoken. Funnily enough, though, the biggest buzz I got was when I made contact with individual members of the audience. I remember a beautiful little girl in her daddy's arms looking up at me once and I looked back at her, smiled and blew her a kiss. The smile I got back lit up her face. Making a difference to someone's life by doing something as tiny as that was great. I loved the fans, and if anyone came up to me when I was out with my mates I'd never turn them away. I just got a thrill out of knowing I could put a smile on someone's face. That's ace. That's what it's all about.

Sometimes I'd lie awake at night in some posh hotel room somewhere, all thanks to Virgin, and feel like pinching myself. Once we'd been signed by Innocent, it was as if we'd been shoved onto a treadmill and someone had pressed fast-forward. I'd think about how far I'd come since the days when Mum and I had racketed around Manchester, staying in the refuges, not knowing what the next day held in store for us. It all seemed such a long way away now, almost like a dream. How I'd made it from there to here was a mystery to me, although I guess my childhood must have pushed me in the right direction, giving me that extra something that Davy T, Andy and the rest of the lads had spotted. When I stopped to think about it, which I didn't have time to do often, the way my life had changed was completely surreal, but bloody fantastic, too.

10

RIDING

HIGH

THE THREE OF US WALKED into the huge film studio not knowing what to expect. Our first single 'Right Now' was due for release in November, so we were set to record our very first video. We found ourselves in a vast warehouse facing a huge, multi-coloured disco dance space. Tash and I were jumping around, screaming with excitement, while Liz, always the more emotional one, quietly welled up. This was all for us. Waiting for us were the director and crew, sound men, cameramen and ten dancers. We'd been shown a storyboard to give us an idea of what would happen, but we hadn't been prepared for this. Of course we'd rehearsed our dance routine in a studio for weeks, but this was awesome. The theme of the video was taken from our logo of three black cartoon bombs with kitten ears, so we each had our own 'cat flap' and there was a big red tunnel with a wind machine at one end that practically blew us away. We were so giddy that the director had to keep telling us to cool down. There were long periods of doing nothing, before we had to get out and explode with energy, then turn it off again and wait while the lighting or camera angles, our expressions, moves and beauty shots were set up. There were endless arguments

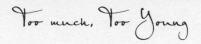

about the dancers as Andy and Stuart insisted the three of us were good enough to carry the video without too much backing from them. Liz, Tash and I kept on calling home and our friends during the breaks to explain everything that was going on – we wanted to share the whole experience. The only thing I can remember going wrong was when I had to slide between Tash's legs. I came up too soon and head-butted her in the pelvis. I felt so bad because I really hurt her, although she was all right again after taking some time out. They fed us can after can of Red Bull to keep us going for twenty hours, by which time our excitement had turned to exhaustion. I'd never felt so knackered in my life, but what an amazing feeling it was, knowing that we'd done our best doing something we loved.

Behind the scenes, Andy, Stuart and Martin were hard at work masterminding everything. Hugh Goldsmith had decided to get Absolute, the outfit who had worked with the Spice Girls and Geri Halliwell, to produce the singles 'Right Now' and 'See Ya'. They didn't want to share the production with Engine Records, so got us in to recreate the whole track and re-do the vocals for 'Right Now'. But because we'd done all the backing vocals and harmonies ourselves, it had taken days to record all the different parts, edit, tune and tighten them up. That's why we had such a distinctive vocal sound. Absolute didn't allow enough time to do all that again, so in the end they did the music and had to take the vocals off Engine's track, mixing them together in a computer. It's amazing what they could do. We were also making a start on our album, which was planned for release in early 2000, as well as keeping up public appearances. As far as I could see, the great thing about us, and the thing that appealed to our audience, was that we were so real. We didn't pretend to be anything more than we were – three girls having a good time. Always being up for a laugh, in your face and down to earth was what made us different from the other girl bands around.

I loved every second of what we were doing. Talk about living the dream. Although it was physically exhausting, we couldn't get enough of it. We worked non-stop during the week, then whenever I could, I went home to Warrington and out to the World with my friends – my days as a glass collector there seemed light years away.

But despite loving our fans and our increasing success, I was discovering that being recognized isn't always pleasant. I began to find it more and more difficult to cope with so many random strangers approaching me, and although I wanted to be nice to them, they were often a bit scary. Girls would accuse me of sleeping with their boyfriend or tell me they knew my dad or my sister. What dad? What sister? And once I had a face-to-face argument with a girl I'd never met before who claimed she'd been my best friend at school. All I can say is that there are some strange people out there. I began to get so anxious about going for a night out in Warrington that I started drinking really heavily when I was at home. I couldn't handle all the attention and found that if I downed a few drinks before I went out, it helped. Anything I could lay my hands on would do. Everyone thought, and still thinks, that I'm very confident, but I'm not at all, and in those days drink gave me the boost I needed to face the world. Back then I could drink whatever I wanted without it having much effect. I never had a hangover and my skin never gave me away – I was young enough to get away with it.

When I was working away from home, though, it was a different story and I didn't need to rely on drink to get me through. In a way, being one of the Kittens was like acting, so because I wasn't being myself I didn't need that confidence boost. Towards the end of the year, we had a crazy week in Japan – our first visit – where Atomic Kitten was being sold as the new Spice Girls and had really taken off. We flew first class, were booked into an ace hotel in Tokyo and ran around doing live appearances on TV and radio for a week. We shared one room, watching loads of films on TV and taking it in turns on the fold-up bed between two singles. Japanese food didn't do it for me, so I'd eat the same thing every night – chicken curry and chips. The Japanese liked us because we were so upfront and outrageous. When we visited Vibe TV, we wanted to do something mad so they'd remember us, so we sneaked into the building, found the programming department, took a deep breath and burst through the door. We all said, 'Konichiwa,' bowed, then leaped onto the table and sang 'Right Now', looking down at the stunned faces of the ten executives. No one behaves like that out there – unless you want to get noticed.

Wherever we went we behaved as we wanted, whether that meant bursting into song in front of hundreds of disbelieving Japanese commuters or Tash and Liz zapping my bum with an electric zit zapper as we were driving down a motorway; mooning at DJs in their glass booths in radio stations or going out clubbing and having fun.

By November, 'Right Now' had had plenty of local radio air time and we'd begun to get some good feedback. The day the record hit the charts we were booked to play at Anfield Stadium, the home of Liverpool FC, who were playing Sheffield Wednesday. At half time, we walked through the players' tunnel onto the pitch wearing Liverpool shirts. Liz and I had to force ourselves to wear them as she's an Everton supporter and I support Man U, but so long as the crowd didn't know... We performed 'Right Now' to the backing track, and to our amazement the 45,000-strong crowd yelled out for more.

Afterwards, Tash had to go home but Liz and I drove to Mum's with Foxy Knoxy, where we switched on the radio to hear the Pepsi Chart Show. The four of us stood in Mum's council flat, listening to the radio and waiting nervously. When we heard the words, 'And at number ten, it's the new girls on the block, Atomic Kitten, with 'Right Now',' the whole of Warrington must have heard our scream. Getting to number ten with our first single was amazing. We couldn't believe we'd done it and were crying, laughing and going mad all at the same time. I couldn't help thinking how fantastic it was that I'd made it despite everything. I just hoped those primary school teachers who had once written me off as trouble just because I was under a council supervision order would remember my name and see what I'd achieved. Perhaps it would make them think twice before judging people next time. I was so proud and excited by what we'd all done. All the hard work we'd put in with Andy, Martin and Stuart had paid off. What we didn't know was that 'Right Now' would stay in the Top Forty for the next seven weeks. A lot of people had thought it was risky to release a single so close to Christmas, but we proved them all wrong.

Apart from touring, we had TV and radio appearances to make, magazine interviews and after-show parties. It was non-stop. We'd been to so many new places and met so many new people,

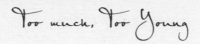

our heads were spinning. One of the highlights of that first year for us had to be appearing on the TV Hits tour that began in August. We were sharing a stage with the big bands like Steps, S Club 7, A1 and Westlife. It was the first time we'd done anything as big and we knew that it would be great for our profile.

Before the show at the Brighton Centre, Liz and I were talking near one of the lifts. I was wearing the outfit I wore for our act – big furry buffalo boots, tiny hot pants and a black off-the-shoulder number with long sleeves. I had my back to the lift when Liz suddenly gasped, her eyes almost popping out of her head. 'Oh my God,' she whispered.

'What's up?' I turned round but couldn't see anything unusual, just a guy coming out of the lift.

'There's one of the lads from Westlife.'

When we'd set off on tour, I couldn't have named or recognized any of them. I was still rubbish when it came to recognizing all the band members because all that stuff had never really interested me. If you'd asked me to name all the guys in Dr Hook, no problem. But I knew Liz was dead excited that we were on the same tour as Westlife. She'd told me all about them: Kian Egan, Shane Filan, Mark Feehily, Nicky Byrne and Bryan McFadden were five Irish lads managed by Ronan Keating and Louis Walsh. They'd already had four number-one hits that year and I'd still never heard of them, which shows how out of touch I was! Whenever we were in the Chrysler, the others wouldn't let me put on my Rod Stewart or Dr Hook, so I'd lie on the backseat, half listening to their music, but I couldn't have told you who was singing it or which of the girls had brought it. Give me the oldies or some country and western music any day!

'Which one?' I was so pleased for her because she was such a big fan of theirs.

'It's Bryan.'

I turned round and saw a tall guy, with brown floppy hair dressed in a round-necked T-shirt with long sleeves. 'Go over and say hi,' I told her.

'I can't, I can't.' She was completely overcome.

I didn't know him and I didn't care what he thought, so I went over. 'Hiya, love. Are you Bryan?' Meanwhile Liz was dying of embarrassment.

'Yes,' he said.

'My mate's a really big fan of yours. Can she come over and say hiya?' Of course he said yes. As we all chatted, Bryan kept looking at me. I didn't think much of it at the time because I was used to blokes giving me the once-over. I suppose I was much louder and more in your face than the others. Next thing we knew, the rest of Westlife appeared – Kian, Shane, Nicky and Mark. When she saw the lads, Liz freaked and ran off, leaving me with them. Thanks, pal! With nothing much else to do before the show began, I went along to their dressing room and sat there at the table, having a can of Coke, while they did a radio interview. Afterwards they started play fighting, rolling around on the floor like puppies. What the hell does Liz see in this lot? I asked myself. They're like kids. Bryan was being really flirtatious but I didn't take it too seriously. Then, when the show started, I went with Tash and Liz to watch them perform and I remember thinking, Bloody hell. They're good.

The after-show party was held in the seafront hotel where we were staying. I snuck into the Gents' with Westlife to have

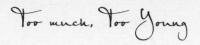

a fag where the fans couldn't see and they were all joking about and asking whether I fancied them and if I'd go out with them. The tomboy in me made me feel great to be one of the lads again, until one of the guys from Innocent came and chucked me out. The record companies' rule was that pop acts couldn't be seen flirting with one another. I went and sat down by the phones around the corner but Bryan followed me. We got on great and I began to think he was quite sweet. He must have asked me out five times that evening and even gave me the pseudonym and password for his room at the hotel in London where they were based. 'Listen, mate,' I said. 'Just because you're in a boy band, don't think I'm going to be another notch on your bedpost. I've never been like that and I'm not going to start now.'

During the tour, I used to see the Westlife lads every now and then, but it wasn't until one night a month later, at a party in our hotel bedroom at the Regents Plaza in Maida Vale, that I began to see there was more to Bryan than I'd first thought. One of the guys in Word on the Street, another band on the tour, had told me that Bryan fancied me, but I honestly didn't take any notice. I'd been going out with Cluke for the last year and I was too wrapped up in the Kittens to have time for anything else. That night Bryan and I sat on the bed together talking and I discovered that he was a fantastic, sympathetic listener. I ended up telling him everything about my upbringing and he seemed very caring and sensitive. Telling someone like him all about the bad things made me feel like I might be able to leave them all behind.

It was late, so he and another boy decided to crash with me and

Tash, and all four of us lay on the bed fully clothed. Bryan's hands were all over me, which really put me off. 'Bryan! Stop it now.'

'But I'm dying to kiss you,' he said as he grabbed me.

'Oh, are you now?' We were laughing as I tried to wriggle out of his way, but then he kissed me. It was absolutely awful, sloppy like a washing machine, and I wasn't impressed at all, but before anything more could happen, Foxy Knoxy burst into the room. She was furious and I knew we were in for it. 'I don't give a shit what Life you're in,' she shouted as she threw Bryan's shoes out of the window. 'Get out of the room now.' Before he left we managed to swap numbers, and the next morning us Kittens took off for more gigging around the country. I lost Bryan's number immediately, just as he lost mine.

The next time I saw him was in November somewhere in Scotland on the Smash Hits tour. I'd heard he was dating Hannah from S Club 7, but we started flirting with one another all the same. We admitted we liked each other, but I pointed out that he had a girlfriend. 'I'm not interested until you're single. So that's up to you. The ball's in your court.' He gave me a kiss on the cheek, went home and finished with her.

At least that's what he told me he'd done during one of our many phone calls. I didn't see him again until 27 November when we were in Manchester and our tour rota coincided. The date's burned into my memory because I was taking a young fan round to get S Club 7's autographs and walked into the dressing room they were sharing with Westlife to find Bryan sitting talking to Hannah. I was so disappointed. He'd obviously been leading me on and they weren't finished at all. 'Oh, sorry to interrupt,' I blurted as I turned round to go back to my dressing room. Bryan

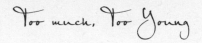

ran after me saying, 'It's over. I was just having a chat with her.' And that's when we had our first proper kiss. Forget the washing machine, this kiss was so sexy.

I'd never met anyone as romantic and caring as Bryan. We had the same sense of humour and were always coming up with one-liners that cracked us up. I just fell head-over-heels, madly, madly in love with him. People would pick him out as the 'ugly one' or the 'fat one' in Westlife, but to me he was beautiful. I wasn't interested in what he looked like. I've never been a looks person and have never gone for the same type of guy the way some girls do. None of my boyfriends have looked alike and I've always gone for the way they treat me. Being looked after is what matters to me most.

Seeing each other was difficult. Not only did we have to hide the fact that we were dating from our bands, our management and our fans, we had a hectic year ahead. Atomic Kitten's schedule had stepped up another level after the release of 'Right Now' and Liz, Tash and I were getting noticed more than ever.

Not long after our first kiss, I took Bryan to meet my Mum in Cabul Close. She was dying to meet him and they hit it off right away. That night we went to the Wheatsheaf with her and her boyfriend, Fox. One of the girls in the pub got jealous of the way her husband was talking to Mum and her mates, and started making trouble. When Mum didn't react, the girl started in on one of Mum's friends, and before we knew it a fight had kicked off and the two of them went for each other. Mum soon joined in and the three of them were rolling around on the floor, hands and feet flying. Nana Betty sat there with our Ange, sipping whisky and muttering, 'It wasn't bloody like this years ago.' In the end, the girl who'd started it all took a good hiding and left with her husband, while we all got back to our drinks. I was mortified inside but played it cool: 'Oh, it's just another Saturday night.' Dead casual. I could see Bryan was panicking. 'It's fine, Bryan. Honest. You'll get used to it if you stick around.'

But why would he want to do that? I'd seen more of the world now and could see how rough my life in Warrington might look to a stranger, but despite everything I still loved living there. I was sure Bryan wouldn't want to see me again, though, and that he'd leave me behind.

To make matters worse, Martin our manager phoned in the middle of the evening. Someone had seen Bryan and me walking around Warrington together, holding hands, and had taken the story to the papers. Martin was absolutely furious. Both of our record companies were terrified that if our relationship was public knowledge it would affect our record sales. Teenage female audiences supported female pop bands provided they weren't snogging the boys they had plastered all over their walls. If the rumour was true, he said, my career with Atomic Kitten could be over. I was devastated. We left the pub and went back to Mum's place, where Bryan and I were due to spend the night on the floor. As soon as we got back to the flat, though, a stupid fight kicked off about whether or not I'd lose my job if I stayed with Bryan. Mum managed to turn the whole argument around to her and what would happen to us if I were sacked. Fox took a swing at Bryan while Mum lashed out at me. It was chaos. I felt so bad for Bryan, but he took it all in his stride as I locked myself in the bathroom and phoned our Angela to come and rescue us. As we left I remember Bryan saying, 'You deserve better than this.'

In the morning he bought me a huge soft toy dog and told me he thought we should end the relationship. 'Look,' he said. 'I've got my career, Westlife has made it, but I don't want to stop you from getting yours. You really deserve it.' But there was no way I was going to break up with him, I loved him too much, so we agreed that we would lie about it and deny that anything was going on. We went back to London to face the music – I was sure I was going to be sacked. Tash was furious that I'd put the band second and risked our careers as a result. That's the only time I ever felt let down by Tash. Looking back, I don't blame her – I expect I'd have felt the same in her position – but at the time I felt I'd given the girls a chance by picking them in the first place and that the least they could do was support me.

By that evening the situation still wasn't resolved. Martin and Innocent had given me a choice: it was Bryan or Atomic Kitten. It was the hardest decision I've ever had to make in my life. Back at the Royal Garden Hotel in Kensington, we both sat on the bed crying. Bryan had made up his mind what we had to do. 'I'm doing this for you,' he said with tears running down his cheeks. 'I've got my career and I don't want you to lose yours.' Then he gave me a kiss and walked out. I was absolutely heartbroken and I sobbed and sobbed into the night, unable to sleep. I didn't want my career to be over, but I wanted Bryan in my life more than anything else. I'd fallen for him fast, but I knew this was the real thing. I think for him I filled a gap in his life, but for me he meant the promise of a proper future.

I couldn't stop thinking about him and how good we were together. As the hours ticked by, I couldn't stand not being able to talk to him, so I called him. He told me that he'd cried in the taxi all the way back to his hotel and couldn't sleep either. We agreed to meet in Kensington High Street. I've no idea why but we climbed over the fence into Kensington Gardens and Bryan carried me so my heels wouldn't get stuck in the mud. We sat all alone on a bench in the cold under the shiny bright stars and talked, and when we eventually got back to my room, he carried me to the bed. I'll never forget one of the things he said to me: 'I've got a circle of life. I've got my career and I've got my family, but there's one bit missing and you're the one that needs to fill it.'

As far as Martin, Andy, Stuart and the management knew, I had chosen the Kittens over Bryan, but the truth was that from that night on, Bryan and I knew nothing would split us up. They may have had their suspicions, but we all played along with it. Our schedules were so manic that we didn't have much opportunity to be together, but if there was a chance we'd grab it. Foxy Knoxy was in on everything and once took me to the back of the Regents Plaza, through the kitchens, to meet Bryan in secret. Liz, Tash and I had done a gig in early December at a school where one of the wires hadn't been properly taped down to the floor. I tripped on it and fell hard on my arse. I'd never felt such pain, and it turned out I'd broken my coccyx, so I came down to London to see a specialist. Bryan had booked himself a room in the same hotel and I was worried he'd want to sleep with me as I could hardly walk, never mind anything else.

When we were alone in my room, he gave me a beautiful little box. I opened it to find a Gucci watch. I was gob-smacked. Gucci and me? It was beautiful but I'd only known him such a short time. 'I can't accept this,' I protested, but I did. He carried me into the bathroom and brought me my pyjamas and some face wash

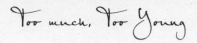

so I could get ready for bed. Then when I came out, the covers on the bed were pulled back and he picked me up and tucked me in. That night, he lay beside me in his T-shirt and boxers, just holding me. He didn't try it on once, we just talked, which I thought was lovely. I was falling deeper and deeper in love with him.

My back was on the mend when Atomic Kitten and Westlife appeared on *Top of the Pops* together later that month. Mum came down to London with our Ange so they could come to the show and the party we threw afterwards to celebrate being in the top ten. Bryan came to see Liz, Tash and me rehearsing 'Right Now' before the show, then when no one was looking, he gave me a sly little wink and mouthed, 'I love you.' He was dead sweet. That night he confessed to Martin that I was the one he was going to marry. Martin could see that we were in love and he agreed to keep our affair secret. I knew that Bryan had booked a room in the Colonnade in London's Warrington Crescent (how weird is that?), and all day I'd been worrying that I was going to have to sleep with him that night. I was petrified because, although I really wanted to, I'd only had two serious relationships before – with Carl and Cluke – and I was worried about what he'd expect or that I might disappoint him, as well as being nervous about having sex with someone new.

Bryan had a cold and sinus trouble, so he had to go to bed early. Liz went out with her family and Tash went out with Word on the Street, but I wasn't in the mood to join them. I was so nervous as the night went on that I had a couple of drinks to give me the bottle I needed. Bryan had given me the key to his room and at last I stood outside, wearing a little black dress with tassels all over it and leopard-skin ankle boots. Taking a deep breath, and with my heart beating a million times a minute, I opened the door to find all the lights off and candles burning everywhere. It was so romantic. Bryan was asleep in bed. 'Hiya,' I said, waking him up. 'You all right?' I sat on the end of his bed and we chatted until I slipped under the covers with all my clothes on and one thing led to another. Halfway through he turned the light on, but I was so embarrassed I turned it off again! As for the rest? All I can say is I needn't have worried.

A few days later, just before Christmas, Liz, Tash and I flew to Japan for a five-day promotional tour and more madness. Bryan and I talked to each other whenever we could and once he played Another Level's 'From The Heart' down the phone to me. The girls and I were knocked out by how romantic he was. Another time he actually proposed to me on the phone, but I didn't take him seriously – we'd only been seeing each other for four weeks, for God's sake. I couldn't wait to see him again. I'd never felt like that about a lad before. Carl and Cluke had been great, but this was different. I'd been so focused on being a Kitten that the whole thing with Bryan had taken me by surprise. I was mad about him.

We got back from Japan on Christmas Eve, and because of the time difference we had two Christmas Eves, one in Japan and one in England, which we thought was brilliant. I was completely hyper, exhausted from the tour and the jet lag, but dying to get home and see Mum and everyone. Bryan had invited me to see in the millennium with him and his family in Ireland. I was so scared about going over to meet them on my own that when Mum dropped me off at the airport, I bought her a ticket too so she could come with me. She only had what she was wearing –

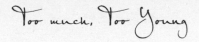
leggings, a jumper and no bra – but I made her come all the same. She'd never been on a plane in her life before and hung on to my hand so tightly I thought she was going to break it.

Because we weren't supposed to be seen together in public, Bryan had got a friend of his called Ray to meet us. As Ray took us out to the car, Bryan jumped out from behind a pillar in the car park to surprise us. It was dead exciting and so wonderful to see him again. I was completely in love with him. I loved the way he made me laugh and the way he cared so much about me. I hated us being apart. Mum stayed in Dublin with Ray while Bryan took me to meet his family. There were loads of people partying at their house, and I met everyone who mattered to Bryan, most importantly his mum Mairead. She was tall and elegant with short, streaked brown hair, but she seemed a bit distant that day. She must have been wondering what her only son's new girlfriend was going to be like. I didn't get the impression she liked me much – perhaps she was worried I might not be good enough for him or that we were taking things too fast. I'll never know. But it didn't matter because as time went on, I discovered the real Mairead. She's such a generous, kind woman who loves her kids to bits and is so proud of them. She welcomed me into their family like one of her own. I love the fact that she says what she thinks and never minces her words, and that she'd take in any waif or stray off the street if she could help them. And later on, after we'd had kids, she helped me out no end by often looking after them while I was working. Bryan's dad, Brendan, a pharmacist, was short, quiet and dead cute while his sister, Susan, was stunning, a really talented singer and dancer and as down to earth as Bryan. They were both dead friendly to me but I was overwhelmed by the number of people I met. As they were organizing a big family photograph, Mairead called me over. I was a bit surprised but pleased that she wanted me in the picture, but then she passed me the camera and asked me to take the photo!

The next day, Mum was happy to fly back home while Bryan and I travelled to Donegal to see in the New Year with his friends Ray and Gary. I didn't have a clue what any of them were saying because their Irish accents were so strong, so I just laughed when they laughed and tried to look as though I knew what was going on. We drove for hours and hours, stopping off on the way to see more of Bryan's family. The family thing was totally new to me. Bryan's dad is one of fifteen and his mum is one of eleven, so Bryan seemed to have hundreds of cousins. Every house we stopped at was crammed with family celebrating Christmas and New Year and wanting to see Bryan. They were all so welcoming, inviting us in and making us sit down for food and drink. I absolutely loved it. Bryan was so proud of me and wanted to show me off, even though no one was supposed to know we were together. His uncles, aunts, cousins, nephews and nieces all came and introduced themselves, but I found it impossible to remember who they all were – I needed them to wear badges so I could sort them all out. We had a great day, but I was absolutely exhausted by the time we arrived at Bryan's cousin's holiday house, a big bungalow in the country, which had been lent to us for the New Year.

As soon as we got there, Bryan said, 'Come on, I want to take you somewhere else now.'

Oh no, I thought, not more family. We've only just got here and I'm knackered. Let's not go anywhere.

So what did we do? We drove to Doe Castle, a big old place by the sea. By now, it was quite late, dead dark and absolutely freezing, with the wind whistling off the water. I hadn't a clue why he'd brought me to the middle of nowhere, but I followed him out of the car and over the fence, into the grounds of the castle. 'Do you know what I've brought you here for?' Bryan asked as he got down on one knee.

'What are you doing?' I started to giggle.

'This is where my granddad proposed to my nana.' My insides turned over. That was the last thing on earth I expected him to say.

'Kerry, you're all I've ever wanted,' he went on, still on his knee while I couldn't stop giggling. A bit of me thought he must be fooling around. 'I know it's soon and I know that I don't know you very well, but I want to spend the rest of my life with you. Will you marry me?'

This couldn't be happening. I had begun to shake now, whether from cold or from nerves, I didn't care. Although we hadn't been together long, I knew Bryan was 'the one' and now he'd popped the question. How lucky was I? I knew immediately that from then on I wanted my life to be totally joined to his and that we would have the happy life I'd always dreamed of.

This was everything I'd ever wanted. This was my chance of having a man in my life who I loved and trusted. I'd seen how Mum had struggled to find a secure relationship, but now I honestly believed I was being offered just that. I thought that from then on my whole life would be different and that I'd be part of a great big loving family with Bryan by my side, whatever happened in life. Who could ask for more? Of course I said, 'Yes, yes, yes. Of course I will.'

After a big kiss, we went back to the car and he opened the boot. Inside was a bottle of champagne and two glasses. Good job I'd said yes! Then he gave me a little box and inside was a ring made of white and yellow gold with five tiny little diamonds. It was so beautiful. He slipped it on my finger and there we were, freezing to death in the pitch dark but engaged.

We both knew we couldn't make our engagement public and had to keep it a secret from our management companies, but right then I could keep the ring on. When we got back to the house, Ray and Gary were waiting. 'Heeeeeyyy,' they shouted; they'd known what was happening all along. For once, I felt embarrassed about being the centre of attention, but at the same time I was so, so happy. Every time Bryan went out of the room I couldn't stop looking at my ring, holding my hand out in front of me and letting the diamonds flash under the light. Oh my God, I'm engaged.

As soon as I could, I phoned Mum, but she'd been in on it from the start, because Bryan had asked her if he could have my hand in marriage. I thought that was such a gentlemanly thing to do. Of course she'd said yes. She was so excited and happy for me and could see that I was going to have everything she'd never had. Isn't that what every parent hopes for for their children? It's certainly what I wish for mine. Afterwards I phoned Lisa as I was dying to share my news with her, though by then I was so excited I could hardly speak.

'Guess what?'

'You're pregnant?' Thanks, Lisa.

'No. I'm engaged.'

'My God,' she shrieked, practically taking my ear off. 'You're mad. You're too young.'

Too much, Too Young

I know that lots of people thought that at 19 we were too young for marriage, but I felt that my childhood had given me an old head on young shoulders and that we knew what we were doing. Besides, the bottom line was that we were in love. I don't know what it was that Bryan saw in me. Perhaps he fell in love with me because I made him laugh. I know that I loved him because he made me laugh, and because of the way he made me feel – wanted and safe. I had never felt like that before. All my life I'd craved love and security, and Bryan gave me everything I'd ever wanted.

11

ON THE
ROAD
AGAIN

HOWEVER MUCH WE WANTED to be together and for the world to know how much we loved each other, Bryan and I had to keep our engagement secret from the public. If any reports appeared saying that we'd been seen together we had to deny them, insisting that pressure of work and the amount of travel involved meant we didn't have time for girlfriends or boyfriends. Announcements were made to the press that Ronan Keating and Louis Walsh had told Bryan he had to break up with me. The idea that the Westlife lads were young, single and available to their fans had to be kept alive, and the same went for the Kittens. Neither Bryan nor I wanted to ruin our careers or for our relationship to affect the others in the bands, so we went along with it.

Westlife and Atomic Kitten both had hectic schedules to keep up, which kept us busy travelling all over the world. Despite that, we did appear at many of the same gigs and TV shows, so we were able to see quite a lot of each other while insisting we were 'just good friends'. We all felt under pressure, but I think the extra pressure on Bryan and me to constantly deny our relationship really told on us. At one point I broke up with him for real. It all got too intense and it seemed like he was always on the phone wanting to know where I was, what I was doing and who I was with. In the end, what with Mum calling me constantly about some problems she was having in her relationship with Fox, and Innocent pressurizing us to get another record in the top ten, everything got too much. I couldn't cope with Bryan's endless questioning, having to listen to Mum and help her sort her life out, as well as dealing with the heavy demands of being a Kitten, so I told Bryan we should finish it. He was devastated, but I was sure that breaking up was the right thing to do. I went on a couple of dates with Dan Corsi, a successful model, and immediately knew I'd made a mistake. Dan was great, but he wasn't Bryan. I phoned Bryan to put it right as soon as I could – I knew that he was definitely the one and couldn't deny it to myself any longer. While he was away on a two-and-a-half-month tour of America, we spoke several times a day to keep each other going through the ups and downs of life on tour. Our phone bills were massive, but we didn't care.

Although, like every band, we were both on a modest weekly wage, we more than made up for it with the side deals and promotions the bands fronted. I found that I didn't want all that much money for myself; what I liked doing was being able to spend it on everybody else, especially my mum. I really wanted to make a difference to her life by giving her things she'd never been able to afford, and my ambition was to buy her a house so that she could have a proper home of her own for the first time – something I managed to do sooner than I'd ever have dreamed possible.

The ball was really rolling for us Kittens now and we began to make appearances in Europe as well as the UK, Ireland and Japan. We released our second single, 'See Ya', in March and it went straight into the charts at number six. For the video we flew to California, where the director had us rolling around like giant hamsters in twenty-foot Zorb balls in the desert outside Los Angeles. We'd thought it would be great, sunny and warm, like being on holiday, but in fact it was freezing and we were so jet-lagged that we spent most of our spare time asleep in the hotel. In the day, we managed a bit of star-spotting, and saw Rachel Hunter, LL Cool J, Patrick Swayze and Goldie Hawn's dad! Bryan was there for a night, too, so we got a little bit of time together.

'See Ya' was picked to front the Fiat campaigns in France and Italy as well as being used in the movie *Bring it On*, so our reputation was spreading. Liz, Tash and I toured everywhere on a non-stop round of appearances, supporting Steps in the UK again, in Europe and Japan, where we were fast becoming one of the most popular international bands. We even had our own outrageous Japanese clothing range with Jassie Tech and shot an ad for a yummy Japanese almondy chocolate called Lotto, as well as releasing our first album *Right Now* months before it came out in the UK. Our singles were coming out every four months, with 'I Want Your Love' in July, along with another great video with a Michael Jackson-style routine I loved where all the dance moves came with kung-fu-style sound effects. This time we went straight to number three, which we were made up about. With every single it seemed like we were getting that little bit closer to the magical number-one spot.

Just as we were riding high, something happened that I hadn't bargained for. Martin had heard that someone was trying to sell a story to the papers about my glamour modelling and lap-dancing days. I had no choice but to go to the papers with the story myself. After all, I didn't see why anyone else should make money out of my past. Martin explained that if I went to the press first I had more chance of controlling what was said about me – damage limitation, if you like. I was proud of being a lap dancer and model and the money had helped pay the bills when I needed it. Now that I was in Atomic Kitten and a bit of a role model for teenage girls, I hadn't planned on letting people see the pictures, but on the other hand, I wasn't ashamed of them either. The lap-dancing stories started the press digging around in my private life, and they soon got wind of my upbringing and began to run stories about my mum and, of course, about Bryan and me. Were we an item or weren't we? The whole incident meant that I was being featured in the papers a lot more often than Liz or Tash. At one stage we did a photo shoot with Beverley Goodway, who I was amazed to find had kept a letter I'd written to him after he'd photographed me when I was sixteen. He photographed us all wearing leather catsuits for the *Sun*, but for some reason they only used the shot of me, alone, on page three. I knew the other two were pissed off about it and felt really awkward, but the *Sun*'s decision had nothing to do with me. I got the impression that Liz and Tash didn't like the amount of press attention I was getting because we were all equal members of the band and not in it to promote ourselves. I completely understood that, but there was nothing I could do to stop it. There were times when I felt I couldn't open a paper without seeing something about me inside.

When you're famous, it's really hard to get your relationship with the press right. In a way you both feed off each other, and there are times when you need them as much as they need you, but it's also impossible to control how far they can pry into your life.

I'd chosen a life in the public eye And I liked the feeling I got from people wanting me or paying me attention – it was something I'd never experienced before – but I felt that meant I couldn't complain when I was splashed all over the papers and magazines. Back then, I was only just discovering what it means to be famous, as the whole obsession with celebrity was just beginning. I had no idea that it would get to the point where paparazzi were sitting on my doorstep every day from nine to five as they do now, taking photographs whether I want them to or not, always there whenever I step outside, following me in their cars. Don't get me wrong, I know they're just doing a job, but sometimes being watched all the time feels too much, and not being allowed to have a private life is difficult. Going out and not being able to have a drink in case you're labelled an alcoholic is plain annoying, and nowadays if I go to the toilet, I never take my bag with me and am careful not to sniff when I come out in case I'm labelled a drug addict.

If only I'd known that it would get ten times worse. Fame brings a lot of good things, but it also brings a fair share of bad. I think the worst thing is the falseness. People look at you differently when you're famous and all sorts of stuff comes back from your past to haunt you. Friends you thought you could trust see a way of making a fast buck by selling stories about you, even when they're not true, while other people who don't want or deserve it, get dragged along on the back of your wave. Some of them love it, but others would rather be left in peace to get on with their lives. At the beginning, though, it was different. Then it was so cool.

MTV decided that they wanted Atomic Kitten to front the MTV Asia Awards in Beijing in June, where we appeared alongside

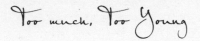

Aqua and Alanis Morissette. On the Heathrow bus taking us from the terminal to our plane, I spotted Lene from Aqua. I looked a mess, travelling comfortably in my trackies and a T-shirt, while she looked beautiful in a miniskirt. She was a stunningly good-looking girl who Bryan had gone out with before Hannah and me. What was he doing with me when he could be with her? I'd heard that she'd discovered she was dumped when she read about it in the papers. Not a good way to find out. When we were on the plane, I went over to say hi, deliberately not mentioning Bryan. We had a good chat but it wasn't until the aftershow party that she asked after him – she had known who I was all the time. She told me she was so mad with him about what he'd done that when she last saw him she'd poured a pint of water over his head. What else could I say but, 'Don't blame you, girl.' And I didn't.

We'd hardly had time to take a breath before the three of us were off again touring Japan, Taiwan, Indonesia, Malaysia and Thailand. This was our sixth non-stop manic trip to Japan. We'd recorded a cover version of the Monkees' 'Daydream Believer' for a Japanese film and had been invited to the premiere. The three of us were having a ball but the constant round of working and play-ing hard was beginning to get to us and we all started to get ill. First of all I had flu, then Tash was admitted to hospital with bron-chitis, leaving Liz and I to appear together at a Bangkok nightclub singing unaccompanied. Then, just as we were about to give an interview on Bangkok's 95.5 FMX station, Liz had to go back to the hotel with earache, so I went ahead on my own, joking that the other two were suffering from alcohol poisoning after a crazy night on the town. For once, nothing could have been further from the truth. Besides feeling run down, I was also finding that I didn't love the non-stop touring as much as I had done when we'd started out. Perhaps I was just exhausted, I told myself, and maybe I'd feel better after a holiday.

The next break in our schedule was in September, and Tash and I flew to Gran Canaria with my mum and her mum, dad and sister. Mum had never flown away on a proper holiday before, so she was really excited and I was so pleased to be able to treat her. We had a great time, even though Tash and I were threatened with the police when we made too much noise jumping in the pool at four o'clock one morning. Bryan had three or four days free, so he flew out to join us. Being with him again was brilliant, but we got totally pissed off with having to sneak around everywhere so that no one would spot us. In the end we decided to set up some pictures of us together, just so people would know the truth. Both the bands had made it so big by now that we didn't believe either of us would be sacked and decided to risk it. Bryan phoned Rav Singh, a London journalist who had known about us from the word go but had kept a lid on the story. In return for keeping our secret, we gave him the exclusive. It was Bryan's last day there, so we told Tash and the others that we were going down to the beach. Rav had sent out a photographer who was there to take pictures of us kissing and fooling about in the sea. Before we could blink, the pictures had been syndicated all over the world and our secret was out in the open. Bryan even bought me a new engagement ring, a platinum band with a solitaire diamond, and proposed again on one knee in our bedroom. I'd been so discreet with the other ring that I was thrilled to have one I could show off properly at last and wore them both together on my engagement finger.

When the pictures appeared, we just acted dumb. I lied to Martin, our manager, telling him that someone must have seen us and called the press, and there was nothing anyone could do except go along with it. But what I found really strange was the amount of made-up stuff that began to appear in the press – I was beginning to learn not to believe everything I read in the papers. There was a huge story about how I'd been jealous of Bryan talking to two girls at a Westlife gig at the Millennium Dome. Apparently I'd stormed into his dressing room where we were heard screaming and swearing at one another. Total rubbish! Another time, I was supposed to have been unhappy because he was flirting with a woman at London's G-A-Y nightclub. I don't know where these stories came from, but they certainly weren't true.

The truth is that Bryan and I hardly ever argued or fought. I found all the stories upsetting to read, but at the same time I was learning that you have to put up with that sort of coverage if you want to stay in the public eye. All that mattered was that I knew Bryan and I were head over heels in love. We just had to turn a blind eye to the negative things that were said about us. He proved his love to me over and over again by the little things he said and did whenever we were together. I thought I had everything a girl could ask for.

Despite the break, the magic of being in the band hadn't come back to me. The thought of another single and going back on the road had lost all its appeal. We'd started working on the next Atomic Kitten single, 'Follow Me', but thoughts were beginning to creep into my mind as to whether I really wanted to carry on in the band. Our schedule was relentless, we were all exhausted and I was finding it hard to cope with all the stuff being written about me in the press. We'd had such an amazing adventure together that in many ways I didn't want it to end, but the excitement I'd felt when we were starting out had long gone. The three of us got on really well. Not surprisingly there were moments when we rubbed each other up the wrong way, though it was never anything serious. Liz and Tash were the sisters I'd never had, especially Tash, my drinking partner, and we stuck together through good times and bad.

Everything came to a head when we were rehearsing at Virgin. In the middle of it all my mum phoned. She was upset because people were giving her funny looks in the street after some story had appeared about her in the papers. I wanted to help her but there was nothing I could do about it. The pressures of work meant I didn't have the time or energy I needed to give her the attention she wanted. I couldn't spend enough time on the phone with her and felt as if I was letting her down, but at the same time, I couldn't take her neediness any more. Suddenly it all got too much: I locked myself in the toilet where I broke down and couldn't stop crying. Eventually Bryan came and kicked down the door, then he took me home to Mum's where I had two weeks off to recover. I was diagnosed with depression and given anti-depressants. I didn't need to be told I was depressed. I recognized all the signs from the times I'd seen Mum struggling with it. The mass of thin white scars on her wrists told the whole story, and there was no way I was going to go down the same path. But although that was the last thing I wanted, I thought that if I took the pills I'd be admitting I had

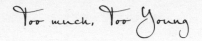

the same problem. I was too frightened to do that, so I threw them away.

By the end of 2000 Atomic Kitten was really feeling the strain. Our schedule was as tough as ever with yet another new single and the *Right Now* album to promote, but we were made up to get Best Newcomer Award at both the *Smash Hits!* Pollwinners' Party and the Disney Awards. I finally decided that I really did want out, and asked Andy, Martin and Stuart to meet us in a pub in Peterborough, where we were doing a signing in a record shop. I think they knew I was unhappy, but I don't know whether or not they expected me to leave. When I told them I'd had enough, the lads were gutted but said they understood, and we agreed that I'd carry on until after the release of 'Whole Again' in February. Tash kept banging her fist on the table, saying, 'We'll carry on. This won't stop us. You replaced Heidi with me, so we can do the same again.' She accepted I couldn't go on and that I wanted my life to revolve round Bryan's now. Liz was much more emotional, and as we left the pub to get in the car that was waiting for us, she ran off down the street in tears. She really thought that it was all over.

Looking back, it probably wasn't the best time to tell them, as there were rumours circulating that we'd been dropped by our record label after our album, *Right Now*, had only climbed to the giddy heights of number 37 in the charts. I found out later that in November Hugh Goldsmith was told he had to drop us. As we were already booked to appear on the *Jim Davidson Christmas Special* on an aircraft carrier in Spain, we went anyway and Martin kept the bad news to himself. Meanwhile, Andy and Sean told Innocent they could keep the last part of the advance for 'Whole

Again' and they'd release it themselves. Hugh Goldsmith thought they must have another licence lined up, so begged Virgin for one last chance. They agreed but gave him the tiniest budget possible.

All we knew was that it was due for release in February. It felt like the bandwagon would never stop. Things finally reached breaking point when Liz and I had a big falling-out. We were touring with Steps again and were scheduled to meet two competition winners. Bryan was with me, so I'd called Carl, our driver, and Foxy Knoxy to ask if there was room in the car for him. They said it was no problem, so we were picked up later and driven off to collect Tash and Liz.

When we arrived at Liz's, I went into the house to get her and saw that her fourteen-year-old brother Joe was all dressed up as if he was coming with us. I said I didn't think there was room in the car and climbed back in, leaving it to our driver – after all, it wasn't my business to say who could or couldn't travel with us. Carl got out protesting, 'Liz, you can't just bring Joe. You need to phone and ask.' She obviously didn't realize that I'd asked if Bryan could come and was furious that there wasn't enough room for Joe. I was sitting behind the front passenger seat, playing Snake on my phone, and Bryan was sitting beside me, trying his best to ignore what was being said. In the end, Joe had to be left behind, but Liz whacked me across the back of the head when she got in the car.

That did it – swiping the back of my head was something Dave always used to do, and it immediately brought back the bad times. I threw my phone on the floor, took off my seatbelt and dived between the seats to get at her. Bryan had to use all his strength to hold me back. Poor Bryan had never seen me lose my temper before and was trying to calm me down while Liz was crunched up in a corner trying to get away. 'Don't you ever do that to me again,' I shouted. 'We all have our problems and we all argue but you never hit, not from behind. If that's how you want to play it, come on then. You and me. Outside, now.' Bryan and Tash were watching, gobsmacked. Once Liz could see that I couldn't reach her, she started laughing at me, and that wound me up even more. 'Carl,' I roared. 'Turn the car round now, before I kill her.'

'I can't do that, Kerry. We've got the Steps gig.'

'Turn it round now. I'm telling you.' He could see I meant business and turned us round.

When we got back to Liz's house, she leaped out of the car and ran into the house, locking the door and pulling down the blinds. We left her there and carried on to the hotel to pick up the competition winners. Without telling anyone, I ran away and jumped in a taxi, driving around for ages, raging inside. Why should I stick around and help the girls promote the new single after what Liz had done? I went over to Mum's and called Martin from there, explaining what had happened. He came over right away. 'Martin,' I said, 'if you put me on stage with her tonight, I'll throw her off it. I swear. We're like sisters and of course we argue, but she knew what she was doing.' He was very understanding and agreed that Liz had been out of order, so we came to a compromise: I agreed to perform, but only on the condition that Liz didn't get in the same car as me or use the same dressing room. Then, just when I felt calm enough to get back to work, Martin dropped a bombshell: telling me that Innocent had never wanted me in the band in the first place. I don't know to this day why he decided to tell me then. Perhaps he meant nothing by it, or perhaps he was just saying that they'd been right about my being a loose cannon. Whatever the reason, it was an awful moment: I felt so rejected, as if everything over the last few years had been a big lie. All the good memories I had of my time with the Kittens – the way being one of them had improved my self-esteem, the independence it had brought me, the fans and the great feeling of being wanted – were overwhelmed by insecurity. My immediate reaction was to think, I'm not good enough; they never wanted me in the first place. They must be so pleased I'm going.

That incident was the final straw. I'd loved being a Kitten while we were clawing our way to success. When no one knows you and you don't give a shit, climbing the ladder's a real laugh. But I was discovering that once people make it, they change, and I really didn't want that to happen to me. I'd loved being with the girls and we'd had great times along the way. We couldn't have asked for better support than having Andy, Martin and Stuart behind us. But now that we were internationally famous, the fun had gone for me.

I'd never been driven by the idea of fame, like some kids are, although I did have a sort of sixth sense that I'd be famous one day. I don't know what it was, but something inside me just told me it would happen, and my friends recognized it too – or at least they said they did. My childhood had taught me what I wanted in life, and fame wasn't the first thing on the list. I had always wanted a job so that I could have my independence – I wasn't going to end up on the dole with nowhere to live. I'd been there with Mum, and once was enough. I also knew I craved love and respect from other people, and that I wanted the sense of security and self-worth a job would give me. I wanted the pleasure I'd found with Atomic Kitten of being able to do a job well, but I'd also learned that nothing lasts for ever. Changing homes and schools all the time meant I'd never stuck at anything for more than a few years, but through that I'd learned that something else always comes along.

Looking back, I'm not sure what direction I thought my career would go in when I left. I was just focused on being with Bryan and on stopping feeling so tired and stressed all the time. I think I probably thought something would turn up – it usually did! Besides, I had other things on my mind...

12

ENOUGH

THERE'S NOTHING like a bit of Ann Summers to spice up your sex life, so one night I turned up at the Conrad Hotel, where Bryan and I were staying, complete with a maid's outfit. I felt really nervous and a bit self-conscious as I went up to our room and waited for Bryan to return. I knew he wouldn't be long because he'd left candles flickering on almost every surface in a typically romantic gesture. When he got back, we drank the little sex drinks I'd bought from Ann Summers – God knows what was in them, but we had a fantastic night... in more ways than one. That was the night our Molly was conceived. I'd always been a bit careless about contraception, and obviously that night was no exception. Of course I didn't know for weeks, and in any case my mind was on whether or not I should stay in the band.

I thought no more of that night in the Conrad until we were being photographed in London's Home House for our official engagement announcement in *Hello!* magazine. Caroline, my make-up artist at the time, took one look at me and said, 'God, girl, your tits are massive. Have you had a boob job?'

'No I have not, thanks very much. They're all mine.'

'Then, you must be pregnant.'

'No, I'm not,' I spluttered. 'I'm just due on, that's all.'

She looked a bit doubtful but I knew better. All the travelling we'd been doing in and out of various time zones had put my periods all over the shop. But a few days later Bryan and I were shopping in Harrods when he accidentally elbowed me in the bust. I couldn't believe how painful it was – I was nearly in tears.

'I bet you're pregnant,' he said.

'You what?' The idea had honestly never crossed my mind.

We carried on browsing around Harrods, but neither of us had our mind on shopping, and eventually Bryan said we should buy a pregnancy test. We got to the car and asked the driver to take us to a chemist. Neither Bryan nor I had any cash on us, so I had to ask our driver to lend me a fiver. We pulled up at a nearby chemist and in I went, baseball hat on and hood up, praying no one would recognize me.

Back at our hotel, we sat down and switched on the TV. Bryan was gripped by something so didn't take much notice when I stood up, saying, 'I suppose I'd better do that test, then.' I don't think either of us really thought I could be pregnant: the implications for us and for our careers were too great. When I peed on the stick, the line appeared almost immediately – I couldn't believe it. I was shaking and laughing, standing up and sitting back down on the toilet while still peeing. When I came out with my pants around my ankles, Bryan was sitting with his feet up on the table just looking at me.

'I'm not lying. I'm not lying. I'm not lying,' was all I could say. I had no idea what his reaction would be and the thought that he might be furious scared the life out of me.

A big smile crossed his face as he stood up. 'Well, we're going to be great parents,' he said, giving me a big hug.

As soon as he let go, I ran off and hid behind the sofa where I started crying. My first thought was that my mum was going to kill me. I knew she'd think I was too young, that I was messing up my career, and she wouldn't be happy to see me following her example. I was in shock, scared by what having a baby would mean to us, but at the same time really excited. I couldn't believe I had a tiny baby in my belly. Oh my God. I'm only twenty and I'm going to have a baby. The idea kept going round and round my head until it sank in. The first person we phoned was Tash. Bryan had to ask her to come round because I was crying so much, and from the way I sounded on the phone, she thought someone had died. She looked so relieved and happy when I told her the real reason.

'Baby Gap!' she said the moment she heard. She was made up for us both.

Bryan ordered us drinks to celebrate and the three of us got into bed together that night. I couldn't wait to wake up in the morning and touch my belly, knowing I was going to have a baby. As soon as I knew, I was determined to give being a mum my best shot and give my child everything I'd never had.

The next morning, the Kittens were due to appear on *SM:tv*. I was playing James Nesbitt's wife in *Chums*, the *Friends* spoof starring Ant, Dec and Cat Deeley. I went through the motions, but all the time I kept asking myself, How am I going to tell my mum? What am I going to say to her?

The night before Bryan and I had decided to wait until the three-month mark before telling Mum, but I knew she could read me like a book and that I'd never be able to hide the news from her for that long. When the first break came, I found a quiet corner and phoned her. 'Hi, Mum. I'm pregnant. Got to go back on the telly. Bye.' I hung up before she had time to say anything, then at the next break I phoned her again. She was screaming and crying at the same time. 'What are you doing? You'll ruin your career? You're only twenty. Are you mad?' As she was speaking, I told myself that everything would be OK. It's a mother's instinct to overreact when their twenty-year-old daughter does something unexpected. I know she had only my best interests at heart but I also knew she'd come round eventually. She wasn't going to spoil this for me. We couldn't talk for long because I had to have my make-up done before going back on to act the next scene as if nothing had happened. I had the surreal feeling that I was two people rolled into one – one who was hugging an exciting secret to herself and another who was the professional, getting on with the job. Whenever I needed to, I could snap back into a role. The story of my life!

I had a heavy work schedule, promoting the single and album right up until Christmas. Then I went to Ireland to spend Christmas with Bryan and his family. We badly needed the break, especially because 2001 was going to be a busy year for Westlife, with plenty of touring abroad, including two months in Europe and another five in the States, while Atomic Kitten would be working harder than ever with the release of 'Whole Again' in February. We'd waited to tell Bryan's parents in person, and if they felt the same as Mum they didn't show it. Mairead was lovely, reassuring me that everything would be fine. 'At least it's with "the one", Kerry,' she said.

I didn't see Mum until the New Year, and by then she'd had plenty of time to come to terms with becoming a grandmother. She was over the moon about my being pregnant and so excited about the idea of a baby in the family. It was while I was staying with her that I had some bleeding at nine weeks. I was so scared I was losing the baby and Mum was no help at all, crying and screaming all over the place. Luckily Lisa was there; she was the one who kept calm and got me to hospital, where I was reassured that sometimes women experience early bleeding. They wanted to check I wasn't having an ectopic pregnancy, though, and the next day they gave me a scan, just to be sure. Even though it was hard to make out what was what at that early stage, seeing the fuzzy white shapes that the doctor told us was Bryan's and my baby moving about on the dark screen – they didn't look anything like one to me – was an incredibly emotional experience and quite a bonding thing for Mum and me. We both cried. It was amazing to think there was going to be one more in our tiny family. I was so sad that Bryan was on tour and wasn't able to be there to share the moment.

What really upset me while I was staying with Mum was receiving a hand-delivered, hand-written anonymous letter call-ing me every name under the sun, saying what a terrible mother I'd be and how the baby should be aborted. I have no idea who I could have hurt so much that they would want to write such vile things. They must have been someone local, but to this day we have no idea who it could have been. Most people know that I'm a good person who would do anything to help anyone. I was only a human being, carrying a baby, trying to do my best. There must be something wrong with a person to write something like that. Of course, Mum was up in arms for me, but there was nothing she could do. Without a name or address, we just had to try to forget about the coward who sent it.

As the reality of my pregnancy sank in, I realized I definitely didn't want to be in the band any more. All my life I'd dreamed of being part of a proper happy family, and now I was on the point of having my own – a wonderful husband, a baby and me – and I didn't want to risk losing any of them. After the bleeding, the doctors had recommended I took time out for complete rest.

When the day came to go back to work, I just couldn't do it. We were due on the Pepsi Show, but when the car came to get me something stopped me. I called Martin and told him that I couldn't perform again. They had already lined up Jenny Frost from a band called Precious to take over from me after the release of 'Whole Again', but luckily she was able to step in immediately. She came on board for the promotion of 'Whole Again', the single that would be Atomic Kitten's first number one, beating U2 to the top spot. I was really pleased for Liz and Tash, but I didn't regret my decision for a moment. I felt as if I'd achieved everything I'd set out to do with Atomic Kitten and that the time had come to move on. I'd had an adventure and would miss the girls badly, but having felt as if my pregnancy had been threatened once already, I didn't want to go there again. I know that lots of women continue with their careers, performing until they're quite far gone, but I didn't want to be one of them. I just didn't want to risk damaging the baby by leading a full-on high-stress life. So I gave it all up for a much quieter existence.

I didn't have an easy pregnancy. My back was still sore from when I'd fractured my coccyx, although I found lying on the floor helped lessen the pain. I felt really poorly at the beginning and my hormones were all over the place, so I was very emotional and would cry at anything, including that ad for Carphone Warehouse where the little mobile gets run over. For some strange reason I found it really sad! Bryan didn't know what to do with me, because I reacted to anything that was remotely upsetting. I also went completely off the fags and couldn't touch alcohol. I just didn't want them any more. My body must have been telling me what was best for the baby.

Bryan didn't want to live in Warrington, so we decided to settle in Ireland where Bryan's family live, and I was happy to give up everything for him. I also felt it was the right time to leave the place where so many bad things had happened to me. This was my chance to start afresh with a new family. I knew Mum could come over whenever she wanted, so leaving didn't feel like too much of a wrench. At the same time I was able to fulfil one of my life goals and used some of my Atomic Kitten money to buy her a small three-bedroom house in Warrington.

Bryan and I found a house in Delgany, a little village just south of Dublin in County Wicklow, near Greystones. It was a show home in the Elsinore private estate and I fell in love with it because it had a dishwasher – something I'd never had before. Second to that were the big pine staircase, the large light rooms and the huge modern kitchen. Bryan was away with Westlife when we moved in, so Lisa came over on the first night to keep me company. As we walked through the front door she burst into tears, sobbing, 'Oh my God, I'm so proud of you!' We wandered around it together in shock. After all the things I'd been through, coming from a council flat to this expensive flash house was unbelievable. I told my mum that I was going to do it all properly – I was going

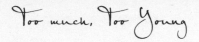

to get a sewing machine and do the gardening and all that stuff. None of it happened, of course, but that was my dream: not to have the money, just the family and everything that went with it.

Although I was poorly throughout the pregnancy, I loved the idea of being pregnant, of having our creation inside me, of having a baby who would want me forever. At the beginning, I had an image of myself pregnant with a dead slim body and a neat little bump in front, looking good, but it didn't work out like that at all. I ballooned to a size 14 and spent most of the time in trackies, looking in the mirror and moaning about how fat I'd got. Not that I really minded. The feeling of a baby kicking in your belly is fantastic, little butterfly flutterings that over the weeks turn into footballer's thumps. The only time it's not so good is at two in the morning when you're dying to get some sleep and the baby's playing drums on your bladder.

The only problem was that the house was a bit too isolated. If we hadn't been in such a hurry to find a home and had thought about it properly, we'd have realized it wasn't ideal. Bryan was on tour for much of the time after we moved in, so I found myself alone, unable to drive and in the middle of nowhere. The house was too big and creepy for me on my own and I'd hear strange noises that would freak me out when it got dark. I think I must have had pre-natal depression while I lived there, because along with all the normal side-effects of pregnancy, like lack of sleep and tiredness, I became very anxious, irritable and sad for no good reason.

To keep me company, our Angela and her husband visited, and Mum was over a lot of the time, managing a good line in jokes to cheer me up.

'Knock, knock.'

'Who's there?'

'Kerry Katona.'

'Kerry Katona who?'

'That's show business!'

Thanks, Mum! But we laughed and laughed.

Of course, the one person I really wanted to see was Bryan, but his work commitments were endless. We did manage to get together for his two twenty-first birthday celebrations though. One was in a London club called Propaganda, but it was so crowded and smoky I decided to go back to the hotel early – places like that aren't much fun when you're not drinking and just want to curl up in bed. Once again the newspapers reported that we'd rowed, which wasn't true at all. Then we had a proper family party in a Dublin hotel. I gave Bryan a black electric piano, wrapped up in a big red bow, so he could go on with his composing at home. When he walked into the room and saw it, he was nearly in tears – it was great having him home again. He loved me pregnant and was so proud of me. He wanted me to wear a short top to the party so my belly was on show, but there was no way I was doing that: I thought it looked disgusting. Mid-party, he sat me on a chair in the middle of the huge function room, surrounded by his family, and sang 'If Tomorrow Never Comes' to me. I was so embarrassed, but that's how romantic Bryan was. He was constantly writing songs for me, including my favourite 'Memoirs of Love'. I love the words about how true love is never taken slowly.

When I was about six months pregnant I flew alone to Italy, one of the stops on Westlife's European tour. I'd been to Cyprus with our Angela for a photoshoot so was dead tanned, but my belly had got really big since I'd last seen Bryan. As I came through the arrivals doors with my case I could see him on the phone, chatting. When he saw me his mouth dropped open in shock. I ran right back into the baggage hall and called him from there. 'I'm not coming out. You think I'm dead fat.' In fact, he wasn't horrified at all. I was afraid he wouldn't fancy me any more, but I was wrong. He thought my belly was so beautiful that he couldn't stop touching me. All the Westlife lads came knocking on the door of our bedroom so they could have a look too.

Bryan was in Ireland when I had to have my next scan, and the gynaecologist asked if we wanted to know whether the baby was a boy or a girl. I wanted to keep it a surprise and said so, but because he'd missed so much of the pregnancy, Bryan said he wanted to know. The gynaecologist wrote the answer on a piece of paper and gave it to me. We went outside and sat in the car. We were dead excited, and I can remember Gabrielle singing 'Out Of Reach' on the radio as we unfolded the paper. It said, 'Female'. Female? For a moment we couldn't think straight, then we both shouted, 'It's a girl.' We were going to call her Molly. Molly McFadden sounds like a real star's name.

Molly was due on 6 September 2001, my twenty-first birthday. Mum was staying with us in Delgany and we had plans to go to the Billy Connolly show in Dublin on 30 August. I hadn't had any pains, but I was sure something was happening, so decided not to go to the show. Mum was really fed up because she'd been looking forward to it. When she went up to bed, I decided to sleep on the big sofa downstairs. I was as comfortable there as anywhere and couldn't face hauling myself up three flights of stairs. Bryan put some cushions on the floor and slept beside me. I couldn't get to sleep, and suddenly I thought I'd wet myself. Then I realized my waters had broken, so I sat bolt upright to wake Bryan, who woke my mum. Bryan was running around like a headless chicken while I sat shaking on the toilet. I was scared stiff; I was about to become a mum. All my worst fears rushed into my mind. What if the baby didn't like me? What if something went wrong with the birth? What if I didn't like the baby? By 1.30 a.m. we were on the way to hospital. Bryan was glued to his phone, telling everyone I'd gone into labour. I was really scared, but Mum was absolutely brilliant at keeping me calm and reassuring me that everything would be OK. Bryan had been away so much during the pregnancy that I hadn't thought there was much point in going to any childbirth classes without him. I thought that was something couples did together. Now I think it would have been more sensible to go alone so that I'd have been a bit more prepared. All we'd done was listen to the doctors we'd met and watch babies being born on TV.

At Mount Carmel hospital we were given a room on the labour ward. Everything's a bit hazy, but I remember that Bryan never seemed to be there; he was always off getting everyone pizza, which was the last thing I wanted. When the pain got too much I had an epidural. By that time Bryan's mum, Mairead, was there as well as mine. When it came to the birth, our mums left the room so Bryan and I could be alone when Molly came into the world. That was the most amazing moment of my life. When I held her I burst into tears. The love I felt for her hit me so hard it took my breath away. She was beautiful, the spitting image of

Filming in the LA desert for the 'See Yu' video

On cloud nine with Bryan just after our engagement

Me and Tash in Gran Canaria as, back home, the news about Bryan broke

Looking really rough after giving birth to our Lilly

Big sister watching over little sister – our Molly with baby Lilly

Happy families – Mum, me, Molly and Lilly

Celebrating Molly's
second birthday

Thumbs up! Bryan with
our gorgeous girls

Bryan's mum,
Mairead, with Molly

Katie (Jordan) and me having our last taste of luxury for two weeks

'We are doomed' – me with Jonny Rotten

Before our jungle challenge – from left to right: Lord Charlie Brockett, Peter Andre, 'Razor' Ruddock, Jonny Rotten, Mike Reid, Tara Palmer-Tomkinson, Mark Durden Smith, me, Diane Modahl, Katie Price, Alex Best and Jennie Bond

Back home to an ace reception in Warrington

With Mum at my Welcome Home party

The best people in the world – my foster parents, Mag and Fred

On holiday in Marbella with Dave (left), Max Clifford (right) and his partner, Jo

With my fiancé Mark who changed my life

My first film role as Denise in *Showbands*

Bryan, and she weighed eight pounds two ounces. She was quite clean, with just a little bit of blood on her head, and looked nothing like the wrinkled bloodstained babies we'd watched being born on TV. She was just gorgeous. It was love at first sight. If I could have bottled the feelings I had when I first held her and could let them out whenever I feel down, I'd be the happiest woman in the world. I stared at her and said, 'Hello, beautiful. I've been waiting for you.'

I think Bryan was in shock. I thought he'd cry like the dads we'd seen on TV, but I don't think he could take it all in. He just stared in disbelief at her in my arms. Mum and Mairead soon joined us and were crying with happiness; I'll never forget it.

While I was still in the hospital, I tried to breastfeed Molly, but she didn't take to it and I was worried I was going to smother her with my huge tits, so we quickly changed to bottle-feeding. After that she became a very contented baby who didn't sleep much but was very happy when she was awake.

Having Molly made me realize just how Mum must have felt about me almost exactly twenty-one years earlier, and understanding that made me feel even closer to her. I knew that just as I was making resolutions for Molly, she must have done the same for me. Things might not have worked out the way she'd hoped, but at least we'd made it through together, which is more than can be said for many families.

The other person I couldn't stop coming into my mind was my real dad. I hadn't given him a thought for years, but now I couldn't help wondering what I would tell Molly when she grew up and asked who her granddad was. How would I tell her about my childhood? I couldn't stop thinking about how he might never see his granddaughter and how she would never know him. I wondered how he would feel about being a granddad.

Bryan was very understanding and patient when I told him my worries; he could easily have brushed them aside, but instead he listened and helped me saying, 'You know you've got my dad.' I thought that was sweet. I loved his dad Brendan to bits, but although I knew he'd make a fantastic grandpop, he still wasn't *my* dad, and there was no getting away from that.

In spite of everything, though, I was never once tempted to contact my real dad. Mum had told me his name years before, and that he came from Liverpool, so I could easily have tracked him down. I've just always chosen not to try because I respect his decision to stick by his family and would never do anything to disrupt that. I comfort myself with the thought that perhaps he knows who I am and that he has watched what's happened to me. I hope he's seen photographs of his granddaughters in the press and is secretly proud of them.

When I got Molly home, I was the most protective mother on earth. At night, I'd sit awake, watching her lying in her bassinet beside our bed. I loved the way her little face screwed up and ironed out again while she slept, the tiny duck-like sounds she made as she breathed and the little sucking thing she did with her mouth while she dreamed. I could watch her little fingers curling and uncurling for hours. I'll never forget that special newborn baby smell, her lightly wrinkled skin and the peachlike down on her cheeks, the smooth soles of her tiny feet with their perfect minute toes. I constantly wanted to pick her up and nuzzle and kiss her. She was like a drug that I'd become completely addicted

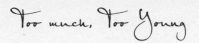

to. Although we were separate, I still felt joined to her, so that when she cried, I felt an almost physical pain.

At times, I'd think I was going mad as I imagined all the bad things that could happen to her. What if she stopped breathing? If she slept too soundly and stopped moving, I'd prod her to make sure she was still alive. Suppose I dropped her down the stairs? I was terrified that she might choke when she coughed or was sick and felt I had to keep guard every moment and be the one to do everything for her myself. All my fears made me really tearful and I'd confide in Mum, telling her how scared I was that I was going insane. 'I'm sick in the head, Mum,' I sobbed. 'I keep thinking someone's going to kidnap her. What would we do if that happened? What if someone hurt her?'

'It's OK, Kerry.' Mum could be so calm when she was handing out advice. 'Every mother's like that with their first child.'

'But I'm going mad. I keep imagining such awful things.'

'Don't worry, love. That's what everyone feels. I promise.'

I've since spoken to friends and have discovered that she was right, but at the time, I was unbelievably anxious. Gradually my fears lessened and I was able to enjoy Molly without feeling panicky that something would go wrong at any minute. Bryan was great with her and absolutely idolized her, although he got bored quickly when it came to the routine things like changing nappies and dressing her – that's when he'd disappear off to his PlayStation. I don't remember him getting up once in the night when she cried. Mind you, I was so protective that whenever he tried to help, I'd sit there telling him how to hold her and feed her. He must have got so sick of me saying, 'No, Bryan, not like that. No, Bryan, you're doing it wrong.'

In the end, Mum was quite firm with me, saying, 'You've got to let Bryan do something with Molly. He might not do things your way, but you've got to let him get close to her too.' I knew she was right, but I found it really hard to let go.

On my twenty-first birthday, soon after we'd come home from Mount Carmel, there was a knock at the door. I couldn't think who it was because we were at home with Mum and Mairead and weren't expecting anyone else. When I opened the door there were all my friends from Warrington, including Lisa and our Angela. I was completely gobsmacked and so were they. All of them were dying to see Molly, but they kept on saying, 'Oh my God. It's so weird seeing you with a baby.' To me, being with my baby felt completely natural, as if I'd been born for it, even though I still wasn't very confident. While they were there, I couldn't relax at all. Everybody was celebrating and getting pissed, but I was up and down the stairs all night with Molly. Mairead was happy to look after her for me so I could party, but I didn't want to leave Molly's side.

As the scary newness of motherhood wore off and we settled into a routine, I soon realized I couldn't just sit around the house on my own with a baby all day. Bryan was away a lot, I had no friends living nearby and I couldn't drive. If anyone did come to visit, we had to make a big thing of it because they'd have to travel so far, so there was no dropping in for coffee or a quick chat. I found I desperately missed doing some sort of work and realized I needed to be out there entertaining, because that's what I love to do. At the same time, though, I didn't want to be apart from Molly.

* * *

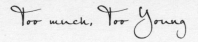

After my experiences on TV with the Kittens, I thought I might be able to make a go of television presenting. I'd already done a little bit and felt quite at home in front of the cameras. The good thing about doing that was that I would be able to organize my work life around Molly. We also decided to move away from Delgany to Dublin where we moved in with Mairead and Brendan, Molly's doting grandparents, until we found somewhere of our own. They are such top people and they really made me feel at home. I adapted quickly to living with them and Mairead was always helping me out with Molly, babysitting her when I couldn't take her with me. In the end she gave up her job as a receptionist to help out whenever we needed her.

My first presenting job was with Bryan when we did the pop interviews on ITV's *This Morning* while it was hosted by John Leslie and Coleen Nolan after Richard and Judy's departure. We interviewed bands like Steps and B*witched, sometimes over the phone and sometimes setting up game shows in the studio. The job was great fun, but we found working together more difficult than we'd imagined. Bryan's a great singer and performer, but he felt quite uncomfortable presenting, whereas I took to it like a duck to water. I think my background helped because I was used to having to get on with people quickly and the job gave me exactly the experience I needed.

Everything seemed to be perfect We were head over heels in love, engaged to be married and had a beautiful baby daughter. Bryan was my knight in shining armour and my best friend, all rolled into one. He had changed my life and I couldn't imagine ever waking up with anyone else beside me. Now all we had to do was plan the wedding.

13

WEDDING DAY

My FIRST THOUGHT had been to run away with Bryan and marry quietly without anyone, not even our mothers, knowing. Bryan's family was so big that I couldn't bear the idea of a big church wedding with all of them crowded onto one side of the aisle and only Mum, Nana Betty and about twenty of our family on the other. Gradually I came round to Bryan's idea of something much bigger, until we both agreed that we wanted a perfect fairy-tale wedding. We wanted the day to go as smoothly as possible, so decided to have a wedding planner to help us – Tara Fay. Tara was so energetic and full of ideas. She completely got what we wanted so that we never had any fallings-out. The most important things I wanted was for everyone to have a really good time and that it would be a day to remember. Because I didn't know Ireland that well, I was happy to go along with what she suggested. We only went to see one church, and as soon as we saw it, we knew it would be perfect. The tiny Church of the Immaculate Conception in Rathfeigh, County Meath was everything we'd hoped for and was really close to Slane Castle, where we would have the reception.

The church had such a romantic atmosphere and enough seats

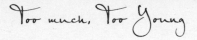

for about 250 people. It was pretty small, so felt very intimate, and on the white walls under the dark vaulted ceiling were fancy framed pictures illustrating stories from the Bible. I dimly remembered one or two of them from school. Under the stained-glass windows at the back of the church was a gallery, which was just the place for a choir to stand and sing. Bryan had been to loads of pop concerts in the grounds of Slane Castle, but I don't think he'd ever dreamed he'd be married there. The square, grey-stoned castle stands in acres of beautiful countryside overlooking the river Boyne and was exactly the magical setting we'd dreamed of.

Although we would have liked to share the day with our fans, what we really wanted was a family affair. With that in mind, we did a deal with *Hello!* magazine, giving them exclusive rights to the coverage. We got a lot of criticism for doing that, but we felt the protection they would give us would help the day go without a hitch, and OK, the money helped too! We couldn't have done it without Tara and her family, who all got involved, with her dad bringing the cake over from England, her mum bringing my dress, her sister booking all the flights and her brother-in-law videoing the wedding. They were brilliant.

Planning the wedding and looking after Molly took up most of my energy. Apart from that there was the small matter of moving out of the McFaddens' into our new home on a private estate in Donaghmede, Dublin: a pair of dead cool penthouse apartments that we planned to knock into one. As for the wedding, there was so much to decide on: from the invitation list and seating plan, which Mairead helped with a lot, to what we were going to wear. Then there was the food – Mairead and I went to a food tasting that Tara arranged and together we chose the menu of melon, vegetable soup, beef, and sticky toffee pudding – the cake and the music. The only little hiccup I had was with my dress that was being made by Neil Cunningham. At five foot three, I was tiny beside Bryan's six foot four, so I'd told Neil I wanted something that would make me look tall and slim. I've never been one for diets, and after having Molly I was a size bigger than my normal size 10. My size 6 days were long gone. I'd had been back and forth to London for fittings, but looking at the photos now maybe I should have gone on a diet – although the dress was gorgeous. Neil made me an ivory satin basque that was covered in glittering crystals over an ivory satin fishtail skirt with a tulle underskirt that flared out at the bottom. At one point, I let slip to Bryan that the dress was a fishtail. He really wanted me to have a big, more traditional dress, so I went back to Neil to change the design, but it was too late. Neil suggested a veil. 'I thought only virgins wore those,' I joked. But I got one all the same, one that was short at the front but trailed behind me, and was held in place by a crystal tiara.

I didn't have time to be nervous until the bridesmaids' dresses were delivered, then suddenly the whole thing seemed over-whelmingly real. My mum and Bryan were both at home when the dresses arrived and immediately sensed something was wrong with me. That night, Bryan tactfully went to watch the football on TV, leaving Mum and I together. I climbed into bed with Mum, which is still one of my favourite places to be when I'm feeling off. 'How come this happened to us, Mum?' I asked. 'Five years ago we were living in a council flat and I was on the dole. We had nothing. I can't believe all this.' Neither could she, of course, but I knew she was dead proud of me, as well as sometimes feeling disappointed and guilty that she hadn't been able to do better for me. But perhaps because of the way she had been with me, I came out a fighter and had achieved this on my own. Now the nerves were kicking in. The idea of walking down the aisle in front of all those people was so scary. What if I tripped up? Suppose something went wrong and Bryan changed his mind now that everything was organized? What if we'd sat everybody in the wrong places and they had a horrible time? Suppose the bands or the DJ weren't any good? Anything could go wrong. And, believe me, I thought of every single possibility.

We'd had our stag and hen nights back in November when Bryan had some time at home. I'd gone for a night out with Georgina (Ahern) and Gillian (Walsh), Nicky and Shane's girl-friends. He'd gone out with the Westlife lads and some of his mates. He'd come back the next day in a weird mood, warning me about people selling stories on us. I had no idea why he was suddenly so worried about that side of things. I reckoned he'd got a cracking hangover, and if he seemed a bit strange towards me, it was because of that. They must have had a top night out, that was all. He was soon back to normal anyway and we were looking forward to what we had planned for the wedding. I didn't think any more about it. There was far too much else going on.

We invited twenty-six of our close friends and family to stay with us in Slane Castle for the week before the wedding, which took place on 5 January 2002. Our parents were there, along with my six bridesmaids – Tash, our Angela, Bryan's sister Susan and my friends Marlyn from Ireland and Michelle and Lisa from Warrington. Fred and Mag came, as well as Bryan's groomsmen,

Ray and Gary, Shane from Westlife, Bryan's old friend and best man Eddie Loughlin and friends Peter Smith and Mark Murphy. We had a brilliant week with all sorts of activities laid on. The boys went off and did quad-biking, clay pigeon shooting, horseriding, golfing and football, while us girls could join in with the boys if we wanted or stay at the castle and be pampered. We'd brought in several beauty therapists who gave us facials, massages, pedicures, manicures and did our hair. Everyone had a fake tan done, except me – I was too scared it might rub off on my dress and I didn't want to look as if I'd been sweating on my big day. I just wanted everyone to relax and enjoy themselves.

One day I went riding with my bridesmaids for a laugh, something none of us had done before, or at least not since we were tiny. The next day we were all limping around the castle. We took it easy after that! There were master chefs who prepared fantastic meals for us, drink was on tap and nothing was too much trouble for the staff. On the Thursday we had a crazy karaoke night. Bryan was in his element, having been a real karaoke kid before he joined Westlife, and when we managed to get the mike off him, everyone else took a turn, belting out their favourite songs. Mine had to be 'I Will Survive', of course! We all got pissed and enjoyed ourselves, with everyone getting to know each other before the wedding.

The night before the big day Bryan and I went for dinner in a little restaurant near the castle, then we said goodbye at midnight. He went off to share a bedroom with his mates for the night – all very traditional – and Marlyn came in with me. Although Bryan was allowed to leave his room, I wasn't allowed to leave mine until the wedding, so she and I lay on the massive four-poster bed chilling. We were so giddy, giggling and joking, but that didn't stop us from going to sleep. I woke up early, my stomach a mass of butterflies. Out of the windows, an Irish mist was swirling across the fields. As I couldn't leave the room, all the girls came to get ready with me. We had a stylist to help them, as well as my own make-up artist and stylist, and the *Hello!* camera crew crammed in as well. We had such a laugh, messing around in slippers and dressing gowns with our hair in rollers, a glass of champagne to steady the nerves while trying to look good for the camera at the same time. Once my hair and make-up was done, I put on my dress, my strappy gold Gina shoes, a dead glam diamond bracelet and earrings a jeweller lent to me for the occasion – and my blue garter!

Everybody fantasizes about having a fairytale wedding dress, but this really was the business, and a million miles away from the white tablecloths I used as a veil when playing getting married at Nana Betty's. I'd wanted my bridesmaids in a Christmassy romantic colour, so they all wore deep-red raw-silk basques and long skirts that buttoned up the back, with matching stoles and silk shoes. The detailing was lovely, including heart shapes embroidered in the same deep red on the top of the basques and skirts, and they carried white roses surrounded by reddish berries and little frothy white flowers while my bouquet was a tight bunch of creamy roses wired with crystals that would glitter in the dimly lit church. Bryan and I had also given each of the bridesmaids a pair of diamanté earrings and a matching necklace to top them off.

Thanks to my nervous bridesmaids, especially our Ange, taking an age to get ready, I was nearly an hour late leaving the castle. With my fantastic foster father Fred, who was going to give me away, we were driven off in a heavily blacked out blue Rolls Royce, with a Gardaí motorbike escort. Although no one could see into the car, we could see out, and there were knots of people standing by the roadside between the castle and the church, hoping to get a glimpse of us. I felt bad disappointing them, but there was nothing I could about it now. There was tight security surrounding the church, thanks to *Hello!*, with a twenty-foot-high black curtain rigged up by the door, which drew around the car when it stopped so the paparazzi couldn't get any shots of us. I was dying to get into the church. Thank God Bryan had waited for me.

As the orchestra started to play, my bridesmaids walked ahead of me down the aisle one by one. Then the music changed as it was my turn. I was still dead stiff from the horseriding I'd done a couple of days before so a tune from a John Wayne movie might have been more suitable. I was proud to be on Fred's arm. I felt a million dollars and couldn't wipe the smile off my face as everyone turned to stare at me. I could see Molly in my mum's arms, looking cute in her ivory silk dress with its red sash. Mum was looking really elegant in a black suit and gold top, with her hair up and a little feathery hat. I could smell the lilies in the arrangements decorating the choir rail of the gallery where they were mixed with white roses and Christmas tree branches. There were even little arrangements decorating the candle holders at the ends of the pews. The atmosphere was perfect, really intimate and loving.

Waiting at the end of the aisle was Bryan, looking handsome in his ivory brocade frock coat, deep red and gold waistcoat and gold tie. He'd been going to wear the traditional top hat and tails, but decided days earlier that they made him look like a hotel porter, so at the last minute he'd commissioned a Dublin tailor to make him something else. Beside him were his groomsmen, their red waistcoats matching the bridesmaids' dresses. When I reached him, he held my hand and looked me in the eyes as he murmured, 'You look gorgeous.'

Before the ceremony started, we lit a single candle each to represent the two of us. Father JJ Mullin, the chaplain at Bryan's school who'd become a close family friend of the McFaddens, led the service with parish priest Father Gleeson. Because Irish wedding masses don't usually include hymns sung by the congregation, we'd had the London Community Gospel Choir fly over especially. When Tara played us their CD, I knew immediately that I wanted them. They were fantastic, especially when it came to a solo of 'The Lord's Prayer', which a woman sang so emotionally that everyone couldn't help but clap. When we had to exchange gold and silver coins, Bryan turned round suddenly and asked the congregation, 'Has anyone got a Euro? I've forgotten to bring one.' Everyone saw the funny side and someone stumped up a coin.

My happiest moment was when we took our vows and exchanged rings. Bryan's was a real diamond knuckleduster while mine was two diamond bands that fitted above and below my second engagement ring. Then we signed the register as the choir sang 'Lean On Me'. From the flames of the two candles we'd lit at the beginning of the service, we lit another single candle to symbolize our togetherness, then we turned to both our mums, who were holding wax tapers which we lit, and they in turn lit everybody else's until the church was ablaze with hundreds of tiny flickering flames and our great friend, Dane Bowers, sang our song 'From The Heart' from the gallery. That was a really

239

emotional moment for both of us, and at last Bryan was allowed to kiss the bride – those three kisses meant everything. We were totally in love and this was the start of our new life together. I believed that we'd stick together whatever life flung at us. I felt so unbelievably happy. But life always has a few surprises up its sleeve, doesn't it?

After the service we all drove back to Slane Castle for the reception. Bryan and I welcomed everyone, standing by a huge Christmas tree while a barbershop quartet sang in the background. The castle looked amazing, with Christmas decorations everywhere, including a giant garland of pine branches, pine cones and white flowers which wound all the way up the main staircase with baskets of white azaleas and narcissi everywhere. The reception started with Kir Royale and canapés like mini pizzas, chicken kebabs and stuff like that. I knew from my touring days what it was like to be faced with food you didn't recognize and what a fool I'd always felt having to ask what something was. I didn't want anyone at our wedding to be made to feel uncomfortable, so kept everything simple, although because Bryan's favourite food was sushi we did have that too.

Two hours later we all moved upstairs for dinner in the ballroom. Gold organza was laid on top of white tablecloths on the round tables so they glittered in the candlelight. Tall brass candlesticks surrounded by little white flowers stood at the centre of some tables, while others had bowls of roses or vases of lilies and roses on them. When I'd snuck up before the service to see the room laid out for the first time, I thought it was the most beautiful place I'd ever seen. We'd asked all our friends and family not

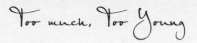

to give us presents, although they could donate something to the National Society for the Protection of Children and the Irish Society for the Protection of Children if they wanted to mark the occasion somehow. Instead of them giving us gifts, we gave each of them a memento of the day on their side plates – a special silver coin with Bryan's and my initials on one side and a picture of the castle and the date on the other.

Bryan and I sat at the top table with our parents, the brides-maids and groomsmen, and as we ate dinner we watched the magician Keith Barry go between the tables doing magic tricks. Bryan and I held hands under the table and had the occasional kiss, but although I was enjoying myself I couldn't really relax. I couldn't stop worrying about whether everybody was having a good time, although they all looked as though they were.

After we'd eaten, we all went back downstairs for the speeches before cutting the cake, which was an amazing fairy-tale castle, just like the one I'd imagine Sleeping Beauty slept in: four pointed turrets, its own drawbridge and fairy lights twinkling in the meringue around the base. Fred spoke first. He got out a piece of paper and said a few words about about how proud he and Mag were of me, though that's not half as proud as I was of the two of them, not to mention grateful for all they'd done for me during a difficult time in my life. He sounded choked up as his voice caught a couple of times, but he managed to keep going. Then Bryan made a beautiful speech about me, although I had to contradict him when he said we'd known each other for three years.

'Two,' I yelled.

He looked shocked. 'Oh no. Am I at the wrong wedding?'

When I tried to interrupt him again, he turned and joked,

'Shut up or you'll be divorced next week.' Then after a moment he added, 'So am I going on my honeymoon alone then?'

No way!

At the end he sang a snatch of 'Can't Take My Eyes Off You' and kissed me.

As you can imagine, I wasn't going to let the moment go without saying something too, so I moved over to the mike and thanked all my family, but especially 'my mum, who isn't just my mum, but my dad, my brother, my sister all rolled into one'. I felt incredibly close to her right then. I couldn't see her, but I knew that she'd be welling up somewhere in the crowd.

With all the formalities done, we partied well into the morning. The Irish might know how to party, but us English can keep right on up with them. Fifteen minutes of fireworks splashed across the sky, ending with Bryan's, Molly's and my names and a big heart. Back inside, Bryan and I led the dancing to my all-time favourite song, Dr Hook's 'Years From Now', which was played by a local band, the Shakes.

By this time we'd both changed: Bryan into a top hat and tails like Fred Astaire and me into an amazing black dress that was an exact copy of my wedding dress. I kept Molly downstairs for the dancing, but she was soon tired and went to bed, where she was looked after by the nanny we'd hired for the night, so we could all relax. The Shakes eventually handed over to DJ George Courtney, who handed over to Paul Harrington on the piano. As the night went on, I exchanged my Ginas for a pair of comfy flip-flops that no one could see under the dress. Mum went one step further and put on her slippers, having changed into one of Shane's T-shirts – a gold one like her top, which she'd spilled something on.

Although there were rumours in the press about Westlife, Ronan Keating and even Atomic Kitten singing, none of them did, although we did do some karaoke. They were our guests, for God's sake, not part of the entertainment. The only interruption was some more food, when burgers, chips, hot dogs and potato wedges were served at 2 a.m. I didn't want anyone having to stop off at a kebab shop on the way home because they were hungry! The party was still going strong when, at about 4a.m., Bryan suggested we went to bed. We were the first to leave and left the others to it.

Bryan had organized the whole honeymoon, right down to the white limo that picked us up from Johannesburg airport with a bottle of champagne on ice and took us to the Palace of the Lost City Hotel in Sun City. Walking into the vast marble-floored six-storey atrium with palm trees dotted around it immediately told us we were staying somewhere completely different. The hotel was a huge palace set in acres of jungle with hanging gardens, bubbling streams, swimming pools and places to sit out and eat or drink. Our room was unbelievable, even bigger than our two penthouse flats in Dublin put together – apparently it was the same room Michael Jackson had stayed in when he'd visited. There were vases of flowers everywhere, a huge four-poster bed, a mirror and marble-lined bathroom with a bath big enough for six and a shower to fit ten. I mustn't forget the grand piano in the living room and the twelve-seater dining-room table – a must on any honeymoon! On the balcony was a lovely hot tub, although I spent half the time running away from the spider monkeys that insisted on jumping over to keep us company.

Westlife were huge in South Africa so we had to be accompanied everywhere we went by a giant of a bodyguard called Ivan, who barely spoke. On safari, seeing elephants and lions in the wild was amazing, although I was a bit nervous of the ranger's gun. Seeing it reminded me that we weren't in Chester Zoo and anything could happen. Bryan was soon recognized and almost immediately made friends with a band called Franklin who were playing in the Sports Bar one night. They all piled back to our room and spent the rest of the evening singing and song-writing, so I left them to it and went to bed.

After four days in South Africa we flew on to Mauritius, which was everything I'd dreamed a tropical island would be – white sands overhung by palm trees, pretty villages dozing in the sunshine and the bluest sky and sea I'd ever seen. Le Saint Geran hotel was on the north-east coast of the island, surrounded by tropical gardens with a beach on one side and a lagoon on the other. We could lie in bed and look out through huge windows across the sea to the horizon. There were a couple of different bars and restaurants where you could sit outside under the sun or the stars. Any thoughts I'd had of us being alone together soon disappeared when Bryan flew out two friends of ours, Mark and Marlyn, to join us. Looking back, I can see that Bryan seemed to be getting more and more bored of being on his own with me. I had begun to feel it when we were in Sun City, but told myself I was just being silly. Don't get me wrong, it was great having the others there, it just wasn't how I'd imagined my honeymoon, that's all. The four of us lazed around, taking a mini cruise together, sunbathing by the pool or going out to the bars in the evening, and sometimes Bryan and Mark might play golf during the day, or disappear into the casino or go drinking in the evening, leaving Marlyn and me to amuse ourselves. There was plenty to do, with an amazing spa where you could get all sorts of treatments, pool, bars and entertainments every night, but all I could do was wonder what Bryan was up to and why he wasn't there with me. Mauritius was a good holiday, but it wasn't romantic, although having some time together without the pressure of work in the background was fantastic. I was a bit disappointed we didn't have more time just the two of us, but I went with it because I'd do anything to please him. If that was the way he wanted it to be, then that was good enough for me. I was too love struck to be able to see the signs that things weren't quite right between us. In the end we had to leave for home a day early because a cyclone was heading for the island. That was pretty scary, but I bet it was nothing like as big as the cyclone that was heading for our marriage.

Despite the honeymoon being suddenly cut short, we were both dying to get back to Molly. Although we rang home every day to hear how she was, it wasn't the same as having her with us. When you don't see your kid for two weeks they change so much – as every mum knows, every second of every day counts when you watch a child grow. Molly seemed so much bigger and more aware than when we'd left her and I was sure her hair had got a bit longer. I promised I'd try not to leave her for so long again.

Back in Dublin, we settled into our new home. I was looking forward to our life together. I knew that our jobs would mean that our marriage would be different from lots of other people's but one of the reasons that I had given up being in the band was so that I could try to be that perfect housewife and mother.

Although I realized that we'd have to keep up a public front at the various charity and music-biz dos that we were invited to, I hoped that in private, when we were at home together, we'd be as normal as Mag and Fred.

With Bryan caught up in a heavy schedule of endless rehearsals, preparing for the next Westlife tour, I was keen to carry on establishing myself as a TV presenter. There was never any question of my being a 100 per cent stay-at-home mum – I needed to work because it gave me the sense of independence I'd always valued. Although I had Bryan, I wanted to be able to pay my own way. I'd been made offers to appear at concerts and had even been offered a record deal, but I didn't have the nerve to perform on my own. Instead, I was dead excited to be given the chance to work as a reporter on Channel 5's *Exclusive*, a showbiz and celebrity gossip programme where I had to interview pop bands like S Club 7 and Steps. It was the perfect job for me because I didn't have to be away from home for long and could even take Molly with me sometimes.

My first big presenting job came when I was asked to front ITV's *Elimidate*, an outrageous version of Cilla Black's *Blind Date*. We went off to a different exotic location for each programme, where four girls went after one guy and four guys went after one girl. The contestants had to do crazy tasks to win and were eliminated one by one until the final couple was left. Molly and Mairead came with me and I loved making the show, meeting the contestants and seeing the world – talk about a dream job.

Molly was turning into a great kid. She was never a problem

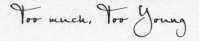

travelling. You'd almost never have known that she was there. She looked more and more like her daddy with her big blue eyes. She had those baby hamster cheeks, a big smile and a round belly. By now she was crawling and loved being held so that she could stand upright, testing how strong her legs were. Although I dressed her up in pretty dresses sometimes, they were never on for long. Expensive clothes for a ten-month-old are such a waste of money. They get dirty within minutes of putting them on and before you've blinked they don't fit any more. I loved babies wearing babygros so Molly was always in them. She'd never slept well so at night I usually had her in bed with me. That wasn't such a good idea because when I tried to put her in her own bed, she didn't want to go. Even at four, she still prefers being in bed with me. She was never into toys, never had a blanket or a dummy, but she loved hearing us sing, especially Bryan. Are you surprised? She looked as if she was hypnotized as she listened to him. If she heard him on the radio or the TV, she'd be clapping madly. Her first word was 'Daddy'. I wish that I'd kept up the baby book that I'd had since she was born, but I always let it slip so I can't really remember all those landmarks. I do know that she took her first steps on her first birthday.

During the previous year, Bryan and I had been able to spend long stretches of time together, but now that our schedules had got busier, we were finding it much harder to be together. Whatever happened, though, family always came first, and we'd get on a plane at the drop of a hat to visit one another.

When Bryan was at home, Mairead was fantastic: 'Kerry, you don't have to be with Molly every hour God sends,' she'd say. 'I'll look after her while you two go out.'

I learned from her that Bryan and I had to put our relation-ship first, making sure we had quality time together. I think you need that in a relationship, otherwise you'll just argue. We spent time as a family whenever we could, too. My childhood had taught me that mums and dads need to be with their children, giving them all the love and security they need. Apart from Bryan's and my relationship, giving love to Molly and making sure her childhood was happy was what mattered most.

I was blissfully happy as Kerry McFadden during those first few months of our marriage. I felt as if I had everything I'd ever dreamed of: a perfect husband and daughter and a promising new career. The only small cloud was when I had an ovarian cyst that made me swell up like a balloon. When it burst, I was in agony. At first I thought it was a case of bad wind, but Bryan made me go to hospital, and once the doctor realized I had a cyst, they wanted to test to make sure it wasn't cancerous. Just hearing the word cancer made me freeze. I couldn't have cancer, not now. Everyone was very reassuring, but just knowing there was a chance made me think about my life, and of course what would happen to Molly and Bryan if there was something seriously wrong with me. The days spent waiting for the results of the biopsy seemed to go on for ever, and the relief when we were told it was benign was intense. I'd had a bad reaction to the operation, which had left me looking as if I was seven months pregnant on my left side, so I had to stay in hospital for several days until it was safe for me to go home. Bryan stayed with me every night – he couldn't have been more caring and supportive when I needed him most.

14

BREAKING UP IS HARD TO DO

THE SUN WAS BEATING DOWN in the Bahamas as we were coming to the end of filming for *Elimidate*. Mum and Mairead were both with me, helping to look after Molly. I phoned my mate Michelle for a chat to let her know how things were going and to check she'd received her tickets to come out and join me on the next leg of filming in Las Vegas. Before I'd even got a word out, she was off: 'I can't believe the story that bitch has sold to the paper.'

'What? What are you talking about?' I was working so hard that I hadn't heard any news from home.

'That bitch. She's saying stuff about Bryan.'

'What?'

'Didn't you get my text?'

'My phone's not working.'

'Oh my God.' For a moment Michelle was silent, then she was back on the story. I couldn't believe what I was hearing. Apparently a lap dancer was claiming she'd given Bryan a blow job on his stag night at Lapellos club in Limerick and that he'd paid her £15,000 to keep quiet about it. As soon as Michelle had finished, I called Bryan, but instead of being reassuring, he had a massive go at me, shouting down the phone. 'If this is what you

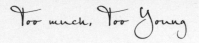

think of our marriage... If you really think I'd do something like that, just go and get a divorce.'

'But Bryan, the paper says...'

'I'm sick of people accusing me of these things,' he yelled.

'But Bryan, this woman's saying that you paid her £15,000 to keep her mouth shut.' All I wanted was some sort of explanation, but instead he hung up on me.

I felt so guilty for badgering him. I knew the woman must be lying or that the paper had made a mistake. I also knew my Bryan wouldn't do that to me. He knew everything I'd been through and how many times I'd been rejected and let down by people I'd trusted. He wouldn't do that to me.

I phoned our Angela, the only other person I felt I could ask, who was much calmer. She had the paper in front of her so I switched to speakerphone and got her to read the article out loud, all the way through. By the time she'd finished, I was devastated. I collapsed, sobbing and screaming on the floor. Mum held me while Mairead made me swallow a couple of Valium. I think my reaction frightened the life out of them. 'Bryan wouldn't do that. I know he wouldn't.' I knew the papers got things wrong, but why would this woman make up something like that? In my heart, I think I knew some of it had to be true. I called Bryan again and this time he wasn't answering his phone. I was desperate to speak to him, so even though I was hysterical, I called Louis Walsh, then the tour manager Paul Higgins, then Kian, Mark and Shane – I phoned them all. Someone must have told Bryan he had to speak to me because finally he answered.

'Tell me the truth, Bryan. Just tell me the truth,' I begged.

He just said, 'Yeah. It's true.'

I felt as if someone had ripped out my heart and trampled all over it. Everything he'd said, everything he'd promised meant nothing. And if he'd lied about this, what else had he lied about? Everyone on his stag night, including all the lads in Westlife, Dane Bowers – our friends for God's sake – must have known and no one had told me. Our wedding had been a sham. The fact that this woman had given him a blow job was one thing, but getting her to sign a gagging contract for £15,000 was another. Somehow, that made it even worse.

In my mind, I kept going over and over the night in November when it had happened. Although I'd noticed he was behaving funnily the next day, in the excitement of the wedding, I'd dismissed it and hadn't given it another thought. Now I found myself going over every detail of what had happened. Bryan had to have his stag night then because it fitted in with his tour dates. I had Georgina and Gillian, Nicky and Shane's girlfriends, coming over. We'd been joking around, but I remembered them saying, no, no, there weren't going to be any lap dancers where the boys were going. I've always been easy-going, never mind being a lap dancer myself, so I'd told Bryan, 'Go out and enjoy yourself. Have a laugh. And when you get there don't keep calling me, just have a good time.' I didn't mean for him to have that good a time, but he obviously had done.

Bryan had called me that evening. He was the worse for wear and told me not to go out with the girls but to go to bed. It was sweet of him to think of me because I'd been having some stomach pains that we later found out were caused by the cyst.

'Just enjoy yourself will you,' I repeated. 'It's your stag night.'

He didn't answer his phone when I tried to call him the next morning, and when he came home, I knew something had

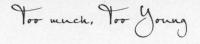

happened because he wouldn't look at me – I could see there was something wrong by the look in his eyes. There was just something different about him. Something had changed. He apologized for giving me a hard time on the phone the night before.

'Don't worry, babe. It's fine,' I reassured him. 'Forget about it. Did you have a good time?'

'Yeah,' he said. 'But I've got to warn you that girls will try to sell stories about us. They will try and destroy us.' I couldn't imagine why he was suddenly coming out with all this, but I went along with it. Looking back, I'm just amazed at how naïve I was. I guess I loved and trusted him so much I didn't think to doubt him; he was my everything.

'I know that and I'll believe anything you say. You know I will.' I promised.

'If it ever happens, we'll have to be strong. We must trust one another or it'll cause havoc between us,' he insisted.

At the time, I'd dismissed the conversation and forgotten all about it. Now, five months later, I saw it in a completely different light.

Putting two and two together, I remembered our honeymoon. Lovely as it had been, it hadn't been what I would call romantic. Then, only weeks before the lap-dancer story broke, we had seven days off together in Belfast. Bryan seemed to have changed towards me. All he seemed to want was sex; he didn't want to be affectionate at all and that wasn't the Bryan I knew. When I asked him if everything was all right, he told me not to be so stupid. Another time, when I'd flown out to Sweden to be with him, he appeared in the hotel lobby with his arms around two fans, then went off without me to go gambling.

They say love is blind, and perhaps that's what I'd been. I had brushed even the faintest suspicion under the carpet because I didn't want to know. Of course I didn't. Keeping my family together was too important to me. After the story broke I had to see Bryan immediately to sort things out. The *Elimidate* crew were fantastic and gave me forty-eight hours compassionate leave. Mairead took Molly back home to Ireland and I flew to Manchester where I was met by Paul Higgins, the Westlife tour manager. Bryan had apparently told Paul to get me into the car and take me straight to the Newcastle hotel where Westlife were staying. My first reaction had been to want to tell Bryan I wanted a divorce, but I would never have gone through with that in a million years. Despite everything I was still madly in love with him and hoping I'd find out the story had all been a terrible mistake.

Paul and I laughed all the way to the hotel. The only way I could deal with the situation was to joke about it, with a few tears thrown in. 'God, Paul. She got fifteen grand for a blow job. What do I get if I give him one? A new pair of shoes. That's it!'

'Now, Kerry. We've got these Americans coming to watch the band so don't hit him, whatever you do.' Paul's first priority had to be the band.

'Hit him? I'm going to kill him.'

'You know I can't let you do that,' he said nervously. 'If you hit him, make sure it's his stomach, not his face. We don't want anything to show.'

I'd booked myself into a separate room at the hotel, and when we got there, Paul was shitting himself because my room was right next door to Bryan's. Imagine what he felt when we opened the

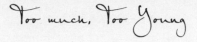

door and saw that it was a themed baseball room. The bed looked like an American car, the toilet was a jukebox and hung all over the walls were various bits of baseball kit, including helmets and, yes, baseball bats. How handy, given the situation. I was so over-tired I couldn't stop laughing. If I hadn't, I'd have cried.

Before I could see Bryan alone, I went down to the gig with Paul. When I saw Bryan on stage he was singing 'Angel' and I just burst into tears. I was so hurt and felt so betrayed, the more so knowing that everyone knew. I couldn't help picturing him and the lap dancer together over and over again, wondering how many other times he might have betrayed me.

Eventually I went back to Bryan's room – Paul was too nervous of us meeting in mine with all those baseball bats – and waited. When Bryan came in, he walked towards me, his face showing how sorry he was. He put out his arms, but I didn't want him near me. 'Don't touch me,' I snapped. Although I'd rehearsed what I was going to say and how I was going to beat the crap out of him, everything flew out of the window. When we were finally in the same room alone together and I could see his expression, all I could do was cry. 'How could you do this to me?' I sobbed. 'How could you deceive me like that? I trusted you. And all those idiots in Westlife knew and let me walk down the aisle.' The idea that so many people knew but hadn't told me hurt almost as much as what he'd done.

He was crying too. We were both heartbroken by what had happened. He explained that it was a stupid drunken mistake and that it meant nothing. He still loved me and no one else. He apologized and I forgave him. I suppose that deep down that's what I'd wanted to happen all along. I didn't *want* anything to come between us, so I wouldn't let it. But patching things up wasn't as easy as that. Whatever we both said, my emotions were all over the place. I wanted to believe Bryan, but I needed time.

The next morning I had to fly out to Las Vegas for the next leg of *Elimidate* with Michelle. I was cracking up and badly needed a friendly shoulder and someone to talk to. One minute I wanted to be with Bryan, the next I never wanted to see him again. Somehow I managed to get through the filming, putting a smile on for the camera and crying as soon as an interview finished. I couldn't tell you what we did, my head was completely taken up by my marriage and what was going to happen to us. Ironically, the last leg of the filming was in Mauritius, our honeymoon destination. By then the paparazzi had tracked me down, so I had to keep smiling and holding up my hand to show my wedding ring, while inside I was dying.

It was hard to keep going. Bryan and I had huge rows over the phone as we tried to deal with what had happened. The incident just wouldn't go away, and every day something new seemed to be written about it in the papers. We couldn't just pack up and go home to sort things out as we both had to keep working, so instead we swept everything under the carpet, just like I'd swept away any suspicions I'd had all those months ago. And there they lay, hidden until the next time. We picked ourselves up, put it behind us and carried on as if there was nothing the matter. Everything went back to normal – more or less.

Not long afterwards, I started to feeling unwell. The symptoms were horribly familiar, but Bryan was away doing a gig somewhere so I asked Marlyn to buy me a pregnancy test. When

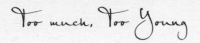

it came up positive I refused to believe it. It couldn't have come at a worse time. I didn't even know if I wanted to be with Bryan any more. Although things had calmed down we hadn't really tried to sort out our marriage or talk about our relationship properly. I made Marlyn go out and buy eight more tests, and every one of them came up positive.

Marlyn was still with me when Bryan came home. He'd just stepped through the front door when I said, 'Can I have a word alone in the bedroom? I've got something to tell you.'

'You're pregnant, aren't you?' He knew immediately. When I told him I was, he just stood and looked at me. I was sure that I could see his eyes fill with disappointment, but, if they were, he covered it up quickly and put on a good show of being made up.

Later, lying in bed, I felt I had to be honest with him. I had so many doubts in my mind and felt very confused about what was happening to us. 'Bryan, I don't know whether I want to have this baby,' I admitted. 'I don't even know if I want to be with you.' As I was saying it, I knew that I could never have gone through with an abortion. After having Molly, I could imagine another little baby just like her and there was no way I could take its life. I'm not against abortions because I know everyone has their reasons, but it was something I could never have done, even under those circumstances.

'No, No.' He was absolutely certain. 'We're having this baby. This is what we need. It will make us stronger and it will make us happy.'

I believed him.

I was still only five weeks pregnant when I began getting pains in my stomach like the ones I'd had a year earlier. I was told it might be a cyst or an ectopic pregnancy, where the baby starts to develop outside the womb, in which case I'd have to have it terminated. Hearing that made me want the baby so bad that nothing would dissuade me. A scan showed that I had two ovarian cysts and would need an operation to remove them, but at least the baby was in the right place. When the doctors told us I might lose the baby because of the operation, I just burst into tears. All my doubts about having another child had vanished and now all I wanted was a healthy baby. Fortunately the op went well, the baby stayed put, and after resting for a short while I was fine again. I say fine, but all through the pregnancy I was tired and sick. Any arguments between Bryan and me – and there were plenty – I just put down to hormones.

Despite everything, I managed to keep on working though it all. I was signed up to present *Britain's Sexiest* with Michael Greco, where the viewers decided who were the most gorgeous men and women in six categories – fitness instructors, teachers, airline crew, builders and plumbers, doctors and nurses, and fire fighters – and was presenting *You're a Star* with Louis Walsh to find Ireland's entry for the Eurovision Song Contest right up to the day before Lilly was born. In *You're a Star* every judge was allowed to play a wild card and put through to the next stage one contestant who hadn't been voted through; when I chose Bryan's sister Susan I was accused of favouritism and got into a lot of trouble. But it was ridiculous, Susan's got a fantastic voice and would have been a great representative for Ireland. Unfortunately, I think having me as a judge really went against her. It was also during that show that I made a joke I've regretted ever since. Why I said that I never sang any of the words when I

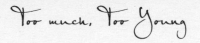

was with Atomic Kitten, I don't know. Of course I did, otherwise I wouldn't have been in the band. It wasn't a very good joke and it backfired on me completely.

Bryan was incredibly busy with Westlife and his work took him away a lot of the time. The band had just signed a massive album deal and Westlife fever looked as if it was never going to stop. The lads had had ten number-one hits in the UK alone since they started back in 1999 and were now huge all over the world. When we could, Molly and I would join Bryan or he'd come home. Things between us were back on an even keel again, with him being as loving and romantic as ever, kissing and cuddling and surprising me with unexpected treats. Once he called me to tell me to get ready because we were going out. When he arrived to pick me up, he was carrying a single red rose as if it was our first date and we went out for dinner and stayed at a hotel. The next morning he was back at work, but he sent me a bunch of red roses. We really did seem to have got over the worst. And perhaps the worst had even brought us closer together.

Bryan would be at home at least every two weeks or so and sometimes I'd go to London to see him. I know it isn't the way most married couples live, but it seemed to work for us. We still liked doing the same things together, watching episodes of *Friends* in bed, looking after Molly and laughing at the same jokes. There were always friends round at the house for parties and barbecues. We'd go to the pictures, to charity and showbiz functions in Dublin and London. I never really enjoyed those glam nights out though, and used to feel dead unfashionable when we went to them. We'd get there, everyone would drink, I'd end up with mascara all over my face, lose my coat or the heel off my shoe and then we'd have to find our way home. Not that much fun. I'd have given anything just to turn up in my 'jamas and slippers. Imagine everyone's faces if I had! Given a choice between one of those evenings and a quiet night in, I'd always choose the night in.

At the same time, the pressure on Bryan and all the boys in Westlife was intense. I think he found the contrast between life on the road and life at home, and adjusting between them, really hard. I could sympathize because I remembered my days with Atomic Kitten and how it had felt to come home to Warrington. Mum would want me to stay at home with her, but I couldn't wind down straight away and always wanted to go out clubbing with my mates, who I hadn't seen for months. Mum would get upset, thinking I didn't love her enough. Bryan was just the same as me and I had to keep reminding myself of that. The day after I brought Lilly home from hospital, he wanted to go out for a meal and couldn't understand why I didn't want to go.

I guess Bryan's like lots of men, who love their kids to bits but don't really enjoy the daily grind of feeding, clothing and washing them, and especially getting up in the middle of the night with them. He was happy for me to do all that, but he was still a great loving dad to the girls. Never having had my own dad, it would melt my heart when I watched Bryan with them. I used to wish that Mum could have experienced the happiness I was feeling and that we'd been part of a proper family. I loved our life together and the way it made me feel so secure. If anything happened to Molly or me then Bryan would look after us. If anything happened to him, I would do everything I could to support and

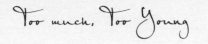

help him. The three of us, and the new baby, were the only pieces we needed to make up our jigsaw. It was complete.

Lilly Sue was born on 3 February 2003. Mum and Bryan were at the hospital with me and this time Mum stayed for the birth. She was really moved at seeing Lilly born, but found it hard seeing me in so much pain – the whole experience brought us close together. This time I was induced because my doctor was going on holiday and I wanted him to deliver the baby. The night before I'd been looking at our Molly's little feet and thinking how tiny she was and how soon it was for her to have a brother or sister. I was scared about looking after two kids. I thought about how Mum had struggled to bring up just one – me – and worried that, even with Bryan's support, I wouldn't be able to handle two. I didn't feel like I'd had enough time with Molly and yet here I was having another one. I was also worried I wouldn't be able to love another baby as much as I loved Molly, or that I wouldn't be able to give Molly enough love once the new baby was born. But as soon as I saw Lilly, I felt a rush of emotion that had nothing to do with how I still felt about Molly. I knew instantly that I'd love them both equally for ever. Lilly was the spitting image of me, tiny with blonde hair, and was every bit as beautiful as Molly had been. We were both so proud of our two gorgeous daughters.

Despite Bryan's growing success, I still wanted to carry on working, and got back to doing some presenting work when Lilly was only a few months old. My own career gave me independence and I wanted to contribute as much as I could to our daughters' financial wellbeing and happy childhood. Mairead was fantastic at helping with both girls, which was great because

I didn't want to hand over my babies to a stranger. I was torn between wanting to see all the little changes they went through and not wanting to miss a minute while also contributing to their future. I based my work around Bryan's, so that whenever I was asked to do something, I would always check where he was going to be so we could all be together as much as possible. As the year went on, more and more work started coming my way. I appeared regularly on ITV's *Loose Women* and performed in *The Vagina Monologues* in Manchester with Jan Shepherd and Ellen Thomas. I had such stage fright that my first line came out croaky and shaking. Come on, Kerry, I encouraged myself. Play the part. It was the first time I'd been on stage since being in Atomic Kitten, and though the experience was completely different I still got just the same buzz. I pretended I knew what I was doing and just copied Jan and Ellen. All the women who came to see us had a great evening out – my mum and all my friends loved it, standing up to applaud at the end – but I knew that when Bryan came to see me, he'd be shrinking in his seat as I started talking about my vagina or faking seventeen orgasms. As far as I was concerned it was a chance to show I wasn't just the dizzy, big-busted blonde some people took me for.

Life was going well again. Westlife were touring all over the world, but Bryan came home whenever he could. We had moved again, this time into our own house in Donaghmede, near Dublin. We'd never got round to knocking the two apartments we'd bought into one and had been living in one of them, cramming all the stuff that wouldn't fit into the other – we badly needed more room for us and our growing kids. The house was on a private estate nearby and the four pillars supporting the porch outside our front door made it look as grand as it was inside. It was a real Hollywood-style place and I loved making it into a family home. My favourite room was our Molly's pretty pink and green bedroom. We went totally over the top and gave her everything I'd never had – a single four-poster bed, a TV and video and loads of toys. As for the rest of the house, we had a snooker room with a bar in it and even a cinema. I know we were lucky to have so much and to be able to travel and meet so many different people, but sometimes I couldn't help wishing, and I think Bryan did too, that we were just an ordinary family living quietly in a nice little house. Celebrity isn't always as much fun as it looks.

We were in Marbella with both the girls when another phone call disrupted the peace we'd worked so hard to achieve. Rav, our reporter friend, called to say that the lap dancer Amy Barker was threatening to sue Bryan for defamation of character unless he admitted publicly what had happened that night. Hadn't she done enough? What was going through the woman's mind that she wanted to try and destroy us? It wasn't just Bryan she was hurting, it was our family, and there were two small children involved. I can't understand how anyone could do that.

Bryan was dead secretive about how he was going to deal with her. I knew he wasn't telling me everything and we had terrible arguments as I tried to get him to tell me exactly what had happened. 'Bryan I need to know. Why is she trying to sue you? What's she got on you?' What she had, of course, was a contract that he had stupidly made her sign. That gave her unarguable proof as to what had happened. Without it she might have left us alone. Then, before we knew what was happening, she was threatening to sue me, too, because I'd called her names in print.

Well, she hit gold: she got her fifteen minutes of fame and a good out-of-court settlement.

As for us? The damage was done. We tried to brush it under carpet again and get on with our lives, but if I'm honest it never really went away. Thinking about it now, there was one positive result for Bryan, it definitely got him his fair share of headlines and put him in the public eye more than the other lads in the band. He wasn't 'the fat one' in Westlife any longer, he was a star, and he loved all the publicity and attention that came with it. Although we continued to have some great times together, as far as I was concerned 'that woman' was always there. She'd shaken my trust in Bryan and we never seemed to get it back again.

15

QUEEN OF THE JUNGLE

I LOOKED DOWN at the round wooden platter in front of me as Ant or Dec lifted the cover. I didn't notice who because I was too busy looking at what was underneath. Three witchetty grubs lay wriggling on their sides. Just the sight of their pulsating short fat creamy bodies and wiggly stumpy little legs made me want to throw up. No way could I pick one up, never mind eating it. On the other side of the table, I could see that Katie (Jordan) felt the same. Her face was a picture.

I had agreed to go on *I'm a Celebrity Get Me Out of Here!* without really knowing what to expect. I'd thought it might be a laugh and I knew it would be worthwhile because part of the cost of each phone call made by the public voting for you would go to your chosen charity. So the longer I stayed in the show, the more money I'd raise. My chosen charities were the Variety Club of Ireland, which helps disadvantaged and disabled children, and the Temple Street Children's Hospital in Dublin, where Molly had been treated for suspected meningitis. That had been one of the worst times of my life – the thought that we might lose our child was unbearable. The hospital staff were so good to us and, thank God, Molly was OK in the end. Raising money to help the hospital would be my way of saying thank you.

Having Molly and Lilly kept me so busy that I didn't watch much TV, so I'd only seen odd bits of the previous series. I remembered seeing Linda Barker and Phil Tufnell getting pissed so I honestly thought I was going to be on the piss with Ant and Dec for a couple of weeks. I certainly didn't think we'd actually be going into the Australian jungle to be at one with nature, especially not the sort of nature that terrified me. I've always hated heights, deep water and creepy crawlies. I knew from the time I'd spent in Kenya working on *Elimidate* that tropical bugs were *not* my thing. Super-sized and noisy, flapping, buzzing and squirming, they scared the life out of me. It had taken me every ounce of courage to allow someone to put a tarantula on my arm once to raise money for ChildLine. I couldn't refuse because it was for such a good cause, so I just gritted my teeth and made myself think of the charity and the money they'd be getting.

Now, I was facing my fears and having to eat them.

We had already munched our way through a series of horrible insects. I'd had a handful (a very, very small one) of shiny-backed mealworms that crunched into something a bit like corn chips. I'd squished the head of a little green-bellied ant so it didn't bite me, then eaten its sherbety body. Yeeeugh! The feeling of a cockroach running around inside my mouth as I tried to bite into it, its legs tickling my gums as it scuttled out of the way of my teeth will stay with me for ever.

By this point in the show, we were all starving. Katie and I knew we had to win as many stars as we could in our bushtucker trial to earn a decent dinner for all of us, and for each kind of insect we ate, we got a star. I would never have been able to do

267

the trial without Katie. She kept me going, willing me on and getting me to go for it with her. We had two more platters to go.

'Come on, Kerry,' I said to myself. 'You can do it. Think of tonight's meal. Think of your charities. Go on.'

But the witchetty grubs were an insect too far. Katie went for it first and managed to get the grub down, but I could see by the look on her face that I wasn't going to like it. I managed to get it into my mouth and chewed down on it. I could feel it squirming, its legs moving against my tongue. It was like biting on a used condom before it exploded in my mouth in a disgusting sour-tasting slime. I gagged and had to spit it out. After that, we were faced with a fish's eye each. I was sure mine had conjunctivitis and said so. They stank so badly that I couldn't even put it in my mouth; Katie managed to get as far as popping it with her teeth but couldn't swallow it. Hats off to her for trying, though. At least we could go back to the others in the camp and tell them we'd won seven stars between us, which meant we'd be eating that night.

When I was first approached about being a contestant, Bryan wasn't keen on the idea of me entering because he didn't want me to be away for so long. I was in two minds about it too, because the filming dates meant I'd miss our Lilly's first birthday. But we were persuaded by my agent and Louis Walsh that taking part in *I'm a Celebrity* was a once-in-a-lifetime opportunity I should grab with both hands.

As the time to leave got nearer, I became more and more nervous until I'd worked myself up into a right state. I couldn't think why I'd said yes to it. I stayed with my mum for a couple of nights

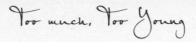

on the way and couldn't stop throwing up from nerves; I had to spend a couple of days in hospital until the panic attack went away. In London, Bryan and I spent our last evening having a meal in our favourite Japanese restaurant in Chelsea followed by a night of passion in the Conrad Hotel. The next morning, I couldn't stop crying as Bryan drove me to the airport. I didn't want to leave him or our girls and kept imagining the worst. Suppose none of the other contestants, whoever they were, liked me? What if I didn't like them? Suppose I was bitten by a poisonous snake or a spider and didn't get to the hospital in time? Suppose I died in the jungle and never saw Bryan, Molly or Lilly again? All the worst things that could happen were whirling round my head. Why had I agreed to go? Walking through the departure gates was so hard. I kept turning back to wave at Bryan until I couldn't see him any more. All I wanted to do was turn round and run back home.

Before we were taken into the jungle, all the contestants met up in a posh hotel where we stayed to acclimatize. None of us knew who else was going to be in the jungle until we got there. I was so pleased to see Katie Price – Jordan – who I'd met before when she was going out with Dane Bowers, and I knew of Alex Best, Peter Andre, Johnny Rotten and DJ Mike Reid, but had never heard of Jennie Bond, the royal correspondent, Olympic athlete Diane Modahl, Lord Brocket or footballer Neil 'Razor' Ruddock. I hit it off with Razor straight away and immediately became one of the lads, whooping his ass at pool. We all got on famously, then just as I was beginning to relax and enjoy myself, we had to trek into the jungle camp. The night before we left I was on the phone in floods of tears to Mum and Bryan, saying goodbye. Then we all had to hand our mobiles over to the production team. We weren't allowed any contact with the outside world.

When I saw the clearing that was going to be our home for the next two weeks, all my fears were confirmed. We'd been warned about the dangerous insects, poisonous spiders and snakes we might come across and told how to recognize them. I could imagine them hiding under every leaf and twig. There was nothing to stop any of them from getting into the camp. We were going to be living in the open on camp beds, once we'd made them ourselves out of criss-crossed logs and canvas with a bit of tarpaulin strung over them to keep out the rain. In the middle of the camp was a fire for cooking and we had to keep that burning. There wasn't even anywhere for us to sit. A little way out of the clearing was the toilet – at least that was private – and the bush telegraph, a little hut where we could be alone and talk privately to the crew. Out of all of us, I was the one who was scared of everything and was reduced to a whinging wreck within seconds of going into the jungle. That first night I was woken by Razor whispering loudly, 'Snake! Snake!'

I sat bolt upright immediately.

'Don't move, Kerry,' Peter said. 'There's a snake under your bed.'

'Oh God. Please come and get me,' I whimpered. 'I want to go home.'

As the snake slid away, Pete came over and I leaped onto him, wrapping my legs round him and hanging on for dear life. 'Please let me go home,' I sobbed.

Going home wasn't an option though so once I'd calmed down and everyone else had gone back to bed, I did too, but not

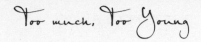

before I'd banged my bed over and over again with a stick to make sure there was nothing in it. I climbed in, keeping my clothes, boots and hat on, wanting nothing more than to get out of there.

Those early days were a nightmare for me. I was totally exhausted from lack of sleep and was missing the kids badly. I kept thinking of them safely at home in Dublin with Bryan or Mairead. I'd get out my luxury – a picture of Bryan, Molly and Lilly with a card from Molly secretly stuffed behind it – and stare at them, wondering what they were doing and what I was missing.

When Mike Reid and I had to follow clues that took us out of the camp to find a 'celebrity' chest, I thought I was going to have a nervous breakdown. I felt as if every branch that cracked, every movement I saw among the trees and bushes, was something coming to get me. All I wanted was to get back to camp. Mike had to climb up a waterfall – I could never have done it – to get the chest while I held the ropes attached to his harness. I didn't even have the energy to hang on to them and broke down in tears again. I was being a complete wimp. Mike did most of the work and then pretty much pulled the chest back to camp single-handedly, with me whinging beside him. No wonder I was called the Warrington Whinger. Once we'd started back, I began to feel dizzy, my chest closed up and I was finding it harder and harder to breathe. I was convinced I'd been bitten by a poisonous spider, though I couldn't see a mark anywhere, or a spider come to that. I had to sit down, sure that I was going to die. One of the doctors on the show was rushed in to see me and it turned out I was having another one of my panic attacks. I couldn't stop crying I was so homesick. I really felt like I'd let myself down. What kept me going was the thought of my mum: she'd kill me if I didn't stay for the first week. I just had to hang on until the voting started, because then I was bound to be voted off. What made it worse was that the chest we'd struggled to find only contained two miniature bottles of port and a cigar. How crap was that?

When it came to the first celebrity challenge, I knew I'd be picked – I was being such a wuss the viewers were bound to vote for me. Sure enough, Ant and Dec appeared in the morning as usual and announced that I'd been voted to do it. I just thought, Fuck. But then I decided I had to give it a go. I can't remember what the challenge was called but I'll never forget what I had to do: I had to climb into a Perspex tank full of leeches, eels and spiders – everything I saw made me jump. The tank was gradually lowered into the muddy water of the lake for three minutes until it was right under. As it went down, I had to fit ten keys into ten locks, and for each one I got right, I got a star – and a meal for the camp that night. I was so disappointed to only get two and felt bad that everyone else would have to go without food because of me.

To begin with I went and sat in the bush telegraph a lot, begging to go home, but the voice would always persuade me to give it a little bit longer. As I talked, I'd think of Mum, Bryan and my girls – remembering that I wanted to make them proud helped keep me going. Then as the days went by I began to find my feet. Getting to know the other contestants was brilliant and Katie and I got on great. The stories she told me about her life made me realize she's the most loyal person you could wish to meet. We had loads of girly chats round the fire and she gave me some great massages and plaited my hair – we even got to dress up as Tarzan

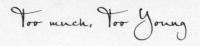

and Jane. Watching her get it on with Pete was interesting as I was kind of piggy in the middle. I used to egg them on and even made them have their first kiss as she and I went off for our bushtucker trial.

I loved Pete. He was so corny, singing his songs, especially 'Insania', but what a genuine guy. Some people thought he was putting on an act, but he has the biggest heart and is just very open with his feelings. It might make you cringe, but believe me when I say he's an absolute diamond. He and I had to go and find one of the celebrity chests together and he tried to be the perfect gent all the time, holding my hand whenever he could. The trouble was he kept falling down all the time. Once he fell, stood up, stuck his middle finger up at the camera and fell straight over again. It was hilarious and we couldn't stop laughing.

When I went with Charlie Brocket to find a chest, we discovered it high up in the trees. He carried the thing back on his own with me trailing behind. I was really pissed off because I badly wanted to help, having fucked up the last chest challenge with Mike. I wanted to prove to myself that I wasn't a wimp, but whenever I suggested helping, he didn't take any notice. So much for teamwork; he was a one-man band. He was a lovely bloke most of the time, though, a proper jack-the-lad and a joker. Sometimes I thought he was trying a bit too hard, but he absolutely loved the ladies. He was all over Alex, especially when he insisted on helping her wash in the river after she'd done her bushtucker trial, where she crawled through a glass tunnel where each compartment contained thousands of different bugs. She had to pick up the stars with her mouth and ended up covered in muck, maggots and chicken feathers. Charlie kept on undoing my bra without me noticing, so I had to be a bit firm with him. I didn't want to end up flashing at everybody at home. Towards the end of the show he turned on Jennie, and I didn't like that at all. She was a kind of mother hen to the group and she made me laugh the way she used to sneak off to put on her make-up. I didn't think he was right to try to turn the rest of us against her. I so respected her for completing a bushtucker trial where she was buried underground with loads of rats running over her in the dark while the tank filled with water. One night Charlie and Jennie were having yet another argument. I was so pissed off and bored and didn't have a clue what they were going on about, so I interrupted them.

'Shhhhhh,' I went with my finger on my lips.

They immediately stopped arguing.

In the silence, I began to sing 'It's All So Quiet'.

Everybody burst out laughing before Charlie and Jennie went back to arguing – nothing could stop them. I felt some of the people in the camp were a bit two-faced over the Jennie/Charlie situation. They'd agree with Charlie to gang up on her, but when push came to shove they wouldn't do anything.

Once we'd got used to the camp, the uncomfortable camp beds, our sweaty sleeping bags, the heat, washing in the lake, being eaten alive by mosquitoes and not having any contact with the outside world – we all went doolally. Apart from the challenges, there was nothing to do except our chores. The team leader of the day would tell us who was collecting wood, making the fire, tidying the camp or cooking. I never did any cooking – Alex and Pete were too good at it! I'm not the greatest cook, so I felt I was doing the others a favour by not having a go and just helping when asked. We weren't eating or drinking properly and we were hot and tired, so we started getting our words muddled up. Anything that was remotely funny we found absolutely hilarious. When Jennie had gone off to find a celebrity chest, Razor asked, 'Where's Maggie with her chest?' The pair of us were crying with laughter. No one else thought it was funny at all, and that just made the whole thing even funnier. Stupid little things like that completely cracked us up. I know I spent half the time talking to myself, acting the goon and playing peekaboo with the cameras we knew were hidden in the nearby waterfall. We spent hours discussing what we'd like to eat and could keep ourselves entertained for ages discussing important questions like 'Why is a fork called a fork?' or 'Who decided to crack open the first egg and fry it?' I still don't know the answer.

We were all so bored that we'd talk absolute dung most of the time, but I loved hearing about everyone's lives and what they'd left behind at home. One night we were given a whole load of champagne, beer and wine. I knocked it back, so happy to have some alcohol that I got completely pissed and Jennie had to help me to bed. I managed to stumble to the bush telegraph to make my nightly report about what sort of day I'd had, but screamed my head off when I saw some horrible creepy-crawly in there.

'I'm not coming in there until you get rid of that fucking thing.'

Charlie came to my rescue, although he managed to shoo it out in my direction. Cheers, Charlie! The next day confirmed what I already knew: beer and champagne definitely don't mix.

I found it hard not being able to talk to Bryan, my mum and the kids, but the others in the camp went out of their way to look after me. When Lilly's first birthday came round, I was so upset not to be there with her that I felt like a really bad mum. Johnny put a load of candlewax on his head, stuck a candle in it and made everyone sing 'Happy Birthday', then we blew out the candle and sang 'Happy Birthday' to Lilly on camera. She must have been scared shitless when she saw him, but I thought it was a lovely thing to do. When times were tough, he and I would sing, 'We are doomed, we are doomed,' and he would call me his 'little bunny'. He took me under his wing, so I was really sorry when he decided to walk. His and Razor's departures were real low points for me. Although the rest of us were good mates, sometimes a bit of a nasty atmosphere would creep into the camp as Charlie began to play his games. He must have been bored and this was his way of amusing himself, but I didn't like what he was doing. When he wasn't stirring, he was a good laugh, though. At one point I went to the bush telegraph and told them, 'I hate it here now. I want to go home.' But as the voice talked to me, I thought of the charities I was trying to raise money for and said to myself, 'God, Kerry. You've got a life of luxury at home. Two weeks in the jungle and you'll raise loads of money for the Variety Club and the children's hospital. If you walk you'll be letting them down as well as yourself. Get on with it.' So I did.

Things really turned round for me once we passed the halfway mark and I could start counting down the days. There was even one challenge I loved. Peter, Jennie, Charlie and I had to try to climb up a giant mudslide while we were bombarded with water and big rubber balls. If all the challenges had been bug-free like that, I'd have been queuing up to do them.

By then we were practically at the end of our time in the camp. Ant and Dec appeared as usual on the last morning. Jennie,

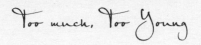
Too much, Too Young

Pete and I were huddled together on a log. I was amazed that I was still there and couldn't understand why. I wasn't as famous as the others; I didn't have a romantic storyline like Pete and Katie; or even an ongoing argument like Charlie and Jennie. I was just being me.

Pete went first, leaving Jennie and me in the jungle for what seemed like ages while he was interviewed. Then it was back to Jennie and me. We sat with our arms around each other, holding tight. I felt completely sick.

'And the Queen of the Jungle is ...'

The silence dragged on and on as I whispered, 'Jennie, Jennie, Jennie.'

And Jennie whispered, 'Kerry, Kerry, Kerry.'

'Jennie, Jennie, Jennie.'

'... KERRY!'

No way! I was absolutely gobsmacked. I was left alone with my thoughts while Jennie got taken away to do her exit interview with Ant and Dec. The next thing I knew I'd crossed the walkways out of the camp, had a glass of champagne in my hand and Tara Palmer-Tomkinson was putting a plastic crown on my head.

'My crown doesn't fit and my legs have gone numb,' was all I could say.

During my exit interview, I had a phone conversation with Bryan. It was so, so good to hear him again. I couldn't wait to get back to Ireland to see him and the girls. I hoped that he'd be really proud of me and of the fact that I hadn't given in to all my fears. Then suddenly, out of the corner of my eye, I saw someone coming onto the set. My God, it was Bryan. There wasn't a dry eye in the house. The first thing he said to me was, 'You stink.'

As if I didn't know. At last we were allowed to go and set off across the bridge towards a hot bath, champagne in hand, tears on my cheeks and fireworks exploding in the sky. Later I learned that 16.7 million people had watched me win – that must be almost as many as watched the World Cup final! – and that I'd won 72 per cent of the vote. Knowing that so many people voted for me was very special and definitely one of the high points in my life.

The first call I made was to Molly and Lilly who were at Brendan and Mairead's. I'd been gutted to discover that not only had I missed our Lilly's first birthday party, I'd missed her first steps, too. When I heard Mairead's voice, I managed to get out, 'Hi. I can't believe I missed you all so much,' before I broke down again. Bryan had told me that whenever our Molly was asked, 'Where's Mummy?' She'd reply, 'In the jungle with spiders.' When Mairead put Molly on the phone, she said, 'Mummy, Queen of the jungle.' That did it; I couldn't speak for ages after that. Then I called Mum. She screamed down the phone, practically deafening me. I got the feeling she was pleased I'd won!

Being back home was great. Having been in the jungle without my family, time with them seemed even more precious. Once I'd had a chance to sit back and think about what I'd done, I realized that the whole experience had taught me I could do anything I wanted if I set my mind to it. It's a lesson I've had to remember several times since.

Although it was tough being in the jungle at the time, looking back now, I'd give anything to go back and relive it. At the end of the day, it's much more of a jungle out here in everyday life, than it was in there.

16

GOING

SOLO

COMING HOME TO BRITAIN was amazing. I had no idea that people had identified with me or liked me so much. I just wished I could have had an out-of-body experience and been able to see how popular the show was while it was on telly. Apparently there'd been posters all over Warrington telling people to vote for me, and in some pubs, if you bought a Smirnoff Ice, you'd get a free T-shirt with Kerry to Win printed on the front. When I went home to visit Mum, the town gave me an amazing reception. A police escort took me to Warrington Town Hall, where about 500 people turned up chanting my name and waving posters of me in my sweaty red fleece and plastic crown with 'Kerry, Warrington's Queen' printed on them. I was overwhelmed by everyone's support and practically crushed as I tried to sign autographs for as many people as possible before going inside for a reception with the mayor.

Suddenly everyone wanted me. One of the first things I was asked to do was present an award at the Brits. Bryan and the lads from Westlife weren't invited because they'd had a big fight with So Solid Crew at the awards a couple of years earlier. I thought it was really funny that I was invited on my own, not as part of

Atomic Kitten, and that Bryan could only come as my husband. My appearance there got reported all over the papers because when I stood up on stage, I said I'd just farted. I hadn't but I was jet-lagged and so nervous that I wasn't thinking straight. I'm always spontaneous and off the cuff, but that time it didn't work and I regret it now. Sometimes my nerves get the better of me and make me say stupid things. The Brits was another occasion where Bryan and I were reported to have had a big row, and once again it's absolutely not true. We'd taken Charlie Brocket as our guest and would never have behaved like that in front of him. I did go home early, but only because I was knackered, and I told Bryan to carry on partying without me.

One piece of news that did shock me when I got out of the jungle was hearing that Atomic Kitten had split up. Tash had had a baby boy with her boyfriend Fran Cosgrove by this time and she wanted to spend more time with him. I could completely understand her wanting to do that, but I'm sure Jenny and Liz must have been gutted that it was all over.

Up until now, my career had always taken a backseat to Bryan's, and I'd been happy for it to be that way. So it was a big shock when I arrived back at Heathrow from Australia to find it full of paparazzi armed with cameras looking for me not Bryan – that had never happened before. Suddenly I was the star, and I got the sense he didn't like it much, although he was dead proud of me. For a while, it must have been difficult for him, particularly when Westlife did the ChildLine concert and, at the press conference afterwards, most of the questions directed at Bryan were about me, our relationship and the jungle. The lads were understandably pissed off and I felt really guilty. It was just like when

I'd been in Atomic Kitten and the press threw me into the lime-light above the others. I wasn't the reason either band should have been mentioned in the press. I'd gone on the show to raise money for charity and to have fun, not to get more work, so I was happy to turn down most of the offers that came my way after-wards, although I carried on appearing on *Loose Women*, debating life in general, because it was a show I loved doing.

While all this was going on Bryan was making his own plans to leave the band. I knew that he'd been unhappy in Westlife for some time, and he'd made no secret of the fact that the constant touring got him down. Although I would have liked him to be at home more, I didn't want him to leave the band and thought he was making a big mistake. I didn't doubt his talent – he's one of the most skilful singer-songwriters I know – but I was scared for him because the public and music business can be so fickle: one bad song and you're finished. I also couldn't understand why he wanted to leave when the lads were still riding high. We rarely saw each other, thanks to his work, and as I'd been away in the jungle, we hadn't had the chance to discuss his decision, even though I'd supported him in his career as much as I could.

Of course I was ready to stand by him whatever he did, but I admit I was really nervous about it. As for the Westlife boys, they said they understood and decided to continue as a foursome, hoping for their fans' continued support.

In March, Bryan announced in a press interview on Sky News that he was leaving the band to spend more time with us, but from that day on I hardly saw him. He rarely called me and I hadn't a clue where he was for much of the time. He went solo straight away, using the kids and me as inspiration for his song,

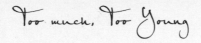

'Real To Me', which stormed to the top of the charts in September 2004. He spent all his time in the studios writing or rehearsing, and I let him do it because I knew it was what he wanted. I didn't want to cross him, but I couldn't understand why he never used to come home.

There was a big charity do in Dublin, where I was due to hand over the half a million pounds I'd raised in the jungle to my chosen charities. I'd told Bryan about the date months before and asked him to clear his diary so he could come with me, but when it came to it, he called to say he was too busy. I was really hurt that he couldn't make time for something that was so important to me. We'd been so lovey-dovey after the jungle, but it hadn't lasted. That was when I admitted to myself for the first time that everything was going wrong between us. We began to argue whenever we saw each other – he was driven to follow his star and I wanted him to see his family more. Rather than being interested in me, he was wrapped up in his solo career and his ambition to be the new Robbie Williams, all of which meant he didn't have time for anyone. I knew that everything we had was being threatened, but never in my wildest dreams did I think it would end in divorce. I felt neglected, but I honestly believed we'd sort the situation out. I'd already learned that marriage isn't the perfect bubble I'd expected: you have to work at it.

Bryan was a changed person; he wasn't the Bryan I fell in love with and married. He decided to change the spelling of his name back to Brian, as it had been before he was in Westlife, he lost weight, grew his hair and a beard and didn't seem to want to be with me. I couldn't understand it. I suppose he was trying to reinvent himself as a solo artist, or perhaps he'd met someone else. I'll never know.

Meanwhile, I was looking forward to starting work on an Irish film called *Showbands*, a two-part drama set in the Sixties, which was being filmed in Ireland. I played the part of Denise, a female singer in a band. The producer, Alan Moloney, had held on to the script for seven years because he couldn't find the right person to play Denise, then when he was describing her to Joanne Byrne, a friend of mine in Ireland, she said, 'That's Kerry.' They called my agent and sent the script, and I fell in love with the show and my character. I knew immediately that it was the perfect first acting job for me. The screen test went well and I got the job. At first Bryan didn't want me to do it because there was a kissing scene and the filming would take me away on location to Galway for five weeks, but I convinced him he was being ridiculous. Although I'd loved acting at school, I had always thought of an acting career as a distant dream and was so excited to get this opportunity out of the blue. I'm one of those people who like to say, 'Been there, done that.' And I don't mean blokes! More than anything, I wanted to prove to myself that I could do it.

The whole experience was great and made me realize that acting was something I'd like to do more of. Acting suits my personality, because you're doing something new every day. I was so lucky to be working with a fantastic professional cast who were really supportive and helped me learn the ropes. I was shitting myself, afraid that they would think I'd only been dragged in because of my name. But if they did, they never showed it and didn't belittle or judge me. If anything they made me feel as if I'd been doing it for years. Liam Cunningham, who

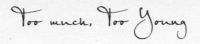

was in *First Knight* with Sean Connery, was my best friend on set. He was about twenty years older than me, but he was great *craic*, laughed at the same things as me and listened to my problems. He'd call me after filming and ask, 'Are you playing out?' and arrange to meet me with the others at Morrisons, a pub somewhere near the set.

On 27 August, I drove home after two weeks of filming. I knew that Bryan would be there when I got back and that friends were flying over to be at a joint birthday party the next day for our Molly and me. I was dead tired but really looking forward to seeing everyone, and I hoped that Bryan and I would have a chance to get over our differences and work on our marriage. I knocked on the door, and after a moment or two Bryan's friend Ray answered. I knew immediately that something wasn't right. Normally, if he was home, Bryan would be the first to the door when I got back, with the kids right behind him, ready to give me a hug and a kiss.

'Where's Bryan, Ray?' I asked.

'Upstairs playing snooker, having a few beers.' Then he disappeared back up there to join him.

I persuaded myself that I was being silly and went straight into the kitchen to unpack the takeaway chicken curry I'd brought home with me. Bryan came down to join me and couldn't stop talking about the new song he was recording. He'd been doing a duet with a new Australian singer called Delta Goodrem, who he kept on mentioning. He didn't seem at all interested in what I'd been doing or how the filming had been going. I don't remember him asking me anything about it. All I do remember is Delta this and Delta that and how 'Almost Here' was coming along. I could tell straight away that he fancied her and I couldn't help feeling a bit jealous. It was as if I didn't know him at all any more and he knew nothing about me. We'd become so separate that I didn't know where to start trying to make it right.

I unpacked the curry and got him a plate, but he didn't want any. He'd obviously had a few beers and was planning on making a night of it in our bar upstairs.

'Bryan please don't get drunk tonight,' I begged him. 'I'm not being a party pooper, but it's Molly's birthday party tomorrow. It's not our day, it's hers.'

Nothing I said made any difference and he disappeared upstairs, not coming to bed until about five o'clock in the morning. What was wrong? Normally he'd have been so pleased to see me and we'd have spent our first evening at home alone together. The next morning Molly was up at the crack of dawn, dead excited about her birthday, so we didn't really have a chance to speak to one another all day. We'd hired a big children's play area for the day and were taking all Molly's friends along, as well as our own friends and family. I was really annoyed to discover that Bryan had organized for a documentary team to follow him around all day. They were already there waiting for us when we arrived, and that was the first I knew about it. I'd thought it was going to be a private family day and he hadn't even bothered to mention that they were going to be there.

While I took the kids on all the rides, Bryan and his friends played crazy golf. I begged him to join in with us: 'Bryan, this isn't about you. It's our Molly's day.' I was so hurt and confused by his behaviour. He'd been so loving towards me in the past and I couldn't understand what had happened. It was as if he didn't

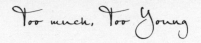

want to know me any more. If I'd done something to piss him off, I honestly didn't know what it was.

That evening, after the kids had gone to bed, all the grown-ups moved on to a nightclub where Bryan had hired a room. I didn't see him all night; we didn't even have one dance together. Once we got home, we all carried on partying and things seemed to get better as he starting talking to me again. Lisa told me that while she and her boyfriend Dave were talking to Bryan by the jukebox, he'd been telling her how much he loved me. Funny that, because that night was the last time we slept together.

Once again our work took us in different directions. He was busy recording with Delta while I finished filming *Showbands*, and then I went to England to make *With a Little Help From My Friends* for ITV. With no budget and a bunch of my old school friends we had to persuade suppliers to provide a digger, hundreds of bricks, soil, cement and tools to build a playground, sensory garden and sports pitch in the grounds of Alder Hey Hospital in Liverpool in five days. I was scared that no one would turn up, but everyone did, including my old teachers. It was like a brilliant school reunion and I got to boss them all around as we completed the task. What a laugh it was, and what a great achievement.

I knew Bryan had gone away for two weeks but I didn't know where. Our relationship had broken down completely. I didn't know why and I didn't know how to make it better, but I hoped that when we were both back home we'd be able to sort things out. It was the first time I'd spent my birthday alone since we'd been together and he sent me a beautiful platinum bracelet. Seeing it made me believe there was a chance we could patch things up between us. As he was away, I decided to take the girls to Mum's, after all, there didn't seem any point staying in Donaghmede without him.

He phoned me while I was there. Mum was ill in bed and the girls were in the front room watching cartoons on TV. I took the phone to the stairs where it was quieter and immediately knew something wasn't right. There was something in his voice that sounded different, strained. He hadn't called me for a couple of days and I was worried.

'Bryan. Are you OK? What's wrong?'

'I don't love you any more,' he said. Just like that. My heart stopped.

'You can't mean that,' I said quietly. I must have misheard him.

'I do, Kerry.' He sounded quite definite.

I felt as though the ground had gone from under me and collapsed on the stairs. 'Bryan, please don't do this. Please. You can't mean it.' I was begging him, desperate.

'No. It's over,' he said. 'It's over.'

I think he hung up on me, then, though it's hard to remember exactly what was said. I remember feeling completely numb. Not wanting to disturb Mum, I went back to the kids and tried to hold myself together while I took everything in. I have three rules that I try my best to keep – never raise your voice, never argue and never cry in front of the kids. From bitter experience, I know how frightening and upsetting that can be to a child. Your parents are the ones who are meant to be in control, the ones who will make everything all right, and if they lose the plot, the world can seem a frightening and lonely place. I learned that the hard way. I'll never forget our Molly coming over to me as I sat down. I had

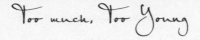

such a lump in my throat that when she asked me what was wrong, I couldn't stop the tears rolling down my face. She looked at me, took off one of her socks and wiped my eyes with it.

'What's wrong, Mum?'

She was just like I had been with my mum and it broke my heart. This wasn't what I wanted for my daughters. For years I'd had to be the adult and look after my mum, and I didn't want that for Molly and Lilly. I wanted to take care of them, not the other way around.

'I've just got a really bad headache, luvvie.' That satisfied her. I never want my kids to feel that sense of responsibility or guilt that I felt while I was growing up.

For the rest of that day I kept phoning Bryan back, begging and begging him to reconsider, but he was having none of it. Nothing I said had any effect; his mind was absolutely made up. I honestly don't know what had happened. At that moment I thought he must be seeing someone else, although he's always sworn he wasn't. That was the only reason I could think of for him behaving like that. I knew that he was capable of falling in love with someone new and immediately finishing with his old girl-friend, because that's exactly what he'd done when he'd met me. The only difference was, we were married. I was so distraught I began to think the very worst possible thoughts. Had our whole marriage been a publicity stunt to big up his career? I couldn't believe that. You can't pretend love, and I knew that he had loved me as much as I had loved him. But when I looked back at some of the more recent things he'd done, I began to see them in a new light. I wondered whether he would have come all the way to Australia to meet me coming out of the jungle if I'd been the first to leave. Did all that fanfare surrounding me winning make him think he'd look good coming out to see me? Or that some of the glory might rub off on him? After all, he knew that he was about to leave Westlife and would need as much positive press coverage as possible to stay in the public eye. He'd made his first solo record and it was looking like it was going to be a big hit; he was composing and singing all the time, establishing his solo career. Maybe he thought he could make it without me now. Surely he couldn't have thought our marriage was just a good career move. I'm not proud to have had such horrible thoughts about the guy I loved, but they wouldn't go away, whirling around my head as I desperately looked for an explanation.

I remembered the night before we got married. We'd gone out for dinner near Slane Castle, just the two of us, when I asked him, 'Bryan, are you ready for this? I've lived my life and you and our family are all I want. Are you sure it's what you want, too?' He was certain. In fact, he was the one who rushed the wedding, I was happy to wait. The one thing I am certain of is that he loved being a dad. He adored our Molly and our Lilly, and still does. Perhaps he just woke up one morning and thought, Fucking hell, I'm married with two kids. Perhaps he felt trapped, with too much responsibility before he was ready for it. Being a pop star is bloody hard work, but it's fun, too, and there are plenty of temptations. Coming home to a family and staying faithful to your wife might seem boring when you have girls offering it to you on a plate. As far as I was concerned, once I was with Bryan that was it. Plenty of guys came onto me while I was in Atomic Kitten, but I was spoken for. That was enough for me. Perhaps he found it harder to resist what was on offer. I don't know because he never told me. Perhaps he'd fallen in love with Delta. He says not, but now, deep down, I think that must have been what happened. They're certainly together now.

I went onto autopilot almost immediately. Apart from the shock, I guess my strong instinct for self-preservation – something I'd had to develop as a child – kicked in. If I wasn't going to be with him in Ireland there was no reason for me to be there. His parents had always been fantastic to me and the kids, but there was only one place I knew I wanted to be, and that was back home in Warrington with Mum and my friends. Mum and Lisa stepped in straight away to help look after the kids while I found somewhere to live. Mum was almost as shattered as I was by our break-up. I found a new house in a private development on what had been the grounds of the old Winwick Hospital, where Mum spent so much of her young life – how ironic is that? – and we stayed there as a temporary measure until the house I really wanted on the same estate came up. Winwick has been our home ever since. Living there is like living in Toy Town: whenever I drive through the perfect streets lined by perfect, exclusive houses, I keep expecting Noddy and Big Ears to pop out.

Now our lives had been thrown up into the air, my first thoughts were for the kids. I wanted to give them a good home and the stable routine I'd never had, so I found a school and enrolled them straight away. I felt really lucky to have enough money of my own to be able to buy us a house, put Molly and Lilly in school and not have to move them from pillar to post. They were not going to have my childhood. I was 100 per cent sure of that.

During that first month, whenever I spoke to him, he was

angry and abusive. I guess that he felt guilty about leaving the girls and his best defence was anger. He probably felt that if he was lashing out at me, then he couldn't be to blame. I didn't understand what I'd done wrong or what he wanted from me, but I knew there was no going back.

When Bryan summonsed me for divorce, I returned to Ireland for the first time, taking the kids to see Mairead and Brendan, who must have missed them loads. I know the girls missed them. Bryan was abroad somewhere, and leaving them with their grandparents, I went back to Donaghmede on my own. Walking through that grand entrance into the home we'd been so happy in really shattered me – I'd thought we'd be living there for years. I crept into bed and stayed there, feeling totally miserable. I phoned Bryan several times, begging and begging him. 'Please, Bryan. Let's at least go to marriage counselling together.'

But he was quite definite. 'No.'

That was the last time I begged him to give it another go, and it was also when I told Molly that Mummy and Daddy wouldn't be living together any more, but that we both loved her and Lilly very much. I made out that we were going to have a big adventure, telling her that I had to go to live in England and that we'd be really near Nana Nou (my mum). She and Lilly would have not one but two houses, with different toys in each one. They'd be going to a different school and they'd be going to stay with Daddy on school holidays. It was going to be so exciting. What on earth could a three-year-old say?

I will never forget how kind Lisa and David were to me during that time. Bringing their young son Callum, they moved in and looked after me as I fell to pieces. Offers of TV and magazine

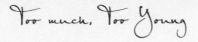

work were pouring in, but I turned them all down and decided to take some time off. I knew I had to be around for my kids, so they'd feel settled, and sticking close to home was the only way I could think of doing that. I felt so alone, especially when our Molly and Lilly went to Ireland to stay with Mairead and Brendan. Losing Bryan felt like a physical ache that wouldn't go away, and I tried to cure it by going out with my mates and acting like I was having fun.

Thank God for my friends, then. Although I was famous, I wasn't especially close to any of the people I'd met when I was in the band or with Bryan because I was always more of a home bird. I'd brushed up against loads of famous people throughout my career, including Tom Jones, Will Smith and the Spice Girls to name a few, but none of them were real mates like the ones I had at home. Once, when I went to see Ant and Dec recording *Saturday Night Takeaway*, I was talking to Robbie Williams when my phone rang.

'Hi, Kerry,' said a voice I didn't recognize. 'It's Victoria Beckham.' Yeah right.

'Fuck off,' I said. 'Who are you working for, love?' I was sure she was a reporter, but she really was Victoria Beckham. I was so embarrassed. She only wanted to say she was sorry about Bryan and me. I thought it was sweet and dead supportive of her, but we hardly knew each other so I didn't really get why she was phoning me up.

I did my best to forget everything and get on with my life, but it was impossible. My dream of having a happy, stable family of my own was in pieces. I was a broken woman and I didn't know how I was going to get through it. I'd go round to my mum's house whenever I could. In her way, she was always there for me, and she more than anyone knew what I was going through – I was finding out the hard way what she'd felt like when she lost Dave. Of course the circumstances weren't the same, but the feeling of loss was just as overwhelming, and she did her best to help me.

I tried really hard to keep positive and hold everything together, but I just wasn't coping. I was in so much pain. It was better when the girls were with me because then I had no time to think, but when they were away I slipped back. When I was at my lowest point, certain friends persuaded me into going out, having a drink and even taking drugs. I hadn't taken drugs since the old days in Warrington, but they told me it would help, and at first they were right. For a few hours I did feel better. I would forget the pain and feel like I wasn't worthless or ugly. I had no idea what I was doing to myself or how it would end and I refused to admit that it was becoming a problem. After all, I was only going out when the girls were away, and I was only twenty-four for Pete's sake. I think I was just hiding from everything. I had so much press attention at the time and felt very pressurized by the photographers – at one point fifteen of them were camped out on my doorstep. I couldn't go anywhere without the cameras following me, and I needed a bit of Dutch courage to smile, stick my tongue out and act like good old Kerry. A few drinks could deceive me into a few hours of believing I'd already bounced back, just like I always had.

But the truth was far from that. I was doing my best to cope, but I was sliding down a slippery slope. I can see that now, but at the time I'd blame everyone else but me. I'd feel so depressed the morning after a binge that I'd just sit there sobbing, 'Poor me.

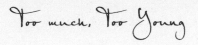

What a life I've had.' I'd do a mum and go through the past, feeling more and more sorry for myself. I used to go over everything that had happened to me and torture myself, thinking about how everyone I got close to rejected me. I kept asking myself why? What was wrong with me? I relived all the bad times that Mum and I had been through and felt as if the two of us were doomed to watch things fall apart. I wasn't yet ready to admit to myself or anyone else that I had a problem, but something in me must have known that I was going down the same self-destructive path she'd taken. That was the one place I couldn't go. I wasn't self-harming in the way she used to do, but what I was doing to myself was just as bad. It took me a long time to see it and admit it, but in the end something made me stop short.

I'd gone down to London where I was being interviewed as a former jungle queen on ITV's *This Morning* to coincide with the crowning of the comedian Joe Pasquale, who'd just survived another two weeks of jungle fun. Bryan had agreed to meet me in the bar of the Conrad Hotel, where I was staying. He could see how devastated I was. He was still my best friend and soulmate, the one I turned to to make everything all right, and seeing him made me confess how badly out of control my life had become. He was obviously upset, but even though I longed for him to say the nightmare was over, he made it very clear that there was no going back.

When he left I felt totally destroyed all over again and stayed up all night crying. I couldn't sleep because Bryan wasn't there to hold me. I replayed our relationship in my mind, trying to work out what had gone wrong. I blamed myself, my upbringing and the insecurities it had given me. I thought about my mum and all the difficulties she'd had. Our split had been just as upsetting for her because it was as if all her dreams for me had been shattered. Suddenly everything hit me and I felt like I couldn't breathe properly.

I called Bryan, who was so worried that he came over immediately. I admitted I couldn't live without him and that I was going to pieces. I needed him to hold me just so I could sleep. I couldn't stop crying. He stayed with me for a while, then in the morning he came back with Paul, his tour manager, and told me I needed to see a doctor. They drove me to Harley Street, where the doctor gave me an immediate referral to the Priory. By this stage I was numb and could hardly speak. I was sure I was cracking up, so for once I just did what I was told.

Everyone talks about the Priory as if it's a health farm, and from the outside it does look a bit like something on the Costa del Sol, but inside it's nothing like that. I can't remember a thing about arriving except that I'd been crying non-stop for about fourteen hours, so someone gave me a couple of tablets – gulp! – and I was out cold. When I came to I was in a single bed in a small room with high ceilings. It was hot and stuffy, with a strong musty smell of medicine and pee, a bit like an old people's home. The only furniture in my room was a wardrobe, a desk and a TV. The curtains were closed over the massive sash windows, so it was very dark, and I kept it that way for the whole week. Most of the time I stayed curled up in bed with my back to the wall. Annoyingly the remote control on the TV didn't work, which meant I had to get up if I wanted to change channels, but the only other time I got out of bed was to go to the toilet or have a fag. Although it's a non-smoking hospital, they let me open the window and smoke out of it because I couldn't leave my room.

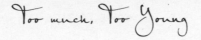

The doctors were nervous that if anyone saw me, they might sell the story to the press. That was why I didn't go to any of the group sessions, I just stayed in my room alone, chilling out.

My manager George was a good friend, visiting me every day, bringing me candles and a plug-in air freshener to make the place feel better. She'd sit on the floor and chat to me. I was desperately worried about the girls and wanted to see them, and I was anxious because Bryan was talking about taking them to Ireland and I thought I might not see them again. I was also terrified that I would be ruined and that my career was over – I'd never be able to support the kids if it was. George listened and talked, reassuring me that I would be all right. When I insisted, she even took me out to their office Christmas party, but she wouldn't let me drink and after an hour or so I just wanted to get back to my room. The only other people who visited were my publicist and friend, Max Clifford, and Tash's ex-boyfriend Fran Cosgrave. Towards the end of the week Fran smuggled me out to the cinema and for a pizza and we rolled back in pissed. I don't think the Priory was too impressed.

I loved the peace I found in that room. I couldn't help thinking that Mum must have felt the same way when she was at Winwick. It was a welcome escape from reality, removing the responsibility of daily life for a while until I learned how to deal with things again. There were times when I wondered whether I was taking the same path as Mum, but I reassured myself I was a good mother, that I'd never self-harm, take drugs or get pissed in front of my girls. At least I'd learned some things from Mum, even if she'd taught them to me in an unconventional way. But obviously I hadn't learned quite enough.

Sitting there thinking and talking to my psychiatrist every day gave me a chance to look at my life again. I was feeling very shaky, but the medication I was given helped me stay calm. I began to look at life in a different way and ask myself some important questions, like what the hell was I doing? What was happening to me? And what was going to happen to my girls? I had a choice. I could go on the way I was, drowning my sorrows, taking drugs and feeling sorry for myself, or I could do something about it. It was up to me. Bottom line? I was the only one who could help me. I didn't want to repeat the patterns of the past and I had to break the cycle by thinking about the positives. I was devastated that Bryan had left me, but at least we had our two gorgeous girls. They were all I had now, and I couldn't let what had happened to me ruin their lives too. I mustn't be selfish. They were the biggest reason for me to beat my demons and get my life back on track. I had to do it for them.

17

MOVING ON

GETTING MYSELF BACK on track hasn't been easy. I'd love to say that I made the decision to make everything better and immediately succeeded, but life's not that simple. Sometimes I've felt that for every step I take forward, I take two back. In the months that followed that first stay in the Priory, I had huge highs and lows. Despite my resolutions to stop relying on drink and drugs, I couldn't resist the way they made me feel better about myself. An argument with Bryan would plunge me back into depression and I'd head straight for the pub. I tried to put a brave face on for the kids, but once they were gone, I didn't know how to cope. At the same time, though, I knew I mustn't stop trying. The one thing I've learned from my past is that no matter how down you are, you never know what's going to happen the next day. Life really can change overnight, so you have to hang on in there, however tough the going gets.

The Priory let me go home to snowy Warrington for Christmas. Bryan and I had been apart for four months and this was the first Christmas I'd spent without him since we'd met. Our Molly and our Lilly went to Ireland to be with him, Mairead and

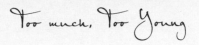

Brendan. Our new house in Winwick was ready, and while I had been in the Priory, Lisa and David had moved all our stuff over from one house to the other and made it ready for me to come home. I don't know where I'd be without Lisa – I've been through everything with her.

Our new home had five bedrooms, a big garden and a view over a big grassy park with a children's playground. I didn't bother putting up any Christmas decorations as there didn't seem to be much point. I borrowed a Collie cross-breed called Tyson from a friend to keep me company and would lie on the couch cuddled up with him. The problem was that Lisa's young son Carl kept sticking his finger up Tyson's bum, so not surprisingly the dog turned into a biter and had to be returned.

On Christmas Eve Bryan phoned. He told me he was dating Delta. I still don't understand why he did that. He was probably scared that some story would break in the press and wanted to tell me himself before I saw it in the papers, but what a time to choose. I was gutted and sat, curled into a ball, on the dining-room floor, feeling so alone. I couldn't stop picturing him and Delta together and asking myself, Why weren't he and the kids here with me? I spent Christmas Day at Nana Betty's with Mum and the family before going round to see Mag and Fred. Afterwards Lisa and Dave picked me up and took me round to Lisa's parents' for the evening. I tried hard not to let what I was going through show, but not having my own family around was hard. All my friends tried to cheer me up and be supportive, but at the end of the day I always ended up alone in my bed, burrowed under the duvet, wishing I didn't have to come out again.

I knew I had to move on and tried to convince myself I was

over Bryan by dating Dan Corsi again for a few weeks at the end of 2004. He called me up and I was flattered by the attention and compliments. He gave me quite an ego boost and made me feel much better about myself. We both knew that it was a rebound thing and much too soon to be anything serious. He was great company, though, and we had a good laugh together. Then Dave Cunningham came back into my life. We'd known each other since Mag and Fred invited him and Mattie Mackay over for barbecued ribs in their garden, and he'd been a good friend ever since, even coming to my wedding. We began an affair in January, when I discovered what sexual compatibility is for the first time.

Not long after I got together with Dave, I had to go to Austria to film *My Fair Kerry*. This was a TV commitment I'd made before Bryan and I split up. I was going to stay with a wealthy aristocratic Austrian family who were going to try to turn me into a lady. Yes, me! I'd hoped that it would take my mind off everything, but I hated being there. Count Carl-Philip Clam was my host and the idea was for him to teach me how to speak proper, dance, walk and mix with the cream of society. Hearing him tell me that so much about me wasn't good enough when I felt so low was horrible. I had to pass myself off as one of the English aristocracy at various events like a dinner, a shooting party, a wine tasting, a spot of target practice and finally, a ball. Talk about a fish out of water! I did my best, but I wasn't really ready to be back at work.

Behind the scenes, Bryan and I were fighting. I might have been in Austria, but he was still only a phone call away. I was furious that he hadn't phoned the girls in over two weeks because I think regular contact is really important and that it ought to be

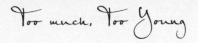

him who made the effort to get in touch. I know what it's like to grow up without a dad and without that sense of security, and I don't want the girls to experience that. I had to threaten to go to the papers with the story if he didn't get his act together.

While I was filming, the Bryan I didn't know any more phoned me during a shoot. He was really angry with me for being there. 'Why don't you get a proper nine-to-five job?' he asked. 'You're a mother and you're supposed to be at home.'

'But Bryan, I have a career, too,' I pointed out. He knew how strongly I felt about earning my own money. And it was a good job I had continued working, otherwise our girls would have had to go without after he left us. Unlike many women who find themselves in a similar situation, I was lucky enough to be able to get work and earn enough to support us. 'Besides,' I added, 'I haven't got enough money if I don't work. You haven't given me anything to help with the girls.' It was true, he hadn't, it was still something we had to get sorted out between us.

I'd obviously hit a nerve because he turned really nasty and threatened to take the girls, who were at home in Warrington being looked after by Lisa and Dave. I'd left the girls with them because I thought they'd had enough disruption and that staying at home gave them more stability. I don't think Bryan meant his threat for a moment, but he succeeded in upsetting me all right. I was in the middle of filming the last scenes when we spoke, so after the call I had to wipe away my tears, get my make-up on and come out smiling. Is there a pattern here? I didn't tell anyone what had happened, but they must have guessed that something was wrong. That's my excuse for getting so pissed at the end of the show and letting down Count Carl-Philip and the other people who had coached me by not being able to go to the ball. I definitely failed to become a lady – all I wanted to do was go home.

Bryan might have tried to make me feel like a rubbish mother, but when I won Quality Street Celebrity Mum of the Year for the second time in a row I was gobsmacked. The award came as such a surprise and really helped lift my spirits. I knew I was doing the best I could to give our girls all the love and security they needed, and it was fantastic to know that other people thought I was doing OK. People I'd never even met wrote to me from all over the country. I was knocked out by all the cards and letters I received. Knowing that support was there really helped me. I was still finding it incredibly tough and couldn't help thinking, If all these people like me, why doesn't Bryan?

The last straw came when I went on a massive bender with Mum in London, where I'd gone to promote *My Fair Kerry*. As always, my low points came when the kids were away and I'd try to make myself feel better by going out on the town. The next day I felt terrible and knew I'd gone too far. I got George to delay all the press interviews I had scheduled, but she insisted I appeared on *Entertainment Today*. Somehow I got through it, despite my belly ache and cold sweats, but I could feel myself going under as I got more and more jittery and paranoid.

I'd arranged to meet Mum at the hotel, but instead I got my driver to take me to the Priory. Even though I'd been seeing my psychiatrist once a week since my first stay there, it hadn't been enough to keep me on the wagon, and as a result my mood swings made me feel as high as a kite one minute and really depressed the next. I thought I was going crazy.

I was put back in the same room as before and George brought

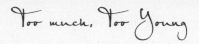

me some clothes and toiletries. I didn't like the food in the Priory so she'd stop off at a chippie on the way over. She was such a support to me. To protect my privacy, I still couldn't go to the group sessions and had to spend another week in my room, being chemically calmed down. My psychiatrist made me recognize that I needed more help to face my problems so that I could overcome them. He also made me realize that asking for help is nothing to be ashamed of and that people often find themselves in situations they can't escape from on their own. He also thought that, apart from my depression, my drug- and alcohol-related problems needed treatment, so he recommended I go to Cottonwood de Tucson, a rehab clinic in Arizona for six weeks. Nobody would know me there, so I could be completely anonymous and take proper advantage of their widely recommended six-week therapy programme.

The girls were in Ireland with Mairead, who agreed to have them for rest of the summer holidays while I got myself better. I didn't want to go away for that long, and nor did Dave want me to. He seemed to think my problems could be turned off like a switch and a few days in the Priory should be enough but I knew they went much deeper and that I needed professional help. I had to get completely better for my girls. Mum was so upset, crying down the phone and refusing to believe there was anything wrong with me. I told her and everyone else that I suffering from depression and nothing else, but nobody wants anything to be wrong with their child and, in this case, nobody knew better than her what depression meant. I went back to Warrington for the weekend, packed a few things and left.

Paul from James Grant, my management company, drove me to the airport. When I wondered out loud about running away when I got to Heathrow, he was very firm with me. 'You're getting on this flight, Kerry. This will be the best investment you'll ever make in your life and the best present you could give to your kids.'

I knew he was right, but at the time I felt so low and ashamed of myself. How had I let things get this bad? It was only the thought of our Molly and Lilly that got me onto that plane.

I phoned Bryan from the airport lounge and told him I had to get away to sort my head out and escape from the press. He reassured me that the girls would be fine with his mum and that he would visit them whenever he could. There were newspaper reports all over the place about how I was losing it. Depression is a complicated thing, I know that now, and at that stage I was having trouble admitting my problems to myself, let alone the world at large. No one should have the right to make money out of my life, least of all the so-called friends I trusted. They claim they talked to the newspapers to help me but their betrayal of our friendship is part of the reason I ended up in Arizona. This is my life, and it's my story to tell when I want to tell it, not theirs.

I arrived in Arizona on 4 July, Independence Day, and when I stepped off the plane, the heat smacked me in the face. I admit that I'd been drinking on the plane – well, it was free champagne – and as the stewardess had poured me yet another glass, she asked, 'Going anywhere nice?'

'Yeah. Rehab.' I smiled back.

Her face froze but she kept on pouring.

The combination of heat and alcohol meant I slept for most of the two-hour drive to Cottonwood. The hospital was once a dude ranch, or holiday resort, in the desert in the middle of nowhere near the foothills of the Tucson mountains. There were

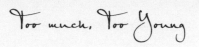

masses of prickly cactuses growing everywhere, just like trees grow over here, and a sharp turn off the road led to the clinic. We were buzzed in through the gate and drove past the car park to the front of the main, low red-brick building, which looked a bit like a primary school. I started out by putting on the cheery 'celebrity Kerry' front, but that was soon knocked out of me when I was completely stripped to make sure I hadn't hidden anything on me. My CDs, Walkman, deodorants, nail varnish, *OK!* magazine, bikinis, perfume, razors and tweezers were all taken away. We were also only allowed to wear skirts that were a decent length and modest tops, because some of the patients are in for sex addiction. As the staff went through my suitcase, I suddenly remembered I still had a huge bag of condoms in there, which I'd taken to London because I was going to a hen night, until I took a detour to stop off at the Priory. I tried to explain, but as they pulled the bag out they looked at me very oddly.

Feeling incredibly manky from the heat and travelling, I was taken round to be introduced to everyone. They were all very friendly, 'Hi, Kerry, how are you?' 'Nice to meet you.' 'Come on, I'll show you around.' 'Hi, Kerry, what are you in for?' But I felt so, so far away from home. I was put in detox for four days, where every new patient is observed as they come off whatever they're on. For the first two or three days, I wouldn't go to any of the classes or talk to my therapist. I felt really uncomfortable and just slept a lot, having the weirdest dreams, or sat outside my room on a little chair, stubbing out my fags in the bucket beside me.

My therapist came to talk to me as I sat there all hot and sweaty, crying and smoking. 'I want to go home. I don't know anyone.'

'I understand, Kerry,' she said calmly. 'I guarantee these six weeks are going to go so fast that you won't even know it.'

'They won't. I know they won't,' I wailed.

'They will,' she reassured me. 'And you're going to make friends.'

'No I won't. I hate it here,' I bawled back. 'I just want my little girls.'

But of course she was right. I started to meet new people and began to relax. To begin with, as I stood in the community meeting that started every day, listening to them all say a little prayer – God, grant me the serenity to accept the things I cannot change, the courage to change the things I can, and the willingness to take action – I thought they were all nuts. But, you know what? Cottonwood was an amazing place. After a while I began to start the day, like the others, 'Hi, I'm Kerry. I'm a depressive.' It look me a little while before I could admit that I had issues with alcohol and drugs. I'd never thought my binge drinking made me an alcoholic. I didn't even like the taste of alcohol and only drank for the kick, not for enjoyment. One of the first lessons I learned is that you don't have to wake up to a drink and drink all day long to qualify as an alcoholic. I only binged when the kids were away and I knew I could stop when they came home. But again, I learned that there are different kinds of addictive behaviour and mine was one of them. My daily list began to get longer and longer as I admitted to being the adult child of a dysfunctional family, the adult child of an alcoholic and then a co-dependent. Co-dependent – at last I had a word for the weird push-pull relationship I'd always had with Mum. For the first time I understood that sticking by her and looking after her had made

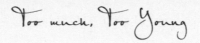

me feel worthwhile and wanted as a kid, but at the same time by looking after her I'd also allowed her to go on behaving in the same old way. As I talked about myself and I learned more and more, everything began to make sense and I felt as if a huge weight was being lifted, until one day I just got up and said, 'Hi, I'm Kerry. I'm a recovering human being.' At least I got a laugh.

My therapist advised me which sessions I should attend over the six weeks and every day began with a seven to seven thirty wake-up and breakfast until eight. After the half-hour community meeting, I went to therapy groups, among them sessions on co-dependency, addictions, women's relationships, trauma and intimacy classes, AA, cardio-boxing and cardio-water exercise. The religious classes made a big impression on me. I've never been religious, but I learned that you don't have to believe in God or in one set religion, just in a higher power that's your own personalized god. I may fuck up every now and then, but there's a greater power out there that will help me get through. I'm not a big reader, but I was given a fantastic book called *Peace is Every Step* by a Buddhist monk, Thich Nhat Hanh, which I read every day. He talks so wisely about how to live in the present. Reading his words was like having a friend with me, helping me. I'd recommend it to everyone. I know I sound as cuckoo as I thought the others were at first, but I was blown away by the whole experience.

Being in Cottonwood was the first time I've ever talked openly and in such detail about my past, including my marriage. I cried my way through many of the sessions as I was made to face myself and what had happened to me. I was made to look at how I felt about my mum's suicide attempts, her decision to stay with Dave rather than me, my feelings of rejection and my relationships with Bryan, alcohol, *everything*. Once I could say how I felt about all those aspects of my life, and acknowledge how difficult it had been and how they'd affected me as an adult, I could start focusing on what I needed to do to get better. I was made to do a lot of what they called 'list work', writing things down to clarify your thoughts and feelings. By confronting and appreciating an issue, I could set myself some goals, and also some boundaries for how I should behave in the future. I wrote letters to my mum and to my real dad. They weren't meant for posting, but for facing up to all the stuff I felt about them but had sat on over the years, and to help me understand those feelings. The one to my real dad is smudged with tears as I wrote about how much I'd always missed him and the times when I would have liked him to have been there for me. After only a week I began to see that I couldn't do anything about the past, I just had to accept what had happened, let go and move on, taking one day at a time.

At Cottonwood, they believe that being alone is another form of escape from the world, so I shared one of the pretty but simple twin rooms with another woman. One afternoon I was so glad to get back to the room after a draining session with the group, where I'd spoken openly about my past and my relationship with my mother and her suicide attempts. My room-mate hadn't been to the class that day, so we were just chatting when she asked me if I had a razor. I thought nothing of it, dug out a disposable I'd bought at the shop and gave it to her. She disappeared into the bathroom and I listened to the water running while I lay on my bed, thinking about the session I'd just been to. Suddenly there was a loud shriek.

I burst into the bathroom to see blood streaming down my room-mate's legs from the cuts she'd deliberately made with my razor. I'd come all this way to get away from stuff like that; it was just like being back at home. At least I knew how to handle the situation without panicking. I bandaged her up and called her a silly billy, just as if she was my mum. Afterwards, I remember looking up at the sky and thinking, What more are you going to do to me? I'm not even with my mum. I'm in rehab, for God's sake.

The fifth week was family week. What family? I didn't dare ask my mum in case they never let her out again! I did ask Bryan, but he was working. Maybe it was me looking for a fairy-tale ending to our marriage, but I would have liked us to confront stuff together, so that we could have a good relationship where we shared the children without any fighting – a bit like Bruce Willis and Demi Moore: that would be my dream now. I'd like us to be able to go to parents' evenings together and share those little things that will mean so much to the girls. In the end Dave and George, my manager, came. They both wanted and needed to confront me about the way I sometimes behaved with them, saying I could be unreliable and that I shied away from commit-ting myself to a relationship. It was hard to hear, but they were both amazingly supportive, and I learned that by behaving unrea-sonably or angrily I was simply rejecting people before they rejected me. A lifetime of rejection dictates its own pattern of behaviour, and that's something I needed to change. During the week, I carried on going to my regular classes while they went to theirs, listening to presentations on family systems, mood disor-ders, addictions, co-dependency and anxiety disorders. After each one we did more list work, which was read out loud, so we could be honest with one another about our relationships and find out how we could improve them and support one another.

When I came out at the end of those six weeks, I was a new woman. I felt so refreshed, so vibrant and healthy. I was really buzzing, although I was shitting myself about going home. You're so cared for in Cottonwood. Other people were dying to go home, but I wasn't. The ceremony where we were all given a medallion and everyone says nice things about each other was a painful goodbye. Against all my expectations I'd survived with no TV (except on 7/7 when London suffered the terrible tube bombings) and no mobile, just a phone card and a public phone where we had to queue. I knew that the reality of putting all my resolutions to the test would be hard, but I was determined to turn my life around. When they leave, every patient places a brick in the low wall outside the clinic symbolizing those who they dedicate their treatment to: mine was to our Molly and our Lilly.

Since Cottonwood I've learned to take responsibility for my own life. My relationship with Mum has changed, and I recognize that although I'm like her in many ways, I shouldn't blame her for the way I've turned out. I see the areas of conflict between us, but also that there's a lot of good going on there as well. Thanks to her, I've learned how to be a good mother. She always listens whenever I'm down and tries to keep out of my business. She's always stuck up for me and is so proud of me, and she's a wonderful grandmother.

Things between Bryan and me have not been as easy as I would have liked. Cottonwood taught me that I had to let go and stop fighting with him over the kids. I've tried my best, but when he doesn't phone them or turn up when they're expecting him, it's hard seeing their disappointment. It makes me really angry. Once a car arrived late at night to take them to him in London. Bryan was furious that I wouldn't let them go, but I didn't want to get them out of bed in the middle of the night to go with a stranger on a long drive to London – I thought it was too much for a two- and four-year-old. I really wasn't being vindictive. If he'd come himself, I would have felt easier. All I want is for us to share the children, being equally responsible for their happiness and security, and I don't think that's too much to ask. Nor do I think it's unreasonable to insist they start the school term on the same day as everyone else, cutting short the holiday he'd planned for them by a few days. I just want them to have a normal life and be the same as their friends. I would never use them to get at him. I know he loves his little girls and they love him, and I certainly don't want to stop him seeing them. I've met Delta and she's beautiful, tall and elegant with a blinding smile, and she has so much in common with Bryan: she's a wonderful singer and he's passionate about his music. I can't blame him for wanting to be with her rather than with me – a brassy, busty, loud-mouthed chav! All the same, I still hope we can work things out and have a friendly relationship, for the girls' sake.

Shortly after returning home from Arizona my psychiatrist said to me, 'I know you don't want to be like your mother, but you're bi-polar.' I know it sounds odd, but I felt relieved and almost happy. I knew that the way I felt so up and then so down wasn't normal. A mood could last for hours, days or even weeks, but then it would change with no warning and I seemed to have no control over it. He was right, of course, I didn't want to suffer like Mum had, but at the same time, if I was ill, then I could be treated. Since then I've been on medication that evens out my mood swings and I visit my psychiatrist regularly to have my medication checked. I'm already feeling much better, as if I can cope with life again.

I'm making it sound as though Arizona was a magical turning point in my life and that everything's been perfect ever since, but of course it's not that simple. All I can say is that the twelve months following my stay there have been a helluva lot better than the twelve months before. Although I've done my best to live by what I learned at Cottonwood, I've slipped up a few times, too, and have had good moments and bad. Perhaps one of the best moments was being a bridesmaid at Katie and Peter Andre's amazing wedding. I was made up when Katie asked me. They are so madly in love that the atmosphere was really special. The whole affair was completely over the top and so Katie and Pete that nobody would have had it any other way. As Katie walked down the aisle, looking beautiful, I was overwhelmed by memories of my own wedding and felt so happy for them. Pete stood there crying and I could see Katie welling up – I bet I wasn't the only person in tears in the church at that moment.

What I want more than anything is to get back to being the old me, the carefree up-for-anything person who went into the jungle. The first step towards that has been to start concentrating on my career again. I've got contracts with Iceland and *OK!* magazine, but I want to find more work that's fun and that will give me a challenge. I still love performing, singing and dancing, so I'd love to pick up where I left off with *The Vagina Monologues* and *Showbands* and get back into the theatre, films or TV presenting. I'm also very proud to be associated with Pink

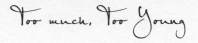

Ladies, the private cab company that began in Warrington, but which now has branches in London, St Helens, Carlisle and Plymouth. Our priority is safety for women, so the drivers are all female and the women or children passengers must be account holders, so no money changes hands. The other area where I'd like to do more is charity work. I was thrilled to raise £500,000 by being in the jungle and would love the opportunity to raise more. I know that there are a lot of children like me, who didn't have the perfect childhood, and if I could contribute something to helping them, I'd be very happy. If nothing else, I hope I've at least shown that being in care isn't the worst thing that can happen to you, and that no matter how bad things get and however low you feel, you can still achieve whatever you want, providing you don't give up.

As for my personal life? Dave and I had a well-publicized break-up. The press made a big thing out of it, but there's really nothing to tell. We had a very public affair that didn't work out – sometimes they don't. He was great with the kids and a huge support to me at the time, but it was a difficult year for me and he had to put up with a lot. When we finally broke up, a close friend of Mum's helped me through. I'd known Mark Croft for about two years – he's a local taxi driver who's ten years older than me – and I often used to go round to his flat and confide in him. He listened to me and looked after me like a brother would. I felt safe with him. Whenever I needed him he was there, and as the weeks went by, I realized that nobody has ever got me the way he does. He totally understands me and we laugh at the same things. He had split up with his girlfriend the previous year and together they have a little daughter, Keeley, who's the same age as our Molly, so we have loads in common. I began to see him more and more often, and I remember telling Mum that I had a really weird crush on him. Then on Valentine's night, 2006, he took me out for a meal and then back to his place, where I jumped on him! The next morning I was so worried I'd ruined our friendship, but far from it.

We haven't spent a day apart since. I love him because he's so down to earth and really cares about me and the girls, looking after me the way I've always wanted to be looked after. He's really affectionate, always kissing and cuddling me, and he doesn't care who's watching – that's what he's like. More than that, he makes me laugh. Nothing's too much trouble for him. He's my best friend and I feel so much safer when he's around, so we go everywhere together.

Mark had been planning to propose to me in front of all our friends and family at a surprise engagement do at the Fir Grove Hotel outside Warrington, but someone let it slip and the secret was blown.

He'd been determined to surprise me because he knows I've hardly ever been surprised in my life. Bryan managed it at Castle Doe, and so did Ant and Dec when they caught me out on *Saturday Night Takeaway*. I was visiting a hospital to give a nurse a cheque from *This Morning*, and Dec was completely covered in plaster while Ant was disguised as the nurse. I kept thinking it must be them, but suppose it hadn't been and the patient was real. I couldn't be sure. Usually, though, nothing gets past me – my childhood has made me far too paranoid, so I'm always on the lookout.

But on 19 March, 2006, Mark came down to London, where I was working, and finally popped the question. I had flu so it

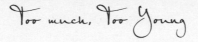

wasn't the most romantic situation, with me blowing my nose and sniffing. He asked me if I still wanted to marry him and when I said yes, he said, 'Well you'd better put this on then.' He got out a ring and made me put it on my finger, but at first I refused to look at it because we'd talked about getting engaged in June. I kept my other hand over it and then took a quick peak. When I saw the gorgeous diamond solitaire, I thought, Yeay! It's absolutely beautiful, although I was disappointed that I didn't have my false nails on to do it justice!

Right now I'm feeling really optimistic about the future. I'm engaged to be married to a man I love and who loves me. I've never met anyone who's so attentive and affectionate – all that kissing and cuddling is just what I need. We're so compatible in every way and so happy. The girls adore him.

Our Molly and Lilly are brilliant. They've settled into their new school and are happy at home. Our Molly takes after me in so many ways. She's always singing and dancing, and she loves showing off, just like I did. Lilly is the spitting image of me but much quieter; she's a real mummy's girl. I'm so proud of them and love them to bits. Every night when they come home from school, we sit in the living room and they take turns performing for me. Watching them takes me back to the days when I used to perform for Nana Ferrier and Nana Betty. All I want is for them to be happy, and I'll do everything I can to make sure they are. Having kids is such a great thing and we all love each other unconditionally. The rewards of a first smile, seeing their first steps or hearing their first words make all the sleepless nights and worry worthwhile. They give me hope for the future. When they're older, I won't push them in any direction because I think it's important to learn from your own mistakes, but I'll always be there for them when they need me. For now, I want them to be two happy free spirits, enjoying the proper childhood I never had.

Molly and Lilly have been the making of my mum, too; they've given her a second chance. Whatever mistakes she made with me, she'll never make with them, and she gives them all the support and love she wasn't always able to give to me. She would die for them. They love going round to stay at 'Nana nou's' and she's the most fantastic grandmother. I'm so proud of her.

Before Christmas 2005, I tried confronting her about all the problems I'd had with her as a mother, just as we'd have done if she'd come to see me at Cottonwood. At first, I think she was very hurt and we fell out big time, which is understandable because she didn't have the benefit of all the background work she'd have been put through in Arizona. But although we still argue, we always make up again, in the end. Now I feel that she's started to be more of a mum to me and is much less dependent on me. But whatever happens, my mum's my mum. She's the only blood family I have, apart from my kids.

All in all, I'm happier than I've been in ages and am looking forward to the future. I'm really happy with Mark and can't wait to be married as soon as my divorce comes through. We've always talked about having a big family, so we were over the moon when we discovered that I was pregnant. I hadn't been well when Max Clifford generously organized a holiday for us in Marbella in July 2006. We had a brilliant time, but while we were there I had a really bloated stomach and got Mark to go to the chemist to buy me some laxatives. I took the ten drops and nothing. Still bloated. I took another five. Still nothing. I couldn't

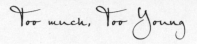

think what was wrong until it hit me that I might be pregnant. We'd been trying for a baby for a couple of months, but I hadn't had any of the symptoms I'd had with Molly and Lilly – I hadn't even missed my time of the month, but I thought we'd better check anyway. When I saw the test was positive, I felt high as a kite. I rushed from the bathroom into the hotel bedroom. 'Babe. I'm pregnant!' Mark was busy chatting to his daughter Keeley on the phone, and when he came off we didn't dare believe the test was accurate, so he went out and bought another seven tests. When every one of them was positive we cracked open a bottle of champagne – a glass for me and Mark polished off the rest. We were both so, so excited.

The next day, we phoned our family and close friends, who were all thrilled for us. I even called Bryan to tell him the news myself because I didn't want him finding out in the papers. Of course, the people I wanted to tell most of all were Molly and Lilly, who were on holiday with Mairead in Ireland. I decided I wanted to be with them when we told them, but I couldn't resist calling them and telling them we had a big surprise waiting for when they came home.

'Is it a horse?' asked Molly.

'Have you got me a castle?' Lilly chipped in.

'No, neither of those.'

'Is it a camel then?' What! Why would it be?! 'Or have you taken the stabilisers off my bike?' Molly was bursting to know.

'No.'

'Well, stick it in an envelope and send it to me!'

They had to wait, but when they got home a few days later they were over the moon to hear that, come February or March next year, they are going to have a little girl or boy to play with. Since then we've been getting in a bit of practice by borrowing Mark's baby niece, Hannah Jane, to look after at weekends – that's been ace.

At last I feel like I can put everything I've been through behind me and we can get on with our new lives together as a family – that's all I want. Mark's mum, brother and sister have been brilliant and make me feel like one of them, and Mark's the most wonderful, caring person I could hope to find. I feel very lucky and am determined to do everything I can to make sure it all works out for us, and I know Mark will too. My own childhood has taught me what I need to provide for Molly, Lilly and whoever else joins them. Whatever happens to me, my children will always come first.